Economic Clarity

or

Political Confusion

The Classical Cure for Keynesian Debt & Deficits

James Malloy

Printed in the United States of America

First Printing 2018

ISBN: 978-0-578-43021-8

Contact the author through the below website

Website: www.econclarity.com

Cover & Back Cover Layout: Larry Holt. Sketchpad Graphic Design

Cover Photo: Zoltan Kovacs. Courtesy of Unsplash

Back Cover Photo: Andy Feliciotti. Courtesy of Unsplash

Dedicated to the Extension of Western Civilization

Contents

Part IV: History

Part V: Today

Part VI: Preparing Ourselves

Introduction

"Beware of little expenses. A small leak will sink a great ship."

Benjamin Franklin

Why do politicians increase government spending when we have enormous deficits and astronomical debt? Can the government spend its way out of financial trouble? Does it sound right to you?

We see supposed conservatives spend incredibly recklessly after attacking left-leaning politicians for it. Similarly, the Democrats, who always push for more spending, often blame the Republicans for increasing the debt. When does this conduct become existentially dangerous?

It's finally time we cut through the confusion and understand why both sides engage in this irrational behavior. Did you know there is a clear theoretical foundation in economics to understand this insanity and the cure?

Do economics and politics mix? One major political party claims that our economic problems and solutions are the opposite of those in the other political camp. Still, the debt keeps rising no matter who's in power. What lies beneath the strange contradictions?

Many politicians tell us we need a healthy respect for the public and the private sectors. We never hear them say we need a healthy respect for the government and the economy separately. What determines the public sector? What defines the private sector? Are these two things distinct, or is there a considerable overlap and interrelation between them? If one listens to financial reporting today, he might think we have two separate economic systems: public and private. So what *is* the economy, and what drives it?

If we look at economic performance over the Obama years, why do some economists forcefully state we did well while others stridently report the opposite? Some cite favorable statistics with seemingly convinced opinions, while others cite data portraying anemic growth over the same years. Does the quote Mark Twain popularized ring true here? "There are three kinds of lies: lies, damned lies, and statistics." These economists can't be politically neutral.

It seems politicians want more government spending to attract voting constituencies and maybe even help the needy, but they argue it's good for the economy. Is this true? If it isn't, why won't the other major political party politicians explain the underlying economic theories clearly to expose it all? Shouldn't we understand why we spend tax money? Are they afraid they can't clarify the principles? Are they confused?

Most politicians seem ignorant of basic economic theory, or they lack character and honesty. Will they say anything to get elected, do whatever they want, or think they must, to rise further in political power and keep it?

It seems academics have convinced themselves and most politicians of economic theories that defy common sense. Do they hope they work only for political expediency or is something more insidious at work? Contrary models can't function together well. Are they all partly functional or in the right circumstances? Do all economic systems have some validity?

Testing the theoretical basics is easy. We can find the real foundation by illuminating what others have done before and looking at how things operate in our lives, especially in our businesses. Given current societal pressures and trends, we must reveal what has worked historically and always works theoretically before things become too dangerous.

Can we reveal timeless truths in economics that lead us to higher, even eternal truths operating in our culture? We must delineate right from wrong and see pernicious theories attacking our society and our children's future.

If we build on a foundation of sand, how long can the structure stand? Shouldn't we first test the theoretical footing? If we create on solid rock as a matter of principle, we can further our understanding on truth.

One side primarily promotes government spending to create jobs. They talk about cutting spending later, but their rhetoric is always for more spending. Will they ever cut spending if they have their way?

Why should they if John Maynard Keynes was right?

"I'm an immoral man. I've always been an immoral man. It's too late for me."

John Maynard Keynes

Part I

Basics

"Every man lives by exchanging..."

Adam Smith

1
Foundations

"All these artisans and entrepreneurs serve each other, as well as the nobility."

Richard Cantillon

WHILE GEORGE WASHINGTON struggled to breathe, his windpipe squeezing closed from a severely inflamed sore throat, his doctors continued letting his blood (Lear, 1799).

Without consensus between them, something like our perplexed politicians and their economic advisors, one doctor wanted no more bloodletting because it would only weaken him, but the others argued for more. The head doctor ended the debate by ordering it a fourth time (doctorzebra.com, 2018).

How much government spending jump-starts the economy? How much achieves full employment? How much maintains full employment? Can increased government spending create a healthy economy?

Is building up enormous amounts of public debt healthy? Is creating and pumping more and more money into our economy like bloodletting the dollar bill? Is over-regulation squeezing our economic windpipe closed?

When I received my economics degree many years ago, the professors told us John Maynard Keynes saved capitalism by charting the middle path between a command economy, or Marxian economics, and a market economy. I didn't know enough back then to ask the obvious question: what happens when you chart the middle path between what works and what doesn't work? Where will you end up?

Will you steer into the channel or onto the rocks? Maybe get stuck in the mud? Any ship's captain will tell you; you better hope it's high tide, and you're lucky.

In 1931, as the esteemed Cambridge professor, John Maynard Keynes, impressed English academia, the London School of Economics invited the young Austrian School economist, Friedrich von Hayek, to give them four guest lectures. They quickly offered him a visiting professorship. The following year they appointed him to the Tooke Chair of Economic Science and Statistics (Hayek, The Road to Serfdom, 2007 [1944], 3). They wanted someone on their faculty who could counter Keynes with his ideas and reputation for intellectual prowess.

Hayek taught his classes, wrote his papers, and debated the English academics, but he couldn't cut through their economic and political confusion about fascism and communism. His concerns led to his most well-received book, The Road to Serfdom, where he tried to enlighten them about this foundational truth: fascism and communism are both socialism and quite similar. His warnings about the totalitarian movements building in Europe seemed fruitless; most of his colleagues believed fascism was a product of capitalism and not socialism. Hayek insisted National Socialism is what it says it is, socialism.

In the introduction to The Road to Serfdom, Bruce Caldwell describes how Hayek began his book as a memo to the director of LSE:

"It began as a memo to the director of the London School of Economics, Sir William Beveridge, written in the early 1930s, disputing the then popular claim that fascism represented the dying gasps of a failed capitalism (Ibid, 1)."

Fascism representing failed capitalism is Marxist propaganda, but unfortunately, many people believe it today. Historically, in Italy, Germany, and Spain, the communists and fascists were political rivals competing for like-minded people, with fascists also calling themselves socialists.

The communists portrayed fascists as right-wing to demonize them, as the fascists attacked the communists as leftists. Today, European and American elitists call fascists right-wing for political reasons because their whole political spectrum represents socialism. Or, they strategically want to disparage capitalism to promote larger government.

Hayek showed that not only does fascism not come from capitalism, it often springs from failing communism. He gave examples and quoted some ideological leftists who admitted it brokenheartedly (Ibid, 78-80). They acknowledged the utopian dream frequently turned into something uncannily like a fascist dictatorship. What happened over time? Karl Marx's futuristic predictions became the reality of Stalin's Russia, Mao, and Pol Pot.

Can't we give many examples of communist legacies today beyond the killing fields? Can we call China communist now? They control industry autocratically, including many nominally private government-connected businesses. It sounds like fascism. What do you call Putin's Russia? Vietnam is supposedly still communist, but in reality, a commercialized dictatorship.

There are numerous examples, and Hayek understood the mechanics, accurately observed human behavior, and saw the patterns many decades ago. The communists and fascists argued for the same followers, although communists used internationalist, but fascists, nationalistic rhetoric. They are both expansionist dictatorships, side by side on the left.

Mussolini, the world's first fascist leader and Hitler's archetype, was a well-known communist until he declared himself anti-Marxian and anti-free enterprise, but "collective" and "totalitarian," or, for the "state (Mussolini, 1932, 7)." He and his advisors created fascism out of Marxism. The truth is, communism and fascism are rivaling socialist siblings, two sides of a coin. Hayek explained the interactions between the two parties in Germany:

"And what is true of the leaders is even more true of the rank and file of the movement. The relative ease with which a young communist could be converted into a young Nazi or vice versa was generally known in Germany, best of all to the propagandists of the two parties (Hayek, The Road to Serfdom, 2007 [1944], 80-81)."

Something Hayek greatly feared took place about two years after he moved to England. The National Socialists won the election in Germany, and Hitler became Chancellor.

Why were the English intellectuals unconcerned? They may have had Karl Marx on their minds, or maybe so much ivory tower Marxist theory in the air had confused them. Marx prophesied that capitalism inevitably leads to socialism (Marx & Engels, The Communist Manifesto, 1998 [1848]). Maybe they realized the fascists were socialists but perceived Germany's vote as the first step in a natural process toward global communism. Professor Hayek understood socialism in its different forms very well. He knew what fascism was, and he knew what communism was, but he was a small fish swimming in a large leftist academic pond.

Nazi Germany became a nationalist collective effort, with many industrial projects undertaken by "following the Fuhrer's will... (German Propaganda Archive, 1938)." He even ordered a "people's car," the Volkswagen, so folks "with limited incomes can afford a car (Ibid)." An elderly neighbor of mine who grew up in Nazi Germany and lived through it as a teenager told me, mostly college kids supported Hitler; they liked his socialist-sounding promises. The government then gave the youth forced conditioning into National Socialism from an early age (the United States Holocaust Memorial Museum, 2018).

Hitler's type of socialism put Germany on a wartime footing in anticipation of offensive combat—if only the Fuhrer and his inner circle understood his plans. He energetically shouted calls for national pride and production, demonized groups of people to conquer and destroy, and got the folks marching to his will.

About five years after he came to power, Hitler's invading armies brought the National Socialist German Workers Party, the Nazis, control of Hayek's Austrian homeland. More invasions of neighboring countries, the mass murder of undesirables, and an awful totalitarian rule followed.

Why did Professor Hayek face such a frustrating task trying to enlighten his contemporaries? Wasn't his position evident? Socialism doesn't come out of ideas of individual freedom, individual striving for economic gain in trade, or the free association of groups of people for exchange in production value. It doesn't embrace the requirement of personal liberty and one's free will for human growth to find one's calling in life. Socialism doesn't naturally evolve from freedom and free-market economic principles, and it doesn't logically follow. It promises preferences to create justice, makes claims for liberty through government protection, and promotes the political class's defined equality. It offers prosperity through government planning and control. Socialism comes out of collectivist ideas.

Not all forms of socialism are the same or equal in severity, but they all attempt to control people in various ways by promising security at the cost of freedom. In the 1930s, Germany became prosperous from a war build-up as the rest of the world struggled through the depression. It's deceptive and unsustainable over time, and it ended in their destruction, not to mention the millions who died. War creates a false economy. Communist governments throughout the world also spent vast resources on their militaries. Still, they had low living standards, and many had enormous death tolls from internal purges besides foreign wars.

It's only freely inspired production and exchange that drives our growth over time. Any sustainable, prosperous economic model must work consistently in peacetime, and freedom within a stable society with law and order is the only way it works. Countries with "Democratic Socialist" politicians and political parties always push for more government control over the economy, which means over the producers. They will even argue their "controls" drive the economy; this is the problem. The academic and political debate becomes what system works for the people, socialism or capitalism. The truth is one "system" is falsity and the other reality.

What does Keynesian economics represent? Is it socialist or capitalist in its operational principles? Does it lead to socialism? If so, what kind?

There are collective interests and some public ownership in all civilized societies, but we all must understand what drives progress and creates prosperity. Hayek's emphasis was on vital economic principles, and he exposed the severe social consequences of controlling governments. The questions to keep in mind are, what *is* the economy, and what drives it?

Keynes and Hayek became academic adversaries, and they debated publicly. They also began meeting for lunch and, over time, had many friendly personal conversations. Years later, in a video-recorded interview, Hayek told Leo Rolston that the brilliant Keynes had "a parochial" understanding of economics. He only knew one school of thought well, the ideas then prevalent at Cambridge. Although intelligent, broadly well-read with much intellectual knowledge, economics was just "a sideline for him." Hayek made this statement partly from quizzing Keynes about work done by earlier European economists. It seemed to him because Keynes could speak and read only English and French, ideas previously experimented with by so many Germans, for example, were inaccessible to him. Hayek believed already exposed errors eluded Keynes (Hayek F. A., 2012).

In the second half of the twentieth century and into the twenty-first, Keynes and Hayek exemplify our mainstream theoretical poles. Hayek stands on the shoulders of giants, notably Ludwig von Mises, his teacher from the Austrian School of Economics. Mises summed up Keynes' ideas this way:

"...salvation through spending and credit expansion," and, "No need to worry any longer about the insufficiency of savings and capital accumulation and about deficits in the public household. On the contrary. The only method to do away with unemployment was to increase "effective demand" through public spending financed by credit expansion and inflation (Mises, 2005)."

***

What proceeds the secular arguments? The foundations run deeper than all these men's ideas, and our fuller understanding rests on context; it's rooted in our better nature and advanced through civilization. Does morality support commerce? What comes first before we flourish?

Timeless economic truths existed when man created value from labor and the land and exchanged it with other men. We see these concepts recorded several thousand years ago in early Bible accounts. Aristotle and other ancient writers broached economic questions. The Greeks and Romans traded with Egyptians and other Africans. Ancient cultures everywhere used forms of money to facilitate trade. Celtic, Germanic, and many other European, Asian, and all people worldwide as far back as we know engaged in commerce. Many cities throughout Europe began as Viking trading posts.

From all this evidence of mankind exchanging value worldwide from the most primitive times, can't we say it's natural for us? Can't we say we should embrace it? Ancient man acquired valuable things by raiding and violently pillaging his neighbors, or he traded with them. Our violence and attempts to control each other are historically unmistakable and rooted in our lowest nature. Isn't associating freely, producing, and exchanging value better?

Stability and freedom flourish through morality. Christianity brought Europe better ethics, education, and quicker advancement. Monasteries weren't just the first colleges for studying and transcribing scripture, but they were self-sufficient economic communities with farming, small-scale manufacturing, and trade.

Industrious monks experimented with crop rotation and allowing fields to go fallow for a season. They made wine for sale outside the community and worked cottage industries to support themselves. They were often very entrepreneurial and tested inventions and better production methods, not for selfish reasons, but for sustenance and money to further God's will in the world. Eventually, with a strong education ethic, many clerics became leading scientists, defining central theories in the coming years (Shea, 2016).

Evangelizing monks planted monasteries in northern Europe and educated the barbarians, and with Christianity came literacy. Knowledge is power. The kings converted to the Christian faith and more orderly societies created more wealth, discovery, and advancement. There is more potential for improvement when the ethical bar becomes the golden rule, and the love of God, neighbor, and self become religious commandments. Not to say people changed overnight as human nature is stubborn, and old ways die hard. Undoubtedly, much unethical behavior persisted, and larger nation-states can engage in warfare just as primitive clan societies can. Human ugliness continued along with much social improvement, but it was the beginning of a paradigm shift in moral, societal, political, and economic advancement.

The Christian era brought artisans with guilds and specialty professions near monasteries and Church communities. They built magnificent basilicas and cathedrals with soaring ceilings, stained glass, and intricate artwork—things much larger and more beautiful than existed before them, or we build today. They invented the university system, the modern scientific method, hospitals, and many other beautiful and practical things as they significantly furthered civilization. They advanced government structures and established chartered towns and cities that became centers of trade within and between themselves and interdependently with farms outside—and with better shipping, with far-off places (Esolen, 2015).

Growth accelerated with new concepts and technologies discovered through international trade. Explorers sailing from the Italian Republics, from Portugal, Spain, and eventually from the Netherlands, France, and England, began exchanging natural resources and finished goods and all kinds of more efficient and better production ideas for everyone involved.

Along the way, Christendom produced economic theorists writing mainly in a theological context as the Churchmen, like St. Thomas Aquinas and other Scholastics, worked to harmonize faith and reason. It led to ethical questions about commerce. Is money lending allowable in any form since the bible condemns usury? How do we define exploitation? What are just prices?

In the sixteen and early seventeenth centuries, theological writers including, Fr. Juan de Mariana, the head of the prestigious University of Salamanca in Spain, wrote about the evils of debasing money, supply and demand, scarcity, and prices. The King couldn't morally steal from the people as he couldn't have monopolies: fairness, just prices, and opportunity require free competition. Justice demanded that any monarch have the people's permission before raising taxes or debasing money (Juan de Mariana, 2011 [1609], 20).

Some historians point to these religious works as the beginning of modern economic teaching, but they addressed essential economic principles within a Christian moral context; they weren't lengthy treatises in full systematic terms. Think of a scholarly composition opening and closing with a crying out to God in heartfelt prayer for wisdom to serve Him and the public good.

Moral questions rooted in natural law arising from the Churchmen and Scholastics led to European scholars questioning our God-given fundamental freedoms they considered separate from what a King and a caste system defined for us. They contemplated philosophy, science, government structures, economics, and the natural rights of man, among other things.

The printing press facilitated much more widespread learning and debate beginning in the mid-fifteenth century and an enormous expansion of Catholic Colleges and Universities across Europe. With the increased diffusion of information also came anti-establishment and dubious scholarship. Printed pamphlets and books spread ideas attacking government and religious authority.

The Italian Renaissance, begun in Florence among Italy's wealthy elite, spread ancient Greek ideas that "man is the measure of all things," which helped create cynicism toward Church authority. "In 1513, Niccolo Machiavelli wrote *The Prince*, arguing that religion was a man-made tool for princes to use for their own political interests (Church History, 2017)."

A large-scale controversy began in 1517, when a German Catholic Priest, Fr. Martin Luther, listed complaints against his religious superiors. There was much Church corruption, but the debate became theological and intensely heated, with secular princes choosing sides. In the coming years, many different religious schools of thought emerged with the Protestant Reformation. The ideas spread quickly with the new printing technology.

Unfortunately, political struggles ensued, and Christianity devolved into horrific warfare between many sects and groups, with some wars lasting decades. There were persecutions with Kings or anti-monarchical forces seizing control and then choosing those preferred and the oppressed.

Much bitterness persisted, with anti-religious sentiment and nihilist philosophers gaining popularity in centuries to come. Ironically, within the religious divisions, the commonly stated goal was better adherence to the Christian faith, and moral principles remained.

Competition and exploration continued in the ongoing Age of Discovery among rival nations, where spreading the gospel and commercial interests drove Europeans to the ends of the earth. Decades earlier, an Italian, Christopher Columbus, discovered the Americas while sailing for Spain in 1492, setting the stage for settlement.

Puritan pilgrims seeking religious freedom from the Anglican church connected English government, who, after being dissatisfied with Dutch society after some time there, struck out to form a pious civilization from scratch. They ventured across the sea in 1620 and started a permanent settlement that eventually led to the American experiment.

The profound statements that "all men are created equal" and are "endowed by their creator" with "unalienable rights" eventually followed in 1776 with The Declaration of Independence. A government declaring, "We The People," protecting religious freedom in the U.S. Constitution, followed in 1789. The United States would set the example for religious liberty, free enterprise, and a large-scale representative government.

In Europe, priests and scholars had advanced economic and political ideas. For Western Civilization, a system of fiefdoms, serfdom, and slavery eventually gave way to the conviction that a just society means more productive free citizens should receive the fruits of their labor.

The natural law taught in a Christian moral context defused into the broader intellectual culture and gave birth to economic and political liberty. America's founding documents express it openly.

Three notable complete economic treatises supplied the ideas for more advancement and affluence. Western Civilization and the world began changing quickly. The new era of prosperity was off and starting to accelerate.

2

Giants

"Free Enterprise..."

"...the system of natural liberty."

Adam Smith

THE THREE GIANTS who laid the solid theoretical economic foundation by writing the first comprehensive treatises were Richard Cantillon, Adam Smith, and Jean-Baptiste Say.

Richard Cantillon wrote the first complete economic treatise, *An Essay on Economic Theory*. He finished it about the year 1730, before the open espousing of laissez-faire and free enterprise.

He came from a wealthy Irish Catholic landowning family in County Kerry, Ireland. But, after the Puritans defeated the Anglicans for control of Great Britain, persecution against Catholics increased tragically, and Oliver Cromwell's government stripped his family of their wealth. As a young man, he escaped the British government enforced Irish poverty and fled to France. There, as a businessman, banker, and speculator, he became perhaps the wealthiest private individual in the world.

According to the Introduction to Cantillon's *Essay* edited by Mark Thornton and translated by Chantal Saucier:

"It (*Essay*) could never have been published under the harsh French censorship laws that prevailed throughout the first half of the 18th century and, as a result, it only circulated privately in hand-copied manuscripts. Only after the censorship laws were relaxed was it published in 1755, and even then, it was published anonymously under the name of a defunct foreign publisher (Cantillon, 2010 [1755], 13-14)."

The French Laissez-faire school economists studied Cantillon's manuscript for years; it brought them together, and they cited him in their treatises (Higgs, Vol. 6, No. 4 (July 1892), 453). Adam Smith spent nearly two years in France and met with these men about ten years before publishing the *Wealth of Nations,* which was his next book. He wrote a letter to David Hume during this time and said:

"I have begun to write a book in order to pass the time (Smith, Letter to David Hume from Toulouse, 5 July 1764, 1986 [1764])."

Smith must have read *Essay* because he referenced Cantillon in *The Wealth of Nations* (Smith, 1991 [1776], 72). Although well known among the top people of his day, because of the danger involved, Cantillon's book became published decades after his death and obscurely, first printed in only French and later in English. Although not as well know as Smith or Say, he had a seismic effect on those advancing economic theory. Some economists consider him the father of modern economics.

In an agrarian economy, a society much less sophisticated than our own, Cantillon uncovered the real key to understanding economics: trade driven by business activity. One of my favorite quotes of his comes from when he discussed entrepreneurship and the circular flow of money:

"...and that all the exchange and circulation of the state is conducted by the actions of these entrepreneurs (Cantillon, 2010 [1755], 77)."

Did you notice how he didn't say consumption or consumer spending circulates money, but it is "by the actions of these entrepreneurs?"

Economics is ultimately entrepreneurially created value from both sides of a transaction exchanged and circulated by entrepreneurs. Cantillon gets credit for giving us the word "entrepreneur." It comes from the French word for someone who undertakes, or takes action.

The next and best-known giant is Adam Smith. The Scottish Professor, first of moral philosophy and later of political economy, most famously wrote, *"An Inquiry into the Nature and Causes of the Wealth of Nations."* He published it in 1776, the same year the Declaration of Independence became America's freedom proclamation and political creed. What President Abraham Lincoln would later call "the spirit of the Constitution."

The Wealth of Nations became, for many, the bible of modern economics. Adam Smith made the term "free enterprise" famous, and he often described "a system of natural liberty." Smith put our economic lives, in a nutshell, this way:

"...every man thus lives by exchanging..." (Smith, 1991 [1776], 29)

The third giant is the Frenchman Jean-Baptiste Say. As Adam Smith became associated with the phrase "free enterprise," Jean-Baptiste Say became associated with the words "laissez-faire." He arguably wrote the fullest work, *A Treatise on Political Economy*. It was a standard economics textbook in Europe and America for many years before the Keynesian era; he first published it in his native France in 1803. Say's most famous quote describes "Say's Law:"

"...a product is no sooner created, than it, from that instant, affords a market for other products to the full extent of its own value (Say, 1971 [1964, 1880, 1821, 1803], 134.)."

It is interesting, and I admit heartfelt for me, seeing how while Smith referenced the English Colonies in America, Say called them the United States of America just a few years later. The United States' birth was into the ideas of natural liberty and free enterprise.

Cantillon described operational business, banking, and trade between people, communities, and states a generation before Smith. While he purposely left politics and government out of it "so as not to complicate our subject," his book is a beautiful description of an "enterprise economy." Smith and Say emphasized the government's impact too.

Smith intricately described the evils of strict mercantilist government policies. Kings and parliaments put limits on production, charged taxes and fees on everything that moved, and paid money to particular industries to give them an advantage, especially against specific rival countries and their producers. It was all in the name of national wealth through government controls. Stiff tariffs were primarily an attempt to make silver and gold money flow into their countries from a positive trade balance.

It all hindered commerce, especially non-favored businesses, those trying to get into business, and the ordinary folks. The general population got hurt by overly cumbersome regulations and high prices (Smith, Wealth of Nations, 1991 [1776], 424-445). Say also described in detail the "bad consequences" from the controlling mercantilist system (Say, 1971 [1964,1880,1821], 149).

Does mercantilist government control remind you of crooked political representation and crony capitalism? Today, many who promote bigger, more controlling government demonize both Smith and Say as if they wanted "reckless, unchecked capitalism" or "a sort of hyper-capitalism."

Is free enterprise for the greedy? Is it true they were economists for the favored few? It may surprise you that although not at all to the degree the political left pushes for today, Smith and Say both came out for progressive income taxes. When Say put it this way, does it sound like someone "all for the rich?"

"Thus, a tax merely proportionate to individual income would be far from equitable; and this is probably what Smith meant, by declaring it reasonable, that the rich man should contribute to the public expenses, not merely in proportion to the amount of his revenue, but even somewhat more. For my part, I have no hesitation in going further, and saying, that taxation cannot be equitable unless its ratio is progressive (Say, 1971 [1964,1880,1821], 455)."

Smith put it this way:

"The subjects of every state ought to contribute towards the support of the government, as nearly as possible, in proportion to their respective abilities; that is, in proportion to the revenue which they respectively enjoy under the protection of the state (Smith, Wealth of Nations, 1991 [1776], 498)."

Here, the classical economists, those most associated with the terms laissez-faire and free enterprise, call for progressive income taxes. Don't be mistaken; they wanted "easy taxes" on all, but neither man favored the rich. As Cantillon did before them, they believed that entrepreneurs drive the economy and high taxes are detrimental, not that there shouldn't be government or taxation. A light tax burden frees up the driving force in economics and helps set the stage for more prosperity for all. Say explains:

"Excessive taxation is a kind of suicide, whether laid upon objects of necessity, or upon those of luxury (Say, 1971 [1964, 1880, 1821], 450);"

Say wrote that no income tax on businesses creates the most employment. A modest progressive income tax on wages wouldn't hurt the economy as much as taxing entrepreneurs would—so they could reinvest and grow their enterprises. The government could fund essential things, but he made it clear that taxing and spending is unproductive.

"Thus, all taxation may be said to injure reproduction, inasmuch as it prevents the accumulation of productive capital (Ibid, 455)."

Say wanted taxes that harm the least:

"Such as are least injurious to reproduction (Ibid, 449)."

Public infrastructure is crucial, but we must build it frugally and intelligently. Government-funded seaports and highways increase everyone's standard of living because so much more trade occurs because of them (Ibid, 201, 443). Say argued that infrastructure is most cost-effective, with less waste, and it better serves the community when done by the local government and not at the federal level (Ibid, 445-446).

Government-funded public schools were substantially in the public interest because the vast illiterate peasantry could add far more to the country's general prosperity if they had at least a primary education. With a reading ability, the commoner could have access to the greatest minds, and who knows how much they could personally improve and contribute? With more prosperous people, you have a more prosperous nation. Say believed the government should educate:

"It would be the more unpardonable in governments to neglect the business of education (Ibid, 436)."

"Academies, libraries, public schools, and museums, founded by enlightened governments, contribute to the creation of wealth, by the further discovery of truth, and the diffusion of what was known before; thus empowering the superior agents and directors of production, to extend the application of human science to the supply of human wants (Ibid, 201)."

Some today demonize the term laissez-faire to denounce those who won't champion government intervention and control as the recipe for general prosperity. At the time, laissez-faire was a statement against the mercantile system, where kings and bureaucrats controlled and micromanaged economic activity.

Laissez-faire is about economic principles; it's a statement against the government governing the economy. It's not a statement against infrastructure or the role of responsible regulation. The government doesn't tell businesses how to operate or produce, but it enforces laws against dishonesty and a public danger. Say answered the attack that "capitalism is a free for all," or "the rule of the jungle," this way:

"...regulation is useful and proper, when aimed at the prevention of fraud or contrivance, manifestly injurious to other kinds of production, or to the public safety, and not at prescribing the nature of the products and the methods of fabrication (Ibid)."

Say expressly said the government has this right:

"...society is possessed of a natural right to regulate the exercise of any class of industry (Ibid, 181)."

Sometime during the seventeenth century, as the story goes, someone from the French government came to a meeting of businessmen and asked how the government could help them. Their response was, you can assist us if you "let us be," hence the phrase "laissez-faire." To let businesses be free to operate with the highest efficiency, thereby creating the most prosperity.

When I was in school, they told us laissez-faire meant "government hands off." The suggestion was a free-for-all, but none of these three giants wanted no government regulation. They taught that government manipulation and interference hurt prosperity and assault our natural liberty. When Adam Smith described the "invisible hand," it meant markets balance through service of others in self-interest, but he also spent much time decrying business corruption. The question is, what causes wealth in nations? What is the driving force in economics?

Keynesian economics proposes a deception: a system where government spending, even social welfare spending, really, spending for spending's sake, stimulates the economy. The truth is we must delineate what drives the economy from government spending for prosperity and fairness. Keynesianism holds that all expenditure is productive, though some may be more practical. The Giants held that unproductive consumption does not replace itself, but if productive, it does.

Productive spending creates value in a production process; the resources destroyed producing goods and services the business replaces with more valuable finished products. Unproductive consumption depletes time and commodities with nothing to show for itself. Productive spending adds value in profits and paychecks from products for exchange in trade, allowing the process to continue and grow.

When we delineate humanitarian expenditure and the economy, we see it for what it is. We can agree to help others because we should, but we must account for the cost when we do it publicly or privately. To say government spending drives the economy is false. Our taxed profits and wages, paid from on-going enterprises, support public expenditures; government spending does not uphold the economy. Keynes flipped economics on its head by asserting that government and consumer spending drive the economy, but how does putting the cart before the horse allow him to pull it?

Cantillon and Smith commented on false ideas that sounded like Keynes would later develop, but Say put it unmistakably this way:

"...since a thing cannot be consumed before it is produced, (they) have confounded the cause with the effect, and laid it down as a maxim, that consumption originates production; therefore that frugality is directly adverse to public prosperity, and that the most useful citizen is the one who spends the most." (Ibid, 407)

The basic erroneous ideas existed before Keynes made them famous (or infamous). Say summed up Keynesian economics and refuted it about a hundred and thirty years before Keynes invented his theories. So, why do we have such low family and personal savings and high government and household debt after about eighty years of putting the ideas into practice?

John Maynard Keynes wrote many articles and several books. His final book, *The General Theory of Employment, Interest, and Money,* countered and tried to discredit the very foundation the Giants and those before them laid. Twentieth-century academia embraced Keynes' ideas and even expanded them lovingly; they gushed over him as a hero.

For decades, many academics snubbed Hayek, considered him a reactionary to their progressive ideas, and treated him as a pariah. He retained a following mainly in conservative circles and right-leaning and libertarian think tanks. His larger vindication came not until the 1980s, Reagan era.

Keynesian economics defines progressive era economics, and with some fits and starts, we're still in the progressive era. Look at both our main political parties. The Democrats claim they are progressives. The Republicans say they are not, but they don't repeal many hindering and destructive laws when they get power. Sometimes they pass additional bureaucratic and reckless spending legislation without the Democrat's help!

Why has the national debt skyrocketed since the inception of progressive era economics? We can chart the spending and regulatory policies, especially from President Woodrow Wilson onward, although their most extensive implementation began in 1931. Keynes published the comprehensive economic theory in 1936 to support the beliefs for much fuller demand-pull theoretical control.

Keynesian thinking became embedded in our understanding. The two opposing schools of thought eventually became the central economic arguments behind our two political parties, but with Keynesian confusion mixed into Republican ideas too. Economics professors may lean one way more than the other, or they may attempt to give opposing theories equal time—almost to say they don't favor one political party over the other.

Do they deny reality for political correctness? Do they think contrary approaches can both be correct? Do they teach things they don't believe, giving them equal time to keep their jobs?

Is it that the Colleges and Universities mainly hire Keynesians, while PhDs with solid economic theoretical foundations must find work in conservative think tanks? Are they only passing along what they've learned?

My college professors mainly taught us economics with a hyphen, Smith-Keynes. Adam Smith was the foundation, but we needed Keynes too. You might describe it as oil-water economics, but how well do things work together that don't mix well together?

Part II

Economic and Political Confusion

"The history of all hitherto existing society is the history of class struggles."

Karl Marx

3

Enter Confusion

"The Proletariat (workers) will use its political supremacy to wrest, by degrees, all capital from the bourgeoisie (owners), to centralize all instruments of production in the hands of the state...of the proletariat organized as the ruling class."

Karl Marx

ADAM SMITH THEORIZED that in a primitive society, the measure of value is in one's labor. In more complex civilizations operating with the division of labor and professional specialties, we are rich or poor in how much of other people's effort we can command, including for services, finished goods, and commodities. Although money and "haggling over commodities" might be the best way to determine immediate prices, over time, it is labor that tells us most accurately what something is worth (Smith, Wealth of Nations, 1991 [1776], 36-38).

Smith wasn't the first to believe in a labor theory of value. Some earlier well-known writers, including John Locke and Sir William Perry, similarly erred. Smith may have gotten ideas directly from Benjamin Franklin. They were reportedly friendly, and while living in Britain, Franklin offered Smith his opinion on drafts of The Wealth of Nations.

Franklin described his view in *A Modest Enquiry into the Nature and Necessity of a Paper-Currency*. He mistakenly argued that all values, whether for silver or other commodities, are labor time derived (Franklin, 1729).

Today, economists rightly consider labor theories of value antiquated and erroneous. Smith summed up his version this way:

"Labour, therefore, it appears evidently, is the only universal, as well as the only accurate measure of value, or the only standard by which we can compare the values of different commodities at all times and at all places (Smith, 1991 [1776], 43)."

Following Adam Smith in what became called the Classical School, the English economist David Ricardo unwittingly lay the foundation for Karl Marx by expanding his labor theory of value and theorizing about class conflict (Skousen, 2007, 54-55). Ricardo personally struggled and never made peace with this work because he tried to prove production costs govern prices instead of realizing utility to the buyer determines them subjectively (Ibid, 59-60).

Another well-known English economist, John Stewart Mill, solidified the English Classical School's errors as economist Mark Skousen describes in his book, *The Big Three in Economics: Adam Smith, Karl Marx, and John Maynard Keynes*:

"It was principally through John Stewart Mill that the next generation adopted this classical model that was more in line with Ricardo's system of "class conflict" than Adam Smith's upbeat "harmony of interests" model (Ibid, 60)."

Karl Marx came on the scene in the mid-nineteenth century and tried to correct everyone with his expanded labor theory of value. He selectively quoted Benjamin Franklin to build an argument for his much more radical ideas in his book, *Critique on Political Economy* (Marx, Critique of Political Economy, 1970 [1859], 56).

Richard Cantillon had it right a generation before Adam Smith as he distinguished between "intrinsic value" and "market value." The intrinsic value was in production costs, as he defined it, costs, "...proportional to the land and labor that enter into their production (Cantillon, 2010 [1755], 103)."

Cantillon went on to describe the "market value of metals, as with other commodities and merchandise" and their utility to the buyer, or "are found useful," this way:

"...as these metals are found useful and employed in everyday life, they will always have a market value corresponding to their abundance or scarcity, and the demand for them (Ibid, 104)."

In continuity with Cantillon, in the Laissez-faire School in France, we see Jean-Baptise Say correcting Smith and the others in plain language in two quotes below:

"Exchangeable value, or price, is an index of the recognized utility of a thing (Say, 1971 [1964,1880,1821], 62) ..."

"...the value of products is not founded upon that of productive agency, as some authors have erroneously affirmed; and that since the desire of an object, and consequently its value, originates in its utility (Ibid, 287) …"

Although Richard Cantillon and then the Laissez-faire School and Jean-Baptiste Say had this right many years earlier, it took what economists call the Marginalist, or the Subjectivist Revolution in the later nineteenth century to correct the mistakes coming out of England.

Unfortunately, Karl Marx, who by this time lived in London, had already exploited it all and took his radical theories to the boundaries of cynicism. Marx founded his whole program on his labor theory of value, worker exploitation, and class conflict.

In another piece to our economic and political confusion puzzle, a generation before Mill, Thomas Malthus, the founder of Malthusian Theory, an Anglican Church clergyman, and David Ricardo's friend, theorized about geometrical population growth compared to food sources increasing only arithmetically. He believed we would run out of food worldwide at an ever-nearing future date.

His theory eventually helped justify rising movements spreading throughout the world in population control, eugenics, and radical environmentalism. Ironically, a religious minister's ideas seeded a campaign against the biblical command, "Be fruitful and multiply," and controlling schemes of redistribution, instead of economic growth, began feeding into these beliefs.

Although Malthus may have had good intentions, his projections were shortsighted. In reality, we need fewer people farming and processing per person because of advancing technology and better methods. We have an increasing abundance of food. Growth, no pun intended, is always the answer, not control and stagnation.

The significant advances in science and technology preceding "The Enlightenment," even the scientific method, came from within the philosophical boundaries of God's natural world working harmoniously. With the stage set, technology continually improved into the nineteenth century and beyond, but science became untethered to divine expression. Civilizations are never all good or evil, but behavior changed.

Charles Darwin and his theory of evolution and many new atheist philosophers and prominent economists around Europe promoted eugenics and selective human breeding. Cynicism ascended, and intellectuals preached about the superiority of some races over others.

Today, some theologians refer to "The Enlightenment" as "The Endarkenment" because traditionally sacred beliefs became challenged, marginalized, and ignored. It's interesting how so much beautiful art, architecture, literature, music, and societal advancement came out of the middle ages, now pejoratively called "the dark ages," because it was a profoundly religious time. If we don't recognize the beauty, we may miss the designs of those who've supplied us with a cynical one-sided story.

Put BBC Spanish Inquisition 99% Myth into youtube, and you'll see a fascinating documentary explaining false accusations and exaggerated numbers regarding execution and torture. The British Broadcasting Corporation, usually no friend of the Catholic Church, sheds considerable light on the subject. As far as bad things we've done to each other historically, the Spanish Inquisition is minimal compared to so much else. How often do we hear this? They say the Inquisition courts were the fairest in Europe; the government courts had the worst record.

Have you ever heard of Anglo-Saxon justice? The British are very proud of their court system, but the truth is, the Inquisition gave them the model for their courts—and by extension, ours. Do you want to go before a barbarian king for justice? If England hadn't adopted the Catholic court system and made it the government model, we'd all have it far worse.

Despite the eugenics thinking "The Enlightenment" produced, secularism didn't evolve humanity. Instead of a religious philosopher like Thomas Aquinas contemplating God as Love, pessimist thinkers like Friedrich Nietzsche pontificated on "the death of God." The societal Christian edifice was cracking from a sustained attack against foundational morals.

The twentieth century not only brought a culmination of atheist communist and fascist governments killing uncounted tens of millions, but even in relative peace after the great wars, the secularists established a pattern of attack. When they couldn't sway popular opinion or persuade the politicians to make the laws they wanted, they sued and used the courts to reinterpret existing laws or judge the Constitution by progressive social mores. It's often easier to persuade judges of elitist beliefs than it is the common man. Another pattern followed. With the judges' modernist rulings, the people fell in line and supported the very different social mores.

Can you imagine a more stark and controversial example of a complete change in mores than this? After decades of pressure from secular influences championing selective breeding and "woman's rights," most Protestant groups and denominations forgot that virtually all Christians had always been staunchly against artificial contraception and abortion. Do you think it's backward even to question these things? Eventually, most Catholics, too, played ignorance and ignored these apostolic teachings against continued Church proclamations. Today, most people believe being against these things is controversial when sixty years ago, being for them was almost unthinkable for most. What happened over time? "Enlightenment" thinking set the stage, and politics and traditional morality, eventually even challenging the family unit, were divorcing.

Eugenics became widely popular among mid-nineteenth and early twentieth-century European and American intellectuals. Adolf Hitler gives us a maniacally evil example of how far such Godless beliefs can go.

Skepticism and secular atheism birthed Karl Marx, the father of socialist economics. He had the ammunition to attack the foundational economic and societal principles, exemplifying how bad it can get.

Man, not God, was master of the universe. Abolish religion, the opiate of the people, and rise to human potential. Adam Smith's "invisible hand," which many understood as the hand of Providence, was only an excuse for exploitation. You could say man's cynicism replaced "natural liberty." Marx declared:

"...it (religion) is the opiate of the people." "To abolish religion as the illusory happiness of the people is to demand their real happiness." (Marx, Contribution to the Critique of Hegel's Philosophy of Law, 1999 [1844]) 126."

All things sacred in bourgeois society Marx endeavored to destroy. No saving the old system for him, with a vengeance, at all levels, he called for cleansing and total reordering:

"The Communist revolution is the most radical rupture with traditional relations; no wonder that its development involves the most radical rupture from traditional ideals (Marx & Engels, The Communist Manifesto, 1998 [1848], 74)."

"Abolition of the family! Even the most radical flare up at this infamous proposal of the Communists. On what foundation is the present family, the bourgeois based? On capital, on private gain." "The bourgeois family will vanish when its complement vanishes, and both will vanish with the vanishing of capital (Ibid, 71)."

"Its complement" meant the proletarian family, which also vanishes as the people become obedient to the state. Your children no longer obey you but the Communist Party leaders. In a tirade, Marx accused the ownership class, the bourgeois, of exploiting the wives and daughters of the proletariat, the working class, wife swapping amongst themselves, and engaging in prostitution while holding up religion and family values. He called the ruling class hypocrites because they objected to a Communist government offering professional prostitutes (Ibid).

"The bourgeois claptrap about the family and education, about that hallowed correlation of parent and child, becomes all the more disgusting...". He goes on to say it's because current society destroys proletariat families as "simple articles of commerce and instruments of labour (Ibid 71-72)."

Marx's pure socialism is very dark. It's all accusations. He uses a pervasive tactic among liars and hypocrites: if some sin gravely, he accuses the whole group of it and condemns them all. He blames others for violence, for prostitution, for brainwashing the kids into their way of life, and then mean-spiritedly declares the Communists will do all these things.

"Do you charge us with wanting to stop the exploitation of children by their parents? To this we plead guilty. But you will say we destroy the most hallowed relations, when we replace home education by social." "The Communists have not invented the intervention of society in education; they do but seek to alter the character of that intervention, and to rescue education from the influence of the ruling class (Ibid)."

Societal overthrow meant flipping social, cultural, and religious institutions on their heads, with an atheist working class becoming the rulers and the former ownership class, the bourgeois, subservient. It's all justification for property seizure and a complete government takeover:

"The Proletariat will use its political supremacy to wrest, by degrees, all capital from the bourgeoisie, to centralize all instruments of production in the hands of the state...of the proletariat organized as the ruling class (Ibid, 75)...

Marx and his partner Friedrich Engels reached an existing socialist movement concerned with indecent working conditions and looking for a better way, organized it, and made it much more radical. They convinced them with writings and rhetoric and told the workers to bring it on. They ended the *Communist Manifesto* this way:

"The Communists disdain to conceal their views and aims. They openly declare that their ends can be attained only by the forcible overthrow of all existing social conditions. Let the ruling classes tremble at a Communistic revolution. The proletarians have nothing to lose but their chains. They have a world to win.

WORKING MEN OF ALL COUNTRIES, UNITE (Ibid, 91)!"

Some may have felt a retributive sadistic justice against the rich. Still, for many profoundly heartfelt naïve people concerned about working conditions, the spin of local Marxist organizers might have sounded good. They may have believed without ever reading or understanding the ideas. There were miserable, even abusive, and inhumane working conditions in many industrial factories in the nineteenth and early twentieth centuries. Much disillusionment remained from Christian groups fighting and persecuting each other for years throughout Europe.

Migrations from family farms into crowded, stinking smog-filled industrial revolution era cities caused working-poor populations to explode. Marx must have struck a chord with many people of all types who had turned away from traditional Christian beliefs to secular humanism as they began to believe in the collective. Some earlier socialists gained adherents using the Bible and Christian rhetoric, but Marx came out even against God.

Not until the twentieth century 1917 Bolshevik Revolution in Russia did we get the first real taste of Marx's theories put into practice when Lenin became Marxism's anti-hero. Eventually, more than half the world's population lived under it, primarily by force, until it receded in miserable failure.

Marx and Engels published their political creed, the *Communist Manifesto,* in 1848. Still, their movement remained a small fringe collection of radicals for many years in various countries, slowly building adherents over time. Almost twenty years later, his magnum opus of high theory, *Capital,* tried to prove his ideas. According to economist Mark Skousen:

"His work culminated in his classic *Das Kapital,* published in German in 1867. *Capital* (the English title) introduced economic determinism and a new "exploitive" theory of capitalism based on universal "scientific" laws discovered by Marx." "Marx considered his work the bible of the working class..." "Marx viewed himself as the Darwin of society (Skousen, 2007, 80) ..."

It's common knowledge very few people showed up at Marx's funeral. Some sources say as few as seven; some give a few more. His family was indeed not religious unless you consider Marxism their faith. His two surviving adult daughters committed suicide at different times after his death.

Neither the *Communist Manifesto, Capital,* nor any of his other writings were successful or substantially well received at his end. He had organized international worker movements, but Communism was still mainly waiting in the wings. Frederick Engels, his longtime comrade, who reportedly often provided him money when he couldn't pay his bills, gave the eulogy at Marx's funeral, lauding and comparing him to the father of evolutionary theory:

"Just as Darwin discovered the law of development of organic nature, so Marx discovered the law of development of human history..." "Marx also discovered the special law of motion governing the present-day capitalist mode of production and the bourgeois society that this mode of production has created. The discovery of surplus value (Engels, 1883) ..."

Marx's whole worker exploitation economics depends on his surplus-value theory. He posited that labor determines value as others erroneously had before him, but he went further, mocking and demonizing entrepreneurs. He described how they struggle to make profits and pay workers subsistence wages so that anything their labor creates beyond that they unfairly forgo. Owner interest, profit, and rent were part of "surplus value (Marx, Capital Volume I, 1887 [1867], 131-138, 148)." In other words, owner profit is theft under capitalism. There is no profit, only exploitation.

The "Liberation School," a Marxist organization, demonstrates surplus value theory in simple terms this way:

"For part of the day, the workers produce the value that covers the cost of their own existence. In essence, what the workers produce the rest of the day is unpaid labor (Liberation School, 2006)."

In reality, there is no "surplus value." Those who dream, design, organize, implement ideas, take risks, execute, and follow-through earn their profits—and they must live with their losses. Entrepreneurial ideas are the driving force for societal advancement, and workers at subsistence wages have the freedom and mobility to move up or move on.

The fuel for Marx's thoughts was class conflict, and he was wrong in theory and practice. He was cynical and controlling, blind regarding natural liberty and the high value in competitive productivity. History shows us the opposite of his predictions. The "workers of the world" didn't unite in revolt; instead, wages increased overall with rising profits. "Capitalism" provides a substantial middle class and the highest societal standard of living. It raises people out of poverty faster than anything else and is self-sustaining, unlike giving people handouts or taking away their freedom for an elitist collective vision. Marx didn't appreciate the enormous benefits from entrepreneurs inspirationally creating better things for their fellow man.

Without exception, wherever Marxism took control, it destroyed prosperity, often horribly lowering the standard of living, stifled advancement, and produced far fewer technological improvements. Sometimes, almost immediately, food shortages and starvation resulted. Usually, an ardent and violent minority forced it on the majority through a military coup and then held it in place through a totalitarian dictatorship.

Marxian economics doesn't work. It never produced prosperity but degradation and poverty. Look at Venezuela today, a formally prosperous nation with starving oppressed people fleeing for food. Shouldn't it shock us that there are economics departments stealthily and sometimes openly teaching it in our universities today? Oddball professors may be poisoning some of your children's minds right now. How is this possible?

It's interesting how Marx countered Jean-Baptiste Say by claiming labor originates value, not the entrepreneur implementing his ideas. John Maynard Keynes opposed Say by claiming consumption drives the economy instead of successful entrepreneurs. The enduring truth is it's our inspired business production that originates the value we exchange from both sides of a transaction; it all starts with an idea and continues with competition through the process of creating and trading.

Today, within muddled minds, leftist beliefs drive sugar-coated movements that influence the naïve. With our societal loss of a moral compass and economic confusion, Marx and Keynes still have mixed-up political proponents crying out for "social and economic justice."

4

Progressive Confusion

"We believe that working people should run both the economy and society democratically to meet human needs, not to make profits for a few."

Democratic Socialists of America

THE NEO-MARXIST YOUTH movement we see today is more confused than ever, but they have an ugly influence, especially among college kids and those susceptible to radical ideas. Believing it can give an angry and confused person meaning in life. They're among the most disturbed young socialists.

They claim they're anti-fascist but use fascist tactics and violence, but their Marxist rhetoric exposes their benefactors. Their cartoonish fraud is that they're communists violently attacking and defending the country from fascists like this is the Spanish civil war.

For the most part, they aren't assaulting fascists but traditional Americans who love freedom. The news media makes a huge hype when they attack a usually much smaller group of neo-Nazis; they call them counter-protesters against a hate group. The truth is they're both socialist punks looking for trouble, but Antifa is a much more prevalent and openly violent problem today. There isn't an American flag that they don't want to tear down or burn up and the mainstream media covers for them.

It seems those behind the scenes, pulling the kids' strings, want agitation leading to anarchy first, to destabilize the system. When they turn up the heat, they're amazingly well organized, with protests popping up in many cities across the country on the same day, holding the same signs, and chanting the same slogans. Do you think kids who can't even explain what they believe or why they're protesting organized it all so well by themselves?

The "useful idiots" are susceptible to these nasty specious beliefs, but the cure is knowledge, strength, understanding, persuasion, and perseverance in the face of it. Better parenting is vital first. Our youth must learn about real economics from early on: productivity, growth, and how we create value and exchange with each other. These movements always use redistribution of wealth schemes, whether they're openly violent or claim they're peaceful. Today, revolutionary socialism is rearing its ugly head in the fringe, but long ago, "progressives" embedded Keynesianism into our system.

Keynes came on the scene when many academics still hoped for a Marxist future. He visited the Soviet Union just a few years after its inception when many called it the new model society. Although Keynes was a quintessential progressive, progress towards the government bringing justice and prosperity in an enlightened society was impossible with brutes steering the ship.

Keynes then openly ridiculed Marxism. He supported the Labour Party in Great Britain, but many of his closest friends were Fabian Socialists. Their goal still today is Democratic Socialism. How much is today's Labour Party in England like America's Democratic Party? How far removed philosophically are either from Democratic Socialism? According to the Democratic Socialists of America's website, they now openly infiltrate the Democratic Party.

"Like our friends and allies in the feminist, labor, civil rights, religious, and community organizing movements, many of us have been active in the Democratic Party. We work with those movements to strengthen the party's left-wing, represented by the Congressional Progressive Caucus (Democratic Socialists of America, 2018)."

Their statement admits they work alongside those other groups to pull the Democratic Party to the left, and their attack is from within. How successful are they? Today, moderate Democrats seem nearly extinct, and in this recent election, several Democratic Socialists won election to Congress as Democrats. How radically left-wing are those other groups? Very.

An exception is traditional religious institutions, but socialists are on the inside working on them wherever possible: they undermine and destroy them by attacking their foundational moral beliefs. They may even believe they're changing them for the better, but in time, if the corroding trend doesn't stop, they first become a hollow shell, then culturally irrelevant, and next, the empty church buildings are sold off.

The Fabian Socialists' Society, still active in England, doesn't officially call for immediate violent overthrow but promotes Democratic Socialism through an incremental societal formation with patient waiting for the right moment. They want to mold the world with collectivist ideas, prepare themselves and the world, and hammer it into proper formation. Their website shows this, their traditional motto:

"For the right moment you must wait, as Fabius did most patiently when warring against Hannibal, though many censured his delays; but when the time comes you must strike hard, as Fabius did, or your waiting will be in vain, and fruitless." (Fabian Society, 2018)

They claim they're peaceful, but the anticipation of warfare before they "strike hard" is their motto. Even before any active assault, "progress" is always toward more control and bureaucracy. The philosophy is collective, by committee, typically lead by a dictator, but it misses the individual's drive to create and stand out successfully. How many historical examples are there of one inspired free businessman changing the world? They would demonize Steve Jobs for building an empire as greedy. They might accuse him of stealing resources from the community, things he bought to make computers for so many people. They might call him a thief, as Karl Marx would.

The Democratic Socialists of America's website introductory video called "Thanks Capitalism" says as much:

"Capitalism is a man-made economic system based on profit. It takes wealth and resources away from the public and puts it in the hands of private capitalists. A few become enormously wealthy on the backs of the many. This consolidated control of profit and political power leads to extreme inequality. These factors all make capitalism profoundly alienating. Which is why everyone and everything seems so distant, so hopeless, so odd (Democratic Socialists of America, 2018)."

It sounds like Marx wrote it for them, but it might be more sophisticated than his starkly driving prose. Underneath their softer words is, disregarding the value of entrepreneurship, social evolution beyond capitalism, and collectivism. You don't need to scratch the surface to see Marxist economic theory but notice something else. Look at the words in those last two lines, "...capitalism profoundly alienating" and "...everyone and everything seems so distant, so hopeless, so odd." They are psychologically praying on the potentially depressed, those young and emotionally vulnerable; it is chilling. Do you want your kids falling into these peoples' hands?

In reality, it isn't "a man-made economic system," but we produce and trade naturally, or we don't eat or improve our lives. We've done it farther back than all ancient records show. People become wealthy because they produce valuable things for others and trade with them, and we can think freely, imagine, and create, so resources are unlimited.

Tactically they work inside societal structures, including our schools, and just like Marx wrote in the *Communist Manifesto,* they have replaced traditional education with "social." Our schools, and especially our universities, couldn't bear this more reliable witness. They attack by accusing their targeted opponents of racism, sexism, and discrimination against LGBTQ and whatever other letters they can add on as a wedge between people. They appeal to young peoples' emotional pain, talking about "safe spaces" and "triggers," and are at war with free speech, especially on college campuses. They think nothing of demonizing political opponents personally and destroying individual lives; it's all part of the ends justifying the means.

It's a design for instability in the short term, to shake things up and break down traditional society. In the long run, they control. What does "wait" to "strike hard" mean? Our leftist politicians use softer precursor buzzwords like the government must "right wrongs" and "level the playing field," but is the underlying philosophy emerging in violent radical kids we see on the news daily?

Who are these youths donning black masks and attacking older folks while blocking the street, smashing their car windows, and derisively mocking their white skin? They look like middle-class white kids. Is this crazy? Have you seen the various images on the news showing kids chanting slogans robotically, with older leaders leading them in what looks like brainwashing sessions? These "heroes" then went out violently "protesting" Supreme Court nominee, Judge Kavanagh. It didn't look like peaceful public dissent but threats and violence. What does this become but domestic terrorism?

The Democratic Socialists of America have now captivated so many of our youth; an enormous number of them voted for Bernie Sanders for President. According to a Washington Post article dated June 20, 2016, about three weeks before Sanders conceded to Clinton and after twenty-one states had already voted in the primary:

"More young people voted for Bernie Sanders than Trump and Clinton combined—by a lot." "Sanders, in fact, won about 29 percent more votes among those under the age of 30 (Blake, 2016)."

Sanders appeals to young people on a very human level. Do you remember his bumper sticker, "Real People Real Power," but what kind of power is this? Is it group supremacy against those they demonize? It isn't a call for individual liberty and free association, but collectivism.

What does "working people should run the economy and society" mean? Does it make any sense? To revisit the heading quote at the beginning of this chapter from their website:

"We believe that working people should run both the economy and society democratically to meet human needs, not to make profits for a few (Democratic Socialists of America, 2018)."

The proletariat (working people) runs the economy and society democratically? Or, as Marx put it, "...to centralize all instruments of production in the hands of the state...of the proletariat organized as the ruling class."

Marx foresaw those sympathetic and educated running the movement in the working class's name, representing them. He and his associates, in other words, run the government. The Communist Party leaders control the people but in the worker's interests. America's creed of "We The People" never meant the government controls the people, but the other way around.

There is no entrepreneurial value in the Democratic Socialist's thinking but only Marxist principles. It isn't mutual production and exchange but socialism. They say they're "Democratic," but communist societies worldwide always claim "Democracy." So, there's a slight structural difference between them and Communists? Their website has the following slogan, all capitalized, on a big picture of Bernie Sanders speaking to a huge crowd:

"RESISTANCE RISING. SOCIALIST STRATEGY IN AN AGE OF POLITICAL REVOLUTION (Ibid)."

Is this what you want for your kids? Proletariat "resistance" against the bourgeoisie and "revolution" in America? "White male oppressors" are now "the ruling class" to target and demonize. They use race, gender, sexual confusion, and disparities in wealth with anything else they can to divide society, or as Marx put it, to "wrest power."

Your kids must understand the underlying economic and philosophical principles. If they know the growth and operational aspects of valuable production and exchange compared with the deterioration of confiscation and redistribution, we can nip it in the bud. We must teach them the history of these ideas, how crazy they are, and how the youth have always been useful idiots for these movements. Bernie is sugar-coating an old story that fails horrifically every time.

Government economic control is never the answer, but how much has this permeated our society? The mainstream media are now propagandists for the left. Today, many are furious about the Republicans controlling the White House, Congress, and the Supreme Court. They say things like, "we need to take back *our* government." I heard some left-leaning cable news anchors recently saying, "Trump is in *our* White House!" "We the People" is an exclusive collectivist concept to them, it seems. Not included are those who believe in the individual pursuit of happiness through business freedom with traditional moral beliefs; we're the enemy; they must attack and marginalize us to take back *their* government.

"We the People" isn't all of us, but only those who agree with them. How could they be so angry if it's only our turn? Without control, they lose progress. They fear their forming of society is slipping. They outwardly proclaim, "Trump is ruining *our* country," when the economic numbers look pretty darn good.

Losing the Supreme Court agitated the left because they fear they can't continue using it to socially form the troglodytes, to hammer us into socialist shape. Although many of them may not be conscious of it, they've received "social" education to function that way. It's eerie like they've had brainwashing or something is working in them they don't understand, yet their odd, bitter, and vicious emotional behavior is before our eyes. Just turn on cable TV if you want to see more than you can stomach.

Bernie and the Democratic Socialists of America believe the federal government should control and do many big things, but according to their website, local control may mean this:

"Social ownership could take many forms, such as worker-owned cooperatives or publicly owned enterprises managed by workers and consumer representatives (Ibid)."

Will it require changing our Constitution to deny individual real property rights to secure "social ownership?" "Publicly owned enterprises managed by workers and consumer representatives?" It sounds like Marx promoting the sympathetic educated class as "representatives" running things for the workers (and consumers). How entrepreneurial is all of this? They openly admit their goal is to eliminate private corporations:

"In the short term we can't eliminate private corporations, but we can bring them under greater democratic control. The government could use regulations (Ibid)..."

Look at the words above: they equate "democratic control" with "government" actions. They aren't liberals but progressively authoritarian—what a twist. It's okay with conservatives if they or anyone else run their business as a cooperative, a sole proprietorship, a partnership, or a corporation; all are free and welcome to experiment in our world. Freedom and experimentation are the answer, not control. It turns out Bernie is a bully! When you scratch beneath the surface, Marxists always are.

Our kids are now socialized to believe moral licentiousness is healthy and collective control honorable. How did this happen? It's backward. People with a strong faith in God are far less likely to act irresponsibly, to hurt themselves or others. How many of these Antifa kids are atheists, I wonder? Whose fault is this? How high must youth suicide rates go before we get it? How many drug overdoses must we endure? Have we gotten morally lazy? Who raised the Bernie bros?

When did they replace Sunday solemnity with watching football? Did their parents stop going to Church, or was it their grandparents? They have no faith and have turned to secular humanism for a reason. They didn't lose it or grow up without it in a vacuum. What underlies a moral and ethical society? Even if you've tried and done the right things, your kids still suffer many deranged influences as good is called evil and evil is called good today.

Our culture is now so confused we have many choices on government forms to claim how we "identify" instead of knowing the objective reality of who and what we are genetically and physically as a man or a woman. I just had to fill one out yesterday at the hospital!

The societal shift into secular humanism and away from our traditional faith has many social and economic consequences—today, an increasing number of people can't say who they are. How does a relativist define morality? The attack against us for holding traditional moral beliefs compared with the exaltation of ideas only a generation ago considered immoral or crazy exemplifies confusion. It's not that society won't let us make judgments because political correctness is very judgmental; the attacks come from those who call us evil to hold traditionally wholesome beliefs. A bathroom is no longer a private place for a woman, even for school kids, in many politicians, bureaucrats, and judges' minds. It seems to keep political alliances so-called "feminists" support it. Our government, college professors, the entertainment industry, and most news media demonize Christian moral values. Our public schools now indoctrinate or socialize our kids. How did it happen, and where is this strange process going?

Can you honestly deny that what "progressives" advocate today is progressing to a further socialist reworking of society? Might you call it a "fundamental transformation" as President Barak Obama did? What could he have meant by that expression on the eve of his election? Can you understand why it made so many of us uncomfortable?

Understanding Bernie Sanders and the Democratic Socialists comes from seeing Karl Marx theoretically throughout their propaganda; their economics is Marxist. Keynes and what's behind his demand-pull theory become apparent because of who embraces him now. Economists try to divorce economics from politics; this is absurd. They want to claim they theorize without bias but follow the different schools of thought, and they lead you directly into the opposing political camps.

Fearing to touch the third rail of economics, politics, only allows crafty politicians the opportunity to confuse the public into voting for them. Some socialists may be true believers, but either way, they prosper by your ignorance, and their plans will eventually trigger our societal collapse.

There's no economic dynamism in collectivism. How can there be any doubt that the driving force in economics is entrepreneurialism? Isn't this how Henry Ford's ideas became Ford Motor Company, with all the people they employ, and with all their purchasing, producing, and selling?

Richard Cantillon gave us a beautiful explanation of an enterprise economy and the "entrepreneur." Adam Smith described a "system of natural liberty" and "free enterprise." Jean-Baptiste Say gave us a practical textbook with the operational benefits of "laissez-faire."

Keynes and Marx didn't build on nature but their imaginations, ignoring natural workings. They didn't shape, clarify, or describe classical economics; they countered it. Marx invented a destructive, radical economic and social theory, but what are we to make of Keynes?

Through implementing his "necessary measures of socialization (Keynes, The General Theory of Employment Interest and Money, 1936, 378)," Keynes offered public investment, credit expansion, and government-created full employment. Marx promised a collectivist society, saving us from exploitative bourgeoisie capitalism. Keynes was to take us partway there.

Today we face a socialist spectrum from violent Marxists to many Keynesian Democratic Party members, but none of them knows what he's doing in economic theory. The laws and policies they ardently support are almost invariably counterproductive; their answers never include freedom.

Marx and Keynes are the underlying theorists for it all. Both men claimed they wanted a man to rise to his potential. Marx wanted a wholly government-owned and collective society leading to utopia, and Keynes a politically managed and controlled economy with progressive secular ideals.

Keynes still has half the political world pushing for him and his ideas. They usually don't call for his complete program, but they use it to change the social structure. Others, it seems, always want more Keynesian theory put in place but incrementally or progressively.

Today we see how so many years of Keynes' false theories lead to Neo-Marxism. We hear both of their rhetoric advantageously mixed into expansionist government arguments with more social and economic control.

Marx was precisely wrong because our entrepreneurial activity is the lifeblood of economics. He didn't value our creative business ideas, and he didn't appreciate the human desire to supply the community or other individuals with something better. Freedom allows inspired creative people to naturally race ahead of the pack implementing their ideas, providing us with all the fruits of their ambition, but collectivist economic schemes hold them down.

Everything man-made around you is the manifestation of someone's thoughts. Will people dream without freedom? What drives the diligence to produce? Can a bureaucrat force it efficiently? Experience shows us people won't continue building things on sheer cooperation with no self-interest. Without something gained, they stop working. They must have incentives.

In claiming consumption drives the economy, Keynes didn't respect entrepreneurship either. Demand doesn't create; it just wants. It can't come first. Production always acts first as it creates value. Supply and demand determine prices that signal producers and consumers when and how to move efficiently, but economics simply defined is trade. Both sides of any exchange must have a commodity or service the other party wants or needs or the proceeds of their previous production in hand for a transfer of value. As Jean-Baptiste Say put it:

"...money is but the agent of the transfer of values." (Say, 1971 [1964, 1821, 1880], 133)

A lower price can increase the demand for something that already exists, but it doesn't create value; it only changes perception. Does this improved opinion or increased demand create more supply? No, it doesn't make anything. The entrepreneur meets needs or generates desires by successfully producing and marketing if he chooses. If he can't get a high enough price to cover costs and make a profit, he won't; he decides what he'll make.

As our national debt grows, central banks in advanced countries now play a dangerous shell game. With printed and borrowed money, they compete in devaluing our currencies. How will this behavior end? When comes instability?

Marxism ends general prosperity much faster than Keynesianism because it pulls life right out of the economy; in fact, it quickly destroys it. Keynesianism hinders more slowly with no driving force in it.

Keynesianism creates a "fizzle" in economic activity through increased government spending. It redirects incomes and redistributes wealth for the social engineer's current vision. The government robs Peter to pay Paul through steep progressive income tax rates. It takes investment capital away from producers to redistribute it through a bureaucratic process to spending non-producers.

Keynesianism allows politicians to claim they're doing something to improve the economy while slowing economic transactions by government hindrances—as the public debt grows over time. The expressed Keynesian goal is a mixed economy for more stability and prosperity. The result is stifled and hindered activity by an ever-expanding government.

Marx's theories are more honest than Keynes': they attack freedom directly. Keynes' ideas are more deceptive than Marx's: they destroy over time as the government grows beyond a crippled economy's ability to support it. This continuing loss of efficiency reflects Keynes' idea of a gradual "socialization" of the economy.

Our impressive high-tech gains don't produce all they should in the face of this progressive loss of efficiency. Still, without the new technologies, our society would likely have already collapsed. Where does it all end? When does the public debt-encumbered house of cards come tumbling down? Who will ultimately take firmer control to quell impending financial implosion and anarchy? Under which form of socialism will we suffer?

How far can the "progressives" in Congress push for more control, spending, and restrictive laws? Radicals from inside our legislature now hide their Marxism in plain sight. Rep. Ocasio-Cortez refers to the Communist Manifesto openly when she talks about a future beyond capitalism. "The Green New Deal" looks like a plan to collapse our economy and force us into a Marxist society. Their new illusory angle is to create green paradise earth through "climate change" fear tactics. How sly. Marx would be proud. We've elected Socialists who conveniently caucus with the Democrats but now brazenly threaten our economy and society. Have you noticed how they rhetorically use Keynes' demand-pull theory mixed with Marxism? There is a constant push for colossal deficit spending.

What happens if we can't produce efficiently enough to stay ahead of our debt payments? Given the amount of our public debt, what if inflation causes interest rates to go up, resulting in interest costs higher than our national tax receipts? How much more would we devalue our currency if we tried to print and borrow to spend our way out of it? Can we justify leaving our kids with this much debt? Do good people readily pass along this kind of problem to their children?

When will all this deficit spending become for us like our founding father's fourth but lethal bloodletting? What would George Washington say of all this?

5

What Keynes Believed

"I shall argue that the postulates of the classical theory are applicable to a special case only and not to the general case...its teaching is misleading and disastrous..."

John Maynard Keynes

M ANY PEOPLE TODAY claim Keynes believed in free markets. They say to employ Keynesian economics during cyclical downturns, but the rest of the time, most of the time, the free market should prevail. Keynes did not believe this.

In the first paragraph of his final book, the book that launched his new theories and, according to him, corrected and clarified his previous books, *"The General Theory of Employment, Interest, and Money,"* he threw classical economics on its head from the start:

"I shall argue that the postulates of the classical theory are applicable to a special case only and not to the general case, the situation which it assumes being a limited point of the possible positions of equilibrium. Moreover, the characteristics of the special case assumed by the classical theory happen not to be those of the economic society in which we actually live, with the result that its teaching is misleading and disastrous if we attempt to apply it to the facts of experience (Keynes, The General Theory of Employment Interest and Money, 1936, 3)."

Keynes, like Marx, believed free markets were inherently unstable. Instability, among other things, meant the inability to create full employment except only briefly, so laissez-faire economic principles couldn't fulfill the peoples' needs. He believed his new ideas could and should be the norm.

"The outstanding faults of the economic society in which we live are its failure to provide for full employment and its arbitrary and inequitable distribution of wealth and incomes (Ibid, 372)."

In Keynes' mind, the government could fix "economic society" by engineering the outcomes and controlling the rewards. Fiat currency and deficit spending were crucial in his plans, along with confiscatory taxes on the wealthy for redistribution, loose credit policies, government-controlled low-interest rates, and more public employees who'd spend their generous paychecks injecting demand into the economy. He imagined he could redistribute wealth more equitably, smooth out business cycles, solve the unemployment problem, and create more general prosperity.

More money flowing into the economy would generate activity from the demand side as the lower and middle classes purchased more with their newfound cash. More government-provided demand creating more employment, more spending, more output, etc.

Government expenditures could help drive the economy, and more public employees could create more jobs overall from their purchasing power. The improved demand drawing new supply would produce "a fiscal multiplier." The economic activity government "controls" created, through spending, would bring in more revenue than the government "invested."

"...we have here established the law that increased employment for investment must necessarily stimulate the industries producing for consumption and thus lead to a total increase of employment which is a multiple of the primary employment required by the investment itself (Ibid, 118)."

Notwithstanding Keynes' convoluted prose, by "establishing" his "law," he contradicted and openly denied the time-tested truths, the bedrock of economic theory summarized in Say's Law of Markets. He lost valuable production, driving the economy, and replaced it with consumption.

Jean-Baptiste Say theorized about how we create value and trade. Once again, he described what became known as "Say's Law" this way:

"...a product is no sooner created, than it, from that instant, affords a market for other products to the full extent of its own value (Say, 1971 [1964, 1880, 1821, 1803], 134)."

According to all three giants, Cantillon, Smith, and Say, entrepreneurial ideas successfully executed through a production process create the value we trade. And no one can spend, over time, without the proceeds from their output. So, let me ask you, how does one trade value unless they have something valuable to trade? How does one acquire things continuously?

Don't you need profits or paychecks to buy what you need or want without running down your wealth or relying on others?

Say never put it this way, but some later economists summarized Say's Law as "supply creates its *own* demand," but it's misleading and allowed for Keynes' misinterpretations. More competent economists use "supply creates demand" because it does in many ways (more on this later). Keynes popularized describing Say's Law as "supply creates *its own* demand (Ibid, 18)," but he went off a cliff by saying that it is "...disastrous if we apply it to the facts of experience (Ibid, 3)." He taught that the opposite works; hence, the oft-repeated Keynesian expression, "demand creates its own supply."

There is no evidence Say ever taught "supply creates its *own* demand," it isn't in his writings, but today, with Keynesians controlling academia, it pops up this way first and most often when you search for "Say's Law" online.

Refuting a strawman, Keynesians argue supply doesn't create its own demand as gluts of goods and services in the short-run, with recessionary "sticky prices" hinder supply and demand equilibrium. Enough businesses don't lower wages and prices to spur recovery and growth, making doldrums.

Their remedies are wrong, as real-world experience shows us that freely seizing opportunities creates recovery. If entrepreneurs produce too much of anything, they discount the price, perhaps take a loss, and move on. Someone else snaps it up and gets a deal! Freedom and business flexibility promotes quick recoveries. Freedom, not control, clears overproduction. Keynes's printing, borrowing, and spending, with artificially low interest rates, endeavor to avoid natural adjustments, pushing prices artificially high. His government manipulation and control cause stagnation and bubbles.

History reveals that government hindrances cause and worsen economic downturns. The intrusion creates inflexibility, hurts business morale, and instills cautiousness. Bureaucrats often keep short-term interest rates too low for too long and then raise them too quickly, fueling booms and busts. They may print or create too much money causing inflation and instability.

Sometimes Keynesians claim supply creates its *own* demand in the long run but not in the short run; capitalism works in the big picture, but we need an interventionist activist government continuously. Keynes believed his system must be in place perpetually, evidenced by the first quote in this chapter, but what about the consequences? His short-term government controls for demand creation don't take care of the long run, but his followers make excuses as we drown in national debt! His dismissive quip, "in the long run, we're all dead," doesn't help our grandchildren! Some say "monetary sovereignty" will save us. Print and spend money to pay the bills!

We must understand that value is the key. If these left-leaning economists read Say's words instead of using Keynes' false definitions, they might notice his intrinsic word *value!* If you create something valuable to others, they can acquire it because of their previous production. We've just defined economics. Say described reality, how things work.

People must perceive value and have the ability to acquire things from their output. Everyone needs something of worth to make an exchange. Successfully produced ideas supply the power to trade.

If you make something all others find worthless, you've wasted your time and will starve unless you can eat it! You'd better do something others value to trade for what you need or want. Do you think you can make everything for yourself? If you try, you won't have much, and in our modern society, it's obvious we can't. To get beyond precarious subsistence, we must trade, but first, we must be productive so we have something to offer.

Who among us can make his cell phone? Can you make your car? You'd be too busy trying to secure food if you attempted to do everything yourself. We specialize, produce efficiently, and trade. Our market-based society allows us to stop by an overstocked store on the way home or at our convenience to easily trade what we previously produced, with money, the medium of exchange we have in hand, to acquire what we need or want.

Say's Law demonstrates how economics is entrepreneurial and value-driven. We competitively make things for others that they need and want then exchange value. It's a reality, indisputable, factual. Real-life and unbiased observation proves it. One must misinterpret it to claim it doesn't work. They can then go off theorizing in the wrong direction as Keynes did.

Keynes' theories rely on assumptions in the "aggregate," meaning all the supply and demand in the whole economy. Instead of understanding business peoples' productive drive, he sees the government increasing demand and spurring output, positively affecting the entire economy. The truth is, individuals and associations of creative people create value, not the government pulling and pushing strings. Free people exchange their productivity in trade because they specialize: we competitively share our gifts and talents.

Keynes expresses his inaccurate assumptions in his cockeyed descriptions of Say's Law below. Besides "its own" added into the definition Say never made, he equates aggregate demand and supply price "for all levels of output and employment," another thing Say never did, this way:

"...that supply creates its own demand in the sense that the aggregate demand price is equal to the aggregate supply price for all levels of output and employment (Keynes, The General Theory of Employment Interest and Money, 1936, 29)."

Compare Say's words, "its *own value*," to Keynes,' "its *own demand*." Say theorized about how we create value and trade it, but Keynes flipped it into a consumer-driven straw man argument. He made up and knocked down definitions and conceptual rules attacking a caricature of Say's Law. It's the basis for Keynesian apologists making their misrepresentations every day. Keynes asserted it again this way, wildly misstating Say's Law:

"From the time of Say and Ricardo, (Ricardo lead the English classical school after Smith) the classical economists have taught that supply creates its own demand; meaning by this in some significant, but not clearly defined, sense that the whole of the costs of production must necessarily be spent in the aggregate, directly or indirectly, on purchasing the product (Ibid, 18)."

In the aggregate, production "costs" must "be spent" "purchasing the product?" Notice Keynes' words, *"costs," "spent,"* and *"purchasing"* are all demand-oriented. Say wrote: "a *product,*" "*created,*" "*a market,*" "for *other products,*" *and* "*value.*" Say meant valuable creation and trade, but Keynes' view was all spending and consumption.

Strangely, Keynes quotes John Stewart Mill's accurate perception of "Say's Law:"

"In J.S. Mill's *Principles of Political Economy* the doctrine is expressly set forth: 'What constitutes the means of payment for commodities is simply commodities. Each person's means of paying for the productions of other people consist of those which he himself possesses. All sellers are inevitably, and by the meaning of the word, buyers. Could we suddenly double the productive powers of the country, we should double the supply of commodities in every market; but we should, by the same stroke, double the purchasing power. Everybody would bring a double demand as well as supply; everybody would be able to buy twice as much, because everyone would have twice as much to offer in exchange (Ibid)."'

The problem with Mill's statement is he doesn't say *valuable* commodities, but he infers it if you understand Say's Law. You can't just produce anything and expect it to sell.

Keynesians famously use charts and graphs with dry mathematical cause and effect to illustrate Keynes' assumptions of how supply changes with different demand. They miss altogether that production *first* creates value. Say's Law demonstrates this operational, entrepreneurial reality, and all business people know it implicitly, if not explicitly. Conversely, Keynes' mathematical and theoretical ideas proceed from the laboratory of his "progressive" professorial mind. Was he a myopic math genius who didn't understand the small picture and couldn't see the big picture?

We could alleviate much confusion by using the word "valuable" in any abbreviation of Say's Law. We might say: "valuable supply creates demand, and exchange, from both sides of a transaction."

With the Keynesian government expenditures driving the economy model, spending to create paychecks leads to production, which theoretically means additional employment, more consumption, increased output, etc. What happened over time? We're drowning in national debt! In reality, valuable entrepreneurial creation is the key. For Keynes, the market was the problem, and the government was the solution, but the opposite is true!

Was Keynes self-reflecting in the Introduction to *The General Theory* when he described how economists could get caught up in "foolish" beliefs?

"It is astonishing what foolish things one can temporarily believe if one thinks too long alone, particularly in economics (Ibid, vii)."

If only his were passing thoughts, and he didn't record them and cause such confusion. The Professor didn't see things with business acumen. He didn't understand the entrepreneur's mindset or all it generates. His incorrect definitions of Say's Law continue below, asserting things Say never did, like, "the demand price is *equal* to the supply price for all levels of output," and "the demand price *always accommodates* itself to the supply price."

We can reference Say's Law, in his own words, and see how Keynes misdefined it, but Keynes was correct that at least its real meaning underlies "orthodox" and "classical theory." Notice how he equates in the first quote below "Say's Law," with, in the following one, "supply creates its *own* demand," and both, in the third with "orthodox economic theory" and "classical theory." Keynes explicitly claimed that Say's Law meant there was "no obstacle to full employment" during a time of high unemployment. Without grasping that government policies caused it (more on this later), his fix was more government control and hindrances.

More misdefinitions:

"Thus Say's law, that the aggregate demand price of output as a whole is equal to its aggregate supply price for all volumes of output, is equivalent to the proposition that there is no obstacle to full employment (Ibid, 26)."

"...that supply creates its own demand in the sense that the aggregate demand price is equal to the aggregate supply price for all levels of output and employment (Ibid, 29)."

"...the statement that supply creates its own demand and continues to underlie all orthodox economic theory... The classical theory assumes, in other words, that the aggregate demand price (or proceeds) always accommodates itself to the aggregate supply price (Ibid, 25-26);"

Remarkably, economist Mark Skousen gives this perspective:

"Interestingly, Keynes never quoted Say directly, and some historians have thus surmised that Keynes never actually read Say's Treatise (Skousen, 2007, 185) ..."

Skousen quotes economist Steven Kates:

"Steven Kates, calls *The General Theory* "A book-length attempt to refute Say's Law (Ibid, 184)."

Keynes' statements don't describe Says Law, and Say never said such things. Throughout Say's treatise, an exchange of production values creates markets. We create for others to trade, benefiting both sides.

There can be many obstacles to full employment, especially government hindrances. Keynes' robotic assumptions in the aggregate don't match the reality on the ground where we make decisions.

Instead of Keynes' assertion about Say's Law, that "the demand price always accommodates itself to the supply price," doesn't the supply price adjust itself to the demand price? Every day in business, we see the buyer's desire for something against the amount available and what the seller can charge or receive in exchange in the open market.

Efficiency is essential, but entrepreneurs usually don't strive to reach equilibrium to maximize profits; they try to grow or increase activity. They can cut prices to move products, produce more efficiently with better technology, improve production methods, or buy materials at lower costs and share efficiencies with customers to increase market share. They can market more unique products or services or better quality and raise prices when they've improved the general perception of what they're selling. They can create or increase demand by changing their customers' opinions of value through effective advertising, better quality, or lower prices.

Entrepreneurs drive the economy, but the seller doesn't dictate; the buyer can negotiate; he has other choices and can walk away. If there is less desire for something, a businessperson must sell it for less. If any producer creates too much of anything, the price will come down until it sells. If he makes things of no value to others, he'll stop producing them because they won't sell; the producer won't replace the resources destroyed during development and business operations; he'll cease production or go broke.

The Giants all made these concepts clear, and we see them working all around us every day. Richard Cantillon illustrated how consumers' wrong perception of value could hinder entrepreneurial efforts when describing silver mining and if property owners and the lower classes (people generally) rejected metals for practical uses on incorrect assumptions. The value decreases from false perceptions, the market price drops too much, and the mining business becomes unprofitable and ceases operations:

"If the property owners, and the lower classes in a state who imitate them, rejected the use of tin and copper, wrongly supposing that they are injurious to health, and if they all used dishes and utensils of earthenware, these metals would be at a very low price in the markets, and the work that was carried on to extract them from the mine would be discontinued (Cantillon, 2010 [1755], 104)."

If businesses must lower prices below production costs, they'll lose money until they're more efficient, meeting expenses, then creating profits, or they'll stop production. Entrepreneurs make valuable goods and services, but they must expose desirable things to others with the power to trade from their output. The more potential buyers want their produce against the available amount, the higher the price.

The seller supplies advertising or makes his products known to potential buyers in the best light; the buyer offers the value of his previous production typically held in a medium of exchange, or money, for what is desirable in the market. The trade occurs when the product or service has more value to the buyer than the cash in his hand, and that money has more value to the seller than the product or service he offers. They make a deal and exchange value.

Say believed that entrepreneurial adjustments balance markets over time as the other giants did from producers reciprocally meeting each others' needs. But Keynes missed the point entirely when he argued against his distortions because he lost entrepreneurs as the driving force in "economic society." He lost what incentivizes individuals. Professor Keynes couldn't see the trees for the forest (or the forest for the trees for that matter), and his big-picture became a deceptive hypothetical that our society now practices!

He may or may not have cared about them from his academic perch high above productive individuals, but he didn't know them, and he didn't understand how the economy works. He lacked insight into practical business applications, so he couldn't extrapolate from the smallest to the largest enterprise and see individual incentives working from the ground up.

Keynes flipped Say's Law on its head but only after getting it wrong. His obsession was consumption driving production. He didn't realize value comes first from both sides before any trade. Producers create markets.

In Keynes' mind, if he could take from the rich and give to the poor, their consumption would drive the economy. His theory of "the marginal propensity to consume" states that although individuals spend more with higher incomes, their savings grow too, hindering overall consumption, but the poor consume the highest percentage of their income. Those struggling indeed tend to live paycheck to paycheck, and the rich accumulate wealth, but if consumer spending doesn't drive the economy, where are we?

Where does a consumer get his money consistently if not from his previous production value, his "supply" that came first? We create and trade, not the other way around. You must start with something valuable to others. In reality, we should tax all entrepreneurs less, and we'll get more reinvestment, productivity, more jobs, and a higher standard of living overall.

Keynes believed we get more overall activity and prosperity by taking from savers and giving to needy consumers because consumption comes first. It supports his assertion that a government-orchestrated redistribution of wealth creates a better economy.

"...the chronic tendency of contemporary societies to under-employment is to be traced to underconsumption; that is to say, to social practices and a distribution of wealth which result in a propensity to consume which is unduly low (Keynes, The General Theory of Employment Interest and Money, 1936, 324)."

Keynes had it backward. Was he serious when he wrote the following?

"If the treasury were to fill old bottles with banknotes, bury them at suitable depths in disused coal mines which are then filled up to the surface with town rubbish, and leave it to private enterprise on well-tried principles of laissez-faire to dig the notes up again (the right to do so being obtained of course, by tendering for leases of the note-bearing territory), there need be no more unemployment and, with the help of the repercussions, the real income of the community, and its capital wealth also, would probably become a good deal greater than it is (Ibid, 129)."

Although he believed it'd be better for the government to build more practical things, this kind of thinking could only come from someone with no business experience; someone locked in the ivory tower too long—his whole life. Capital wealth will increase with income from government printing and hiding money in bottles, then taxing people through permits and fees to let them engage in government-provided "laissez-faire?" How do you define unproductive? Ridiculous? His scenario creates nothing valuable with nothing produced but printed money found orchestrated by the government.

Why do we spend tax dollars building turtle tunnels so they can get across the street safely, on research for shrimp running on treadmills, and on what bugs do near lightbulbs? Is this our way of printing cash, putting it in bottles, covering it with rubbish, and paying people to uncover it to get the economy going? Do you remember Obama's stimulus package? What was the point of all the reckless spending? Could the politicians justify spending your confiscated pay on absurdities without Keynesian economic theory?

The classical approach has always appreciated savings as a primary source of capital formation. Keynes argued redistributing income from the rich to the poor could increase investment capital.

"...measures for the redistribution of incomes in a way likely to raise the marginal propensity to consume may prove positively favorable to the growth of capital (Ibid, 373)."

Keynes espoused "the paradox of thrift." He wanted fewer savings and more spending to drive the economy, especially in slow times. In his mind, saving money was a societal problem because it affected consumption in the aggregate. Below he expresses how it "necessarily defeats itself."

"For although the amount of his own saving is unlikely to have any significant influence on his own income, the reactions of the amount of his consumption on the incomes of others makes it impossible for all individuals simultaneously to save any given sums. Every such attempt to save more by reducing consumption will so affect incomes that the attempt necessarily defeats itself (Ibid, 84)."

In Keynes' mind, individuals must spend more and save less. Businesses must spend and invest more and not hoard money, but government spending programs would be the difference in bringing about "something approximating full employment."

In driving the economy, additional government spending is more efficient than tax cuts in Keynes' mind. Government "investment," or expenditure, produces more than individuals or businesses when they accumulate, leverage, and use capital. Tax cuts put money in individuals' hands and into business coffers, but some people save while the government spends all it has (more than it has since Keynes). The classical understanding of savings expressed by Benjamin Franklin, "a penny saved is a penny earned," became antiquated, inefficient, and passé.

Princeton Professor Emeritus Paul Krugman is one of the best-known modern-day Keynesian economists and a left-wing media darling. Besides writing an intensely political New York Times column, he appears on CNN Business, Bloomberg TV, and ABC News Roundtable, among many others.

Krugman condenses these Keynesian points in a New York Times youtube video interview when he describes the Obama stimulus package. According to classical economic theory, he gets it all precisely wrong, proving how Keynes and his disciples put the contrarian theories into practice.

Notice his pecking order: Direct government spending is best, handing the states money is second, giving people money directly third, and tax cuts last; he considers business tax cuts "money down the drain." Although he includes tax cuts to help get the economy going in slow times, Keynesians typically push for higher taxes in good times as part of the regulation, control, and redistribution of wealth they promise.

Krugman sees everything through demand creating its own supply:

"What's clear, is you get the biggest bang for the buck by actually having the government do something...you've directly created demand...and most of the estimates say that a dollar spent by the government on infrastructure or some other form of government direct spending generates at least a dollar fifty of GDP. So that's the thing that's most effective...and that's clear; you want to do every shovel-ready project that makes even a bit of sense right now... The second thing you can do is you can provide aid to state and local governments...they are actually slashing spending, and one very quick way to increase spending is to prevent it from being cut... The third thing you can do...then you get into the realm of actually giving people money... That's a little more questionable aside from...well, because it's not clear they will spend that money. They might use it to put in their savings account, to pay off credit card debt, but to the extent you can target that on people who are in distress...that's a pretty effective form of stimulus... Then the last thing is cutting people's taxes...that can be done fast, but there is a high likelihood people won't spend the money... When I look at this stimulus plan, about two-thirds of it is clearly good stuff. I don't have a problem with it, the two-thirds that's spending... The rest is business tax cuts which all look like they are extremely ineffective...it's just money down the drain (Krugman, 2009)."

Professor Krugman calls himself a capitalist, but he writes and speaks against how free markets work every day. His prescriptions are not economics but left-wing politics in disguise—always and only justifying big government—and so many of our leftist politicians and media parrot him.

With a fully Keynesian system in place, we won't have a free enterprise system anymore. What Adam Smith called the free market's invisible hand becomes the government's hand. We now have an economy fighting against headwinds, and the business culture, the political mentality, and the individual's frame of mind become accustomed to many new government controls. Keynes introduces "socialization of investment" this way:

"The State will have to exercise a guiding influence on the propensity to consume partly through its scheme of taxation, partly by fixing the rate of interest, and partly, perhaps in other ways. Furthermore, it seems unlikely that the influence of banking policy on the rate of interest will be sufficient by itself to determine an optimum rate of investment. I conceived, therefore, that a somewhat comprehensive socialization of investment will prove the only means of securing an approximation to full employment (Keynes, The General Theory of Employment Interest and Money, 1936, 378) ..."

You tell me, how much "state" "influence" is "comprehensive socialization?" How much government control does this represent? Keynes continues with something to make any free enterprising person shutter:

"Though this need not exclude all manner of compromises and devices by which public authority will co-operate with private initiative (Ibid, 378)."

Just how much authority will he give to "public authority?" Is this kinder, gentler fascism? What kind of mindset will the public authorities have? A free enterprising one or a bureaucratic one? Does any of this help create an inspirational business environment? Where does it lead? What do you call bureaucratic government manipulation and control for prosperity?

"But beyond this, no obvious case is made out for a system of State Socialism which would embrace the economic life of most of the community. It is not the ownership of the instruments of production for the state to assume. If the state can determine the aggregate amount of resources devoted to augmenting the instruments and the basic rate of reward to those who own them, it will have accomplished all that is necessary. Moreover, the necessary measures of socialization can be introduced gradually and without a break in the general traditions of society (Ibid, 378)."

"It's not ownership of the instruments of production (communism)...if the state can determine the...rate of reward to those who own them (fascism)." The "measures of socialization?" He champions a progressive intrusion, and since Keynes, the government has grown irrepressibly.

"The instruments of production," so coolly stated, means your business Mr. & Mrs. America. If you own a business, I think you should be feeling sick right now. He's the most influential economist in the last eighty years? He's the reason our politicians say stupid things about economics, they implement destructive control-oriented laws and policies, and they can't stop deficit spending! Do you want government bureaucrats to manipulate your business through their mechanisms, even if they're trying to help?

Is Keynes' program a moderate "socialization?" Is Democratic fascism possible? Does it become an envious mob willing to take away others' pursuit of happiness to satisfy their jealousy? He claimed he didn't embrace totalitarian socialism and falls short of "an obvious case for state socialism," but is the operative word "obvious?" Was his a desire for stealthy socialism?

"The authoritarian state systems of today seem to solve the problem of unemployment at the expense of efficiency and freedom. It is certain that the world will not much longer tolerate the unemployment which, apart from brief intervals of excitement, is associated—with present-day capitalistic individualism. But it may be possible by a right analysis of the problem to cure the disease whilst preserving efficiency and freedom (Ibid, 381)."

Did he "solve the problem" and "cure the disease" or "preserve efficiency and freedom" with "necessary measures of socialization?" Isn't "the disease" really creeping government instead? He wades into semi-authoritarianism while claiming it's the cure for an authoritarian state system. Use principles that don't work to save us from their further implementation? Does more government control create a prosperous economy? Leftists love his "central controls" so they can progressively change society.

"The central controls necessary to ensure full employment will, of course, involve a large extension of the traditional functions of government (Ibid, 379)."

Classical economics is reality, just life. Natural liberty is something we breathe in every day to create and trade. Rogue economic theories cause and support political movements that can quickly destroy societies, grow over time, become monstrous, or get administered like slow poisons. Keynes had one thing right when he wrote the following:

"Practical men, who believe themselves to be quite exempt from intellectual influences, are usually the slaves of some defunct economist (Ibid, 383)."

Keynes builds a contrarian theoretical skyscraper in the *General Theory* while pulverizing the classical rock foundation. He tips his hat at market efficiencies, attacks proved truths, and flips upsidedown economic and even moral principles. His result isn't just nonsense: it leads to disaster over time.

6

Antecedent

"We must either repair the defects in the old economic structure or accept communism, community of property. There is no other possibility."

Silvio Gesell

WHAT SIMILAR ECONOMIC ideas preceded Keynes? He referenced Silvio Gesell in, *The General Theory,* who he said theorized about an "anti-Marxian socialism" in his book, *The Natural Economic Order.* Both men mocked Marx while they championed the socialization of the economy in varying degrees. To get there, they threw economics on its head by claiming demand is the driving force. Their mechanisms were somewhat different, but the demand-pull theory each espoused is uncannily comparable.

Keynes commented on his predecessor, Gesell:

"It is convenient to mention at this point the strange, unduly neglected prophet Silvio Gesell (1862-1930), whose work contains flashes of deep insight and who only just failed to reach down to the essence of the matter (Ibid, 353).

He goes on to summarize Gesell's book:

"The purpose of the book as a whole may be described as the establishment of an anti-Marxian socialism, a reaction against laissez-faire built on theoretical foundations totally unlike those of Marx in being based on a repudiation instead of on an acceptance of the classical hypotheses, and on an unfettering of competition instead of its abolition. I believe that the future will learn more from the spirit of Gesell than from that of Marx (Ibid, 355)."

How would Gesell create demand first? By what he called free money and free land. He wanted to unleash competition in workers and producers by bringing interest rates to zero and nationalizing all real estate for the public good, thereby allowing for "a natural economic order."

"To take away the privileges of money and land ownership, with free money and free land. The economic order here discussed is a natural order only in the sense that it is adapted to the nature of man (Gesell, 1918, 1)."

Denying ownership rights forces merit-driven productivity?

"Competition among men can be carried on equitably and in accordance with its high purpose only if all special private or public rights over land are abolished (Ibid, 36)."

Gesell believed leveling the playing field meant everyone earned income actively unless the government took care of them. Abolishing passive income opportunities in lending and owning real estate meant removing structural unfairness and excessive disparities in wealth caused by ownership. There could only be higher or lower incomes through performance—accentuating "the nature of man" and "equity."

"The abolition of unearned income, of so-called surplus-value also termed interest and rent, is the immediate economic aim of every socialistic movement (Ibid, 8)."

On the other hand, Keynes' mechanisms for redistributing wealth were mainly through high taxation, government growth and social spending, jobs programs, long-term public employment and benefits, and "social justice" policies, but not in direct land confiscation. Keynes championed easy fiat money— not tied to the value of any precious metal. Like Gesell, the government could spend it into existence through public works projects designed to create full employment. Both men wanted easily printed money spent quickly, conceptually creating demand.

Gesell's program included government "nationalization securities," compensating former landowners fully within approximately twenty years by reducing the interest rate to zero over time. The government paid off what it said it owed them.

"We propose to introduce the money reform simultaneously with the nationalization of the land. Its effect will be to reduce the market rate of interest, so the rate of interest on the nationalization securities will also be automatically reduced, from 5 to 4, 3, 2, 1, - and finally 0% (Ibid, 38)."

Gesell called for putting his new depreciating money, which lost value through regularly added tax stamps, into circulation initially by buying back the old coinage, dollar for dollar. After this, increasing or decreasing the money supply by lowering or raising taxes, theoretically speeding up or slowing the economy (Ibid, 124-125).

"Free-Money loses one-thousandth of its face value weekly, or about 5% annually, at the expense of the holder. The holder must keep the notes at their face value by attaching to them the currency stamps mentioned above. A ten-cent stamp, for example, must be attached every Wednesday to the $100 note...one stamp for each week since the beginning of the year... In the course of the year 52 ten-cent stamps must be attached to the $100 note, or, in other words, it depreciates 5.2% annually at the expense of its holders (Ibid, 123)."

What if people are too busy, have an emergency, or forget Wednesday is stamping day? I find it hard not to laugh when I read the above paragraph. Can you imagine living like that? Gesell's demand-pull theory made the money supply the economic gas pedal: push it down, or increase it to go, and let it up, or reduce it to slow down.

Correspondingly, regularly dropping money's value meant people spend more quickly to get it out of their pockets, theoretically creating demand and increasing supply in response:

"Free-Money forces its holder to buy: it constantly reminds him of his duty as a buyer through the losses it causes him if he neglects to buy. Purchase therefore at all times and under all possible circumstances follows on the heels of sale. And when everyone is obliged to buy as much as he has sold, how can sales slacken (Ibid, 134)?"

"Sales, sales, that is what we manufacturers want; steady, assured sales, with long-term orders in advance. For industry is dependent on regular disposal of the product; (Ibid, 133)"

"Under Free Money... Our production, the supply of goods, is the order for demand, and the National Currency Office executes the order (Ibid, 134)."

Can you imagine the required bureaucracy to facilitate all this besides the National Currency Office pushing down or letting up on the stamped money gas pedal? The government drives the economy this way besides doing many other things. Gesell thinks the economy is so consumer-driven it's all worth it. The government pulls strings, and the people jump!

"Demand no longer depends on the will of buyers, bankers, speculators; for money has now become the very embodiment of demand. The possessors of money are now kept under discipline; money holds the possessor of money like a dog on a lead (Ibid, 134)."

Keynes didn't buy the entire program. He saw other money, precious metals, or commodities "stepping in the breach" and hindering the depreciation scheme, so in practical terms, it might only work on a small scale; but he liked the stamped money concept to create "effective demand:"

"The idea behind stamped money is sound (Keynes, The General Theory of Employment Interest and Money, 1936, 357)."

Gesell posited, as Marx and Keynes did, that his system could lead to world peace. He thought money interest and land ownership caused wars. Stop warfare and save capitalism by taking the capital out of it?

"Everyone would, of course, like to enjoy the blessings of civil and international peace, and at the same time live on capital-interest. But those who have discovered that the possibility of doing so is a Utopian fantasy, an illusion of naive minds; those who recognize that war and interest are inseparable, must choose one or other of these alternatives: Either interest and war, or earned income and peace (Gesell, 1918, 203)."

Marx's radical revolutionary socialism, on the other hand, meant state indoctrination and control. Full socialism meant a command economy and bringing about world peace by destroying capitalist exploitation (owner profits). Marx put it this way in *The Communist Manifesto*:

"In proportion as the exploitation of one individual by another is put an end to, the exploitation of one nation by another will also be put an end to. In proportion as the antagonism between classes within the nation vanishes, the hostility of one nation to another will also come to an end (Marx & Engels, The Communist Manifesto, 1998 [1848], 73)."

"Domestic policy," for our third fanciful visionary, Keynes, meant redistributing wealth more evenly through government "controls" or "socialization." He advocated high progressive income tax rates and a steep inheritance tax on the wealthy (Keynes, The General Theory of Employment Interest and Money, 1936, 94, 372).

Aside from "dictators and others such, to whom war offers, in expectation at least, a pleasurable excitement... (Ibid, 381)," Keynes points to "economic causes of war, namely, the pressure of population and the competitive struggle for markets (Ibid)."

Friction between countries trying to create full employment through a positive trade balance, or as he saw it, mercantilism in his day, could end with government-created full employment. Without an unemployment problem, a more efficient international division of labor with less hostility would result among nations (Ibid 382-383).

"But if nations can learn to provide themselves with full employment by their domestic policy (and, we must add if they can also attain equilibrium in the trend of their population), there need be no important economic forces calculated to set the interest of one country against that of its neighbors (Ibid, 382)."

Not falling into the sway of these nonspiritual dreamers shows us that countries become hostile for many reasons: ethnic, religious, economic, and others, but control-oriented governments don't cure the problem. History reveals they usually exacerbate it. Leftists often blame or demonize something so they can replace it with their utopian schemes. If there are ethnic hatreds, can we get rid of ethnicity? Cultural pride is healthy societally among all groups. If people misuse religion, does it mean it's all bad? Good religion brought us Western Civilization, our hospitals, our court system, school systems, etc., as well as showing us "God is love (1 John 4:8, 1987)."

Keynes' remedies didn't bring anything close to full employment during the depression, and government spending became unsustainable; it began our debt spiral. Plentiful job opportunities always come under times of less government control, except in war, which is also unsustainable. Government-caused activity creates a debt buildup if the real economy, which is value freely exchanged between producers, isn't firing fast enough to pay for it.

The truth is, free and fair trade makes us interdependent, starting with individuals, families, and groups of free people within and across national borders. We freely associate and exchange goods and services, which helps us get along. We naturally become friends and allies because it's in everyone's interest. Keynes throws this on its head by saying a government-manipulated economy with stagnant population growth is a key to international peace.

How would these three men evolve humanity? Marx, by radically controlling and educating society into cooperation. Like Keynes, Gesell saw himself as an economic scientist in an age of eugenics. He would manage it through his designed competition, called "eugenesis (Gesell, 1918, 1)."

"We are here on a higher plane. We are confronted with the problem, to whom is the further evolution of the human race to be entrusted (Ibid, 134)?"

Like Marx's, Gesell's and Keynes' theories sprang from secular humanist philosophy, where man is autonomously the highest being, without God. Unlike Cantillon, who left the government out of it "not to complicate our subject" and showed us how the economy works, these three men wanted the government in and God out to create further human evolution.

Today, Keynesians typically call themselves behavioral economists. Keynes described what he saw in human behavior as "animal spirits."

"...our decisions to do something positive, the full consequences of which will be drawn out over many days to come, can only be taken as the result of animal spirits - a spontaneous urge to action rather than inaction, and not as the outcome of a weighted average of quantitative benefits multiplied by quantitative probabilities (Keynes, The General Theory of Employment Interest and Money, 1936, 161)."

Before Keynesianism became dominant in our society, the standard behavioral analysis was the "economic man model." The economic man was rational and planned for what was in his best interests. Some people complain it is too dry conceptually and not realistic, that we make decisions more freely within the general popular psychology or the current business climate, or even intuitively.

It's correct that business people and consumers alike make big decisions on gut instinct, but isn't this before or after a careful analysis? Wouldn't it be better to understand how our sub-conscience and conscious minds work together through crucial decisions? It seems to me Keynes saw people in a very two-dimensional way. It works well with his demand-pull theory. Put money in impulsive, needy peoples' pockets so they'll spend it to drive the economy. Gesell's system forced impulsivity mechanically to create demand.

Earlier than the Economic Man model, the scholastics and the Churchmen, the priests and scholars, saw our economic interests related to God's will for our lives and the lives of our neighbors around us. Are we fair and honest in competition with our neighbors? Are our decisions and actions moral or immoral, charitable or uncharitable, good or evil? Interestingly, we separated the Christian worldview from our economic thinking and embraced a rational man model selfishly interested, only to slip to an irrational animalistic man model with Keynes. It seems when we separate our faith from practice, we detach our thinking from morality.

Imagine attempting to improve business competition under Gesell's program? Confiscate everyone's property and make them renters while weekly decreasing the value of their money. People spend their pay quickly to avoid its continual devaluation, theoretically circulating it rapidly. Would it cause business activity in a rush to supply all the demand? What citizen wants to be Gesell's "a dog on a lead?"

What happens to the people? Do they become like gerbils on a wheel running faster and faster? They can't hope or strive for property ownership. A rat race of non-owners. Would there be a heart attack epidemic? Would the stores quickly replenish their shelves with better or cheaper goods to keep them moving? Wouldn't the consumers reach exhaustion and max out on what they could buy?

Some small communities experimented with Gesell's ideas and claimed success; you can see several youtube videos with fanatical "free money" advocates. Worgl, Austria, is one well-known example. The mayor employed Gesell's ideas to create economic activity during the Great Depression. They would only accept the special stamped money in their community as a protectionist measure, but they claimed some increase in local business activity (Complementary Currency Resource Center, 2007).

The Austrian courts and central bank shut the experiment down after about a year. What was their great fear? Was it a big government power grab over a local community? Maybe to some degree, but they may have had very legitimate concerns.

Government control of the economy causes many ancillary problems. It's always a push out of equilibrium because it doesn't create value first. Are you concerned about the idea of running an economy on printed funny money? For Gesell, business people didn't create value first but reacted to cash; he equated printed currency with demand. Keynes similarly saw businesses responding to demand but with "animal spirits."

It seems Keynes thought of business decision-makers reacting with greed and avarice, with a killer instinct, like emotional animals. They strike at money and profits. Did he see humanity with smug cynicism coldly? Did he perceive this behavior as a reflection of himself?

Keynes believed there is a "psychological justification" for controlling peoples' incomes and wealth. It's wise to allow some "significant inequalities of wealth and income" to keep the peace by keeping our animal instincts at bay. Making money was an addiction related to a lust for power over other men (Keynes, The General Theory of Employment Interest and Money, 1936, 374).

"It is better that a man should tyrannize over his bank balance than over his fellow citizens (Ibid)."

Keynes's government "controls" would manage our animal instincts, but not to be confused with his eugenics ideas to further human evolution:

"The task of transmuting human nature must not be confused with the task of managing it (Ibid)."

It's interesting how Keynes received and read so much information from Gesell's fanatical followers but then claimed it didn't influence his ideas:

"...his devotees bombarded me with copies of his works; ...I entirely failed to discover their merit...their significance only became apparent after I had reached my own conclusions in my own way...I treated his profoundly original strivings as being no better than those of a crank (Ibid, 353)."

Gesell's "Free Money" movement got a small, ardent cult-like following; some people claim he's a biblically connected prophet. No kidding, some claim he was the second coming of Christ! Several youtube videos depict these things. If his theories seem bizarre, please realize that they are only a bag of tricks and devices behind the idea that demand creates its own supply.

The truth is, our entrepreneurial drive and improvement come through working on getting and keeping customers by providing them value. It's the need to create efficiencies, make a profit, or survive while doing something for others that enhance the products and services we trade with each other.

We develop new technologies and better production methods in this struggle by making a living competitively serving others through our ideas put into practice. It's what raises our standard of living: we exchange a higher value or increased utility more quickly over time. Consumers can't do this for us. Creating and trading value reciprocally does. We grow more prosperous as we specialize (excel in our vocations) and share our efficiencies in trade.

Production and exchange are what economics is, but perceived valuable supply necessarily comes first from both sides of a transaction. Gesell's system never became mainstream, but the future did embrace another demand-driving production theory because of Keynes.

The controlling Keynesian theories coldly smack of inhumanity and do nothing but push a string through a government forced redistribution of wealth and incomes on the one hand while detracting from efficient production on the other, and they build debt over time. Marx's ideas went into practice in more than half the world, but the amount of evil they caused, so much wealth and human life destroyed, are almost incomprehensible. Gesell's theories never became widely popular, so we don't know what damage his form of socialistic control might bring large scale; inflation, government debt, disincentives to hard work, and stagnation might be observable outcomes.

Keynes still affects us immensely. What will the future bring as our government debt builds and our business freedom wanes? Whether they know it or not, the political left uses his ideas to drive Western Civilization financially and morally toward a potential fiscal and societal Armageddon.

Keynes, Gesell, and Marx show us control is antithetical to prosperity, and I hope exposed, all three seem wacky. Any theory that doesn't hold economics is creating value first for trade from both sides of a transaction is, at best, a house of cards. If you want to use the term "supply-side economics," you better understand it's two-sided—supply from both sides; any valid consumer or business transaction is an exchange of worth; it's making a deal. Entrepreneurs and free productive people with their creativity and drive, through efficiencies in systems and machines, drive the economy because only those with something others want in hand can trade.

Part III

ECONOMICS IN THE REAL WORLD

"...everybody must buy, the objects of want or desire, each with the value of his respective products transformed into money for the moment only." "Thus, to say that sales are dull, owing to the scarcity of money, is to mistake the means for the cause;"

Jean-Baptiste Say

7

Economics Simplified

"...and that all the exchange and circulation
of the state is conducted by the actions of these entrepreneurs."

Richard Cantillon

WHICH CAME FIRST, the chicken or the egg? Could this be the most critical question you ask yourself today? Most people get it right when I ask them within an economic context because I think it's common sense. When I ask them without referencing economics, they either chuckle or get that blank look. Some say things like, "that is the question, isn't it?"

Regarding economics, the chicken must come first. If there were no chicken to produce the egg and do the necessary work to incubate and hatch it, feed it, keep it warm and protect it until it could defend itself, no next chicken could exist. Unless the chicken comes first, no more chickens, that's it; it's over for all chickens, or at least that line of them.

If the chicken comes first, we're in business! It causes value through the stages of production, the business operations that must occur in producing any product or service.

If the egg comes first, but no chicken exists to incubate and take care of it, what then? You may say, but the egg itself is valuable! Well then, you better devour it quickly before it rots because once it is gone, no more eggs.

Putting the egg first is like Keynesian economics. If the consumer doesn't produce something valuable, it's gone once he spends what he has. On the other hand, the producer keeps creating value, and he trades with someone else who produces, so they both have the goods. Putting the consumer first is like the proverbial cart before the horse.

Business production has multiplicative economic value. Acquiring materials, equipment, and money paid vendors and employees create economic activity in different directions. The entrepreneur, his employees, vendors, and everyone he trades with through production become consumers after exchanging the value of their previous output. Profits and paychecks further production, but the engine of commerce creates value and transfers it for what you need or want. Thereby, chickens, eggs, and many other commodities follow in business and consumer transactions.

The resources spent on manufacturing or business development must create more valuable products and services than all the costs of making them. When completed merchandise sells, all the money fronted during the production stages plus a profit returns more value to the entrepreneur for future production and trade. The revenue over costs, cash on hand, and credit lines bestowed on successful businesses facilitate more investment, creation, and commerce. Entrepreneurs create multipliers.

Keynesian economics doesn't work in theory or practice because, in reality, valuable production comes first. Keynesianism only works in the minds of those who want to promote it for political reasons. I say, beware of things that sound too good to be true, i.e., "we can spend our way out of financial trouble!"

The good news is we can create our way out of financial trouble! It means understanding what the economy is and what drives it, and correspondingly, fully grasping how the Keynesian deception produces inefficiencies and debt traps.

Supply drives the economy because it is the action of the economy. No one can act on any need without value for exchange. Demand does not even actually exist without supply. People can have wants and needs, but there is no economics without the answer to the need. Supply creates demand as demand follows.

We hear our Keynesian espousing politicians tell us we should give people jobs or put money in their pockets to drive the economy. So why doesn't it work? Businesses create jobs; jobs don't create businesses. Jobs come after a business needs work done in producing products or services.

Supply comes first when finding or creating the need or want through testing and advertising. An entrepreneur's creative action starts the production process. It begins with his thoughts and dreams, and economic transactions follow in the implementation. Demand does not create its own supply, but supply creates demand. The economy is not consumer-driven but entrepreneurially driven.

Imagine this: There are two prehistoric people, the valley people and the hill people. The valley men hunt expertly, they provide their people red meat and animal skins abundantly, and their women produce lots of well-made clothing from the animal skins and fur. They have a big problem though; they don't know about fruits and vegetables.

The valley people are malnourished, resulting in awful breath, physical pain, and short lifespans. They need fruits and vegetables, but that need does nothing by itself. If they had no food at all, they would want it, but they would starve to death without a food supply. Even though they have enough food to survive now and have things to trade for the type of food they need, they don't know it, and no one else does either, so there is no actual demand.

On the other hand, the hill people live amongst trees that bear fruit, and many years ago, they found that eating fruits and vegetables with their meat meant better, longer, and happier lives. The hill men also hunt expertly, providing for their people abundantly, but the hill women detest making clothes. The hill men hate winter more than they should have to because of their ragged clothing.

One day, a hill man looks down into the valley and observes the valley people. He can see their clothing and how warm they seem as he shivers; he also realizes they look unhealthy. He knows how eating fruits and vegetables makes him feel, but he understands the valley people don't know about them. He has an idea! Economics just began, at that moment, as quiet as it was. The economic process has commenced!

He starts planning a way to help them if only he can get some of their warm clothing. He gets some fruit and vegetables together on a flat piece of wood and goes down with his samples; his sales display! Approaching them slowly, he greets them, "Hello, I'm here on friendly business, don't kill me, I won't kill you." He eats first, showing them it's okay to try it.

Think about how good that fruit must have tasted to the valley people when they accepted his offer. Think of all the health benefits when they began this relationship, but what about the social rewards?

Both tribes now have adequate nutrition and warmth, but they also have good reasons to get along. Many more real opportunities arise for trade to make all their lives better. They may even improve on each other's inventions and production methods.

The valley people had to make more clothing for trade with the hill people. The hill people had to collect more fruits and vegetables to exchange with the valley people. They all lived much longer, happier lives! The valley people because they were not now malnourished, and the hill people because they were not getting sick and dying unnecessarily from being cold.

They became friends and allies with more safety for their people because the hill man followed through on an idea. The valley people didn't even know what they needed, but after interacting with the hill man and experiencing how it made their lives better, they desired and sought increasing amounts. Wouldn't the world be a better place if we all engaged in open and honest free trade?

They both had more children as they prospered. More people came up with new inventions, more people to trade with, a multiplier effect on supply and demand, present, and future, caused by following through on an idea.

Supply creating demand accelerates with more advancement and increased productivity. How much consumer demand followed from inventing the automobile? It's mind-boggling to consider the amount of industrial production, like, metal mining and forming, rubber and glass, plastics, cloth, vinyl and leather, electronics and wiring, designing and manufacturing, packaging, delivery, sales, and the servicing of it all. Demand results from supply through all the stages of production and when consumers trade for the finished product's perceived utility with their previously produced value held in a medium of exchange, or money.

How much demand resulted from inventing the computer? How many people want and need one or more? Think about all the parts and the workers involved. Supplying CPUs meant providing the printer, the mouse, the wiring with all those tiny internal components, the ink cartridges, software, lots of paper and packaging, and many other business-related things from transportation to sales and on. Today one computer may have parts in it from many different countries. These individuals, throughout the world, cooperate in the production process. They rely on each other for their income, peace, and security. The same is true for all kinds of products and services; there are many ways supply creates demand.

Consider how much more we get done with high-tech equipment, including handheld devices. How much faster and more efficiently all kinds of transactions occur compared to two hundred years ago because of the computer and transportation technology, and the supply of many other things. Some new inventions create almost limitless demand. Demand that previously didn't exist even though people had needs.

The supply of all these things creates consumers from entrepreneurial profits. Entrepreneurs and their employees can now buy many more things or trade the value they previously produced held in a medium of exchange; money represents their productive contribution. We have more to spend and invest depending on how much value we create for others. New technologies and efficiencies raise our standard of living because we get more done in any given period, so we have more value to exchange for other things.

Equipment and tools help create and increase demand, from burrowing wood with a sharp rock to hand-cranked drills to electric ones, to computer-driven assembly line machines allowing us, with further advancement, to create more and more value in any given time. People and products go around the world in hours instead of months because of the supply of jet planes. Larger trucks, massive ships, more powerful and efficient locomotives, pulling many more rail cars, farming equipment, and improved production methods supply many more products quickly. All these increase our wealth because we can trade for increasing amounts of other things. We hold this value from trade in money or other assets.

Today even people with a modest income often have more food than they need, and low-income people in our society are often obese. What a problem for the poor if you know the long history of mankind, too much food! It may be the same lack of discipline that hinders their income and willpower while surrounded by such abundance.

More technological advancement begets more economic progress in a free society. Highly controlled countries improve by trading with more free nations. China produces and exports, exchanging with foreigners but has significant domestic growth limitations. North Korea doesn't create much value for exchange with the rest of the world, and they are poverty-stricken. South Korea produces and exchanges internally and externally and has a much higher standard of living than the same ethnic people in the controlled society up north. Germany and Japan should have higher living standards because they produce and export much value, but their overly controlled domestic economies hinder their prosperity.

Freedom and creative actions are the mother and father of invention; economic progress is slow without freedom; the exception is wartime. Controlled countries may invent much weaponry and wartime technology in a life and death competition with their enemies. Authoritarian governments often fund wars with slave labor and the resources they took in conquest.

Free countries usually fund wars by borrowing, but economic booms may follow when entrepreneurs adopt the new wartime technologies and production methods to create a higher standard of living after the war.

After World War II, the U.S.A. experienced this economic paradigm, and it got us out of the depression. Going to war to create new inventions and new production methods is morally bankrupt and maniacally insane. Freedom within a stable society, law, order, stable government, and entrepreneurial action is how a free nonwartime economy advances.

Does demand fulfill the need? No. Supply is economic action; its fruit trade in the creative process and then the exchange of value in the finished product. The creative process provides things then consumed, but it also creates consumers.

Do crops plant farmers, or do farmers plant the crops? When the farmer is hungry, does the product feed him, or does he eat it? Yes, the farmer must do something from the very beginning; someone must do something! If you argue Keynes sees the farmer planting crops because people need food, I reply, not necessarily. He decides what he grows.

It's not the need that plants the crops; the entrepreneur's production follows contemplation. The farmer can plant other things, like tobacco, sod, or flowers. His activity creates food if the farmer chooses to grow food; it's then available for consumption. The farmer sees the need and fills it if he wishes. If the hungry people do not create anything valuable to get food in exchange or they don't grow food, they will not consume anything unless someone else supplies it from charity; from other peoples' previous production.

Over time, the farmer can't supply food without a return supply in value, typically held in money, which is the value of something else produced and sold or traded for its value. He can't only do free things from the goodness of his heart without eventually running out of resources and going out of business.

Someone must trade with the farmer to continue production; he must receive from someone else's supply in exchange for him to keep providing. We see here economics is supply and supply.

You might argue, but demand exists too! Economics is supply and demand! Supply and demand are essential concepts relationally; they allow us to produce and trade efficiently. We arrive at prices, which aids us in other crucial things like budgeting, forecasting what and how much to create, inventory purchasing, marketing purposes, and industry analysis, including government compiling and data analysis. Still, it is not what economics is, fundamentally. Economics is an exchange of production value, or trade, with many crucial ancillary component analyses.

Measuring demand is also measuring consumption activity or predicting a frame of mind. Still, economics is perceived value freely traded, usually through a medium of exchange, or money, rather than by direct barter. Demand can't create its own supply for many reasons but principally because it is not what economics is: the economy is trading, which means valuable supply and supply in exchange. It begins with an idea, and then to production, and on. Repeating this foundation sheds light in many areas.

Was there a demand for alcohol before someone invented it or supplied it? No. Here we see demand as a frame of mind or a desire leading to action that supply creates. You might say there was already a need for human escape. Maybe, maybe not, but aren't there healthier ways to escape? There is a health benefit to rest, but there are much better ways to relax than alcohol.

Is there some intrinsic human need for cigarettes? No. Is there an inherent human need for candy bars? No, but people will trade their hard-earned dollars, representing the value of their efforts, or, what they produced and exchanged, for cigarettes no matter how high taxes go on them, it seems. They will buy candy with their last dollar because the supply of candy has created an intense demand.

When one economic sector slows, some economists and financial writers say they perceive a lack of demand. Keynesian apologists argue for more government spending to increase demand. If producers were free to produce better products, cut prices, or provide less expensive versions of products that meet their potential trading partners' needs, there would be no perceived lack of demand. The answer is not more government printing and spending. The answer is entrepreneurial, not governmental.

If a housing bubble exists, homes are too expensive: lower the price, and they will sell if people need the houses you have. If you build a home where no one wants to live, say in a toxic waste dump, as an extreme example, there is no value for a trade at all, and no one will want to trade their hard-earned money from their previous production for the down payment or future production to make loan payments, with you.

There must be perceived value for exchange between free and competent parties in approximating fair market value. A vibrant economy requires free trade between rational players.

We've seen irrational exuberance and how dangerous this crazy thinking is to society and individual net worth. When the perceived value goes beyond reason, the fundamentals can help bring us back to our senses. When the perceived value is not reasonable, greed usually has deranged general perceptions—moral and ethical fundamentals, economic basics, consistent central banking, and government policy help. In response, the government should never over-regulate business, overprint money, push crazy liberal lending guidelines, or force interest rates too low. Natual adjustments repair negative equity, sustaining healthy housing and other markets.

The many economists and pundits today who say an overall lack of demand is our problem tell us who they are. Keep listening, and Keynesian theory will follow. One economist I just read said the Eurozone economy suffers from pockets lacking demand.

If people in those economies produced valuable products and services, they'd sell them to other productive people who perceived the value. Those in other European communities who made desirable things would have Euros in their bank accounts because they had exchanged goods and services with others. The European Union is, above all, supposed to be about free trade among those in member countries.

Our world continues getting smaller. With technology and freedom, industrious people can trade value with others in distant places if they don't have productive neighbors with value in hand, increasing prosperity locally.

If there isn't enough trade in any locality, it would mainly be from the people in those countries not having valuable things to sell, unless from government hindrances, which is often the problem today. Those societies don't suffer from a lack of demand but a lack of valued supply. They require successful creativity followed through consistently. They need desired production and effective marketing and sales for trade if no one appreciates what they've made or if no one knows about it.

There can be many reasons why once valuable products become obsolete. Newer technology and more efficient production methods often make older products too expensive with reduced utility than newer, more efficient ones, but this benefits society. When an oppressive government causes problems, it hurts many people. The government can control us out of prosperity because our production becomes too arduous and expensive. When they take away our freedom by force, success becomes illegal.

8

Supply Creation Demand Creation

"…it is production which opens a demand for products. Should a tradesman say, 'I do not want other products for my woolens, I want money,' there could be little difficulty in convincing him that his customers could not pay him in money, without having first procured it by the sale of some other commodities of their own."

Jean-Baptiste Say

WE HEAR KEYNESIANS tell us all the time, "The government needs to gin up demand." Responsible business-friendly political leaders can inspire demand creation, but they aren't the creators. The government doesn't gin up demand, but it can hinder business and usually hurts morale when it tries to. Ginning up is a false way to look at demand creation, but it's fair to analyze the concept of demand.

What is demand? Among other things, it's useful for price theory. If you have a lot of something and not many people want it, the price is low. If you have little of something and a lot of people desire it, it's high. The product or service's value is relative to its availability and subjective to the potential buyers' desire.

Supply and demand determine prices, which helps signal buyers and sellers how to act efficiently, guide markets, and provide better quality and availability (Sowell, 2001, 2). Analyzing and forecasting demand is different than creating demand. Economic transactions require a willing buyer with his previous production value in hand, even an employee who exchanged his labor and skill with his employer, ready and willing to buy from a seller of a valuable commodity or service. The executed trade transfers this value, usually through a medium of exchange or money. Adam Smith said:

"Every man lives thus by exchanging or becomes in some measure a merchant, and the society itself grows to be what is properly a commercial society (Smith, 1991 [1776], 29)."

Understanding demand creation requires us to see it as an active desire. How do potential consumers get to this state of mind? Who creates demand?

The idea of the government ginning up demand depends on Keynes' theory of "animal spirits." On the consumer side, the government should redistribute wealth and income to put money in needy people's pockets and let their emotions and desires or instincts take over. The more they need or want things, the faster they'll spend. It looks at humanity cynically to think the government can make people react to base instincts or greed.

You can say intuition is essential. We should pay attention to the gut instinct, but without careful consideration and thoughtful analysis, even for personal needs and wants, "animal spirits" sounds like only animal instincts, or even emotionally reactive human foolhardiness. Some activity may occur in an economy of mostly alcohol, cigarettes, and candy bars, but not many big-ticket items would sell. Contrarily, in truth, good citizens need discipline!

On the business side, "animal spirits" imply recklessness. Could embracing it generate irrational exuberance? Doesn't it suggest reckless gambling? Is addiction to money sustainable? In reality, entrepreneurially created utility or value, not greed, drives improvement and creates demand.

We must realize demand doesn't exist until a supply someone values and can act upon does. Remember the example of the valley people? They didn't know about fruits and vegetables yet; they needed but without actual demand. Supply draws those with something to trade after they know about it and then fulfills a need or want; we see demand as a measurable response to perceived value.

As a small businessman, if I send out business postcards advertising a product or service, how many people will call me to ask about it? If I spend $5,000.00, can I make $10,000.00 gross sales to cover costs and make a profit? How would you define market demand?

It's a response to advertising, successful selling, and other entrepreneurial incentive and creative activities. Invent a better iPod, and people will line up to buy it. Supply advertising and a quality innovative product, and create demand; a good reputation helps further it, even for the future. Put up a colorful billboard of a dripping juicy cheeseburger along the highway with your Exit number and brief directions, and hungry families will pull into your restaurant fifteen minutes after driving past it. We see who creates this state of mind.

Demand as an indicator of activity is like a voltmeter in your car. Does your gauge show a positive number? Is it barely charging? If it's negative, you're in trouble; how long can it run down your battery before your car doesn't start (or your business fails)? The voltmeter measures, but it doesn't create the charge. Overall, healthy demand indicates many prosperous producers, willing, able, and in fact, trading as they purchase each other's goods and services with the value of what they previously produced.

The suppliers of valuable products and services create the demand measured; inventing the need or want, and communicating, establishes the state of mind. Entrepreneurs generate demand, and economists gauge it.

Advertisers know it's partly emotional and partly rational. Refinance, and you'll save thousands annually! The ad has big green $1,000 bills all over it! Or, you'll have this much with our easy savings plan! In a TV commercial, you may flash to an older woman waitressing during her retirement years, rubbing her lower back in pain, and then the same woman relaxing by a pool reading a book with the investment company information across the top.

Advertisers typically cause a problem in someone's mind and give them the solution; they create fear and provide a comforting answer. The TV commercial shows thieves breaking into someone's home with young children in bed. What does the innocent family do? On cue, a voice comes through an intercom asking who is there, letting them know the police are on the way. It flashes to a concerned-looking professional group at the security company monitoring station taking action, listening, quickly conferring, and calling the police. Then back to the thieves running away or being cuffed and put in a police car. It ends with a happy, safe family at the breakfast table with a voiceover quoting a small monthly monitoring fee. It's all safety, smiles, and peace of mind.

It's an engagement of imagination through the description, often using word pictures. The point is, it's creative and entrepreneurial. Businesses create demand by supplying advertising and a quality product or service, and they deliver value. At least hopefully, or they won't stay in business.

If the government puts spending money in people's pockets, it will amount to an economic fizzle of activity because there is no production causing it. The government took money away from others in one way or another to give the spenders spending money. Once they consume, it's gone. There is no production value to trade going forward. No multipliers, only destroyed resources the destroyers did not replace and growing public debt!

How does economic activity flourish? Looking at how a small business creates demand, we'll extrapolate upward to giant corporations and the whole economy.

All the individuals involved in production and trade are economic engines aspiring to perform their functions efficiently. This description, "economic engines," may sound cold or even inhumane, but the truth is the more humanity the workers and the dreamers have, the better they work together; the better they create and meet other peoples' needs and wants. Economic growth, in many forms, is celebrating human creativity. When done honestly, it's celebrating humanity.

An economy consists of individuals and groups of individuals working together to support, and perform, trade within their business functions, resulting in the trading of a finished product or service. It may sound simplistic, but it is foundational to understand economics and comes before all valid economic theories.

Keynesian theory is alien to this concept at its foundation. All government-controlled attempts to create prosperity fail this first test. Economic socialization hinders; it doesn't produce.

One main reason public ownership of the means of production, a so-called command economy or a fully socialized economy, isn't an economy at all? Communist societies sap their people's creativity and undermine their dreams. It eventually becomes all stick and no carrot; it's not trade, but force! Conversely, American prosperity represents attempted and realized dreams and the free exchange of our products and services.

Socialism as a means of production isn't economics at all because it's not freely inspired exchange. It's the government forcing people to produce, and taking from some, and giving to others. Even if the government pays employees well and makes something for sale to the public, there is no free competition: it removes individual initiative and dream fulfillment from production. There is no economic engine, but instead, it can devolve to a bureaucrat with a whip enforcing scheduled quotas. What's called compassionate and humane (socialist ideas) in practice become cold and inhumane in reality; people become functionaries instead of creators.

There is no engine in Keynes' view of government controlling "the instruments" from the demand side because there are two supply sides from which we trade. "Demand-side" economics is a fallacy.

The government supposedly ginning up demand doesn't work, nor does hiring more public employees for a theoretically more prosperous society, nor with Government bureaucrats controlling the means of production even if they leave the nominal ownership in private hands. These things don't represent freedom; the owners and the workers become slaves to the government. The most prominent owners become cohorts with the government bureaucrats as they need each other to control the system. Keynesian crony capitalism-fascism, you might say.

A controlling government starts with the premise of meeting people's needs, not with incentives, invention, and betterment. Is there dynamism in a government agency? Who does better, those who get high satisfaction freely competing to build something they dreamed of or those who plan only to meet needs from a list? Do government planning and control beat free individuals and their associations, racing toward an inspired goal? There is no personal profit through a government bureaucracy of confiscation, procurement, and redistribution without corruption or theft.

With free enterprise, the real economy, you must find better ways to do things; your efficiency and creativity are the difference between profits and losses, success and a good life, or failure and poverty. It can be exhilarating or painful, but your hard work best comes from the inspiration of doing something profoundly beneficial or enjoyable to others.

If you open a restaurant, you better choose the right location and create a more attractive atmosphere than your competition! Is yours the better tasting menu with a better price point for comparable food and drinks? Is your staff consistently efficient and courteous? You better advertise and promote efficiently, among many other things.

You better create something that works, or you will not produce consistent customers; you will not have created a demand for your product. Flexible creativity is an entrepreneurial requirement. All these stages of production have a role. Once your supply produces the customer's frame of mind, then the profitable transaction, your valuable trading follows.

Economics is a free action, starting with the idea, the creation, and following through to the facilitation, sales, and maintenance, which leads to more sales. Facilitating the business begins with the individuals, the economic engines as part of the whole, getting out of bed in the morning and showing up on time ready, willing, and able to work each day.

Economics runs on creativity, consistency, inspiration, and implementation, all requiring freedom. Even employees who must follow the rules and perform specific duties to keep their jobs are free to leave, get another job, or start their own business. Hopefully, each day, their inspiration includes their family's well-being; they usually want to advance and improve their situation to pay for their loved ones; their discipline and consistency are part of this formula that creates results.

The entrepreneurial function creates demand from its first move toward production. From the initial investigations, ordering of supplies, and the first space rented, trading occurs from the beginning to the final sale. The many activities within the stages of production begin, maintain, and facilitate business operations and create demand with each step. It all results in trade of the finished product, which at the sale, makes potential reinvestment and more commerce as the proceeds mean continued paychecks for employees and owners who then trade in their personal lives.

All entrepreneurs must attract those with the power to buy their goods or services to create demand. An illustration of supply creating demand in action with which I am familiar is a small mortgage brokerage and real estate sales business. The broker first contemplates, plans, and gains knowledge, gets licenses, acquires bank funding approval for potential loans, and employs know-how, among many other things.

The broker, the mortgage salespeople, or the loan officers must then create viable or effective (demand for) loans to stay in business. I've done this for years, and I know when I've done it well and haven't. It can be risky, and if you aren't good at it, you can quickly put yourself out of business.

There are many different types of advertising and all kinds of salespeople calling and e-mailing every day trying to get you to pay big bucks for their advertising system. Advertising can become a black hole and put you out of business quickly; most of what they sell, in my experience, doesn't work well or not at all. They make a sale, but it may end my production if I buy too much of something that doesn't work.

Contacting first-time buyers, high-end buyers, investor buyers, second home buyers, different types of sellers, refinance applicants, or purchase applicants, takes strategy, efficient execution, and follow-through. It always means a different approach and creativity in individual situations.

The strategies and actions I've employed, when successful, have created all kinds of economic activity, but it's often from angles or tactics I figured out myself. Effective marketing companies are valuable, but you must stay on top of the campaign and watch them closely. It takes talent and risk to create demand. You must appeal to their imaginations in advertising to get them to inquire. I don't want to sell them anything in the first step; I try to trigger their dreams, unleash their imaginations, get their hopes up, and push the right buttons to make them contact me.

Once we're on the phone, I color their dreams and describe a road to their new home. I calculate their monthly payments, taxes, and required down payment, something I know they can afford after I conversationally asked them a few questions about their job, credit, and current debt payments.

The stages of production already started, and my vision, planning, and creativity in action set up dream fulfillment and turn them into needs and wants. Production continues as I qualify them financially, do the loan application paperwork, and find a house for them with online MLS tools. We both then search for their new home. I show them homes, write offers, and cajole the listing agents on the places they like.

Sometimes I write a heartwarming cover letter with their offer to persuade and comfort the seller and the listing agent. In the loan approval letter, they find out that I know personally of my client's excellent credit; I give comfort and confidence to a seller and their agent in what I write and say with well-presented facts. They accept my client's offer against the competition. Any seller I represent wants me to create demand through effective marketing. You could call this creating compelling value.

In my experience, the government does many things to hinder this demand. It hurts the most with excessive regulations. A potentially prosperous society needs law and order with stable banking and real estate laws with fair enforcement, but these things allow for they don't create demand. The government doesn't create or gin up demand but hopefully sets out a conducive environment for entrepreneurial creativity.

When a real estate salesperson or a mortgage loan officer creates demand through their creativity and expertise in action, many more people go to work. Title company people, real estate appraisers, and the associates at the appraisal company go to work. A home inspector, an insurance agent, and the other employees at the agency and the insurance company go to work. The listing agent and everyone involved with the seller go to work too. Many others, including moving companies and all their employees on both sides of the transaction, maybe even repair contractors, clean-up people, landscapers, handymen, roofers, and many others.

Eventually, future home buying and selling follow, and all the trade in the next transaction as the sellers move up to a new, more expensive home with the first purchase's equity. When the buyer's or seller's reason for moving is a job transfer, we help facilitate their new business activity— business ripples out into multiple current and future events. Multipliers come from all this supply that creates demand with all the value exchanged. Qualified buyers can help cause home construction.

Cynics may complain here: the buyers I got into new homes would probably have bought later, or I merely took the business away from another real estate agent or loan officer. This kind of thinking lacks creativity, and it doesn't value, nor does it understand entrepreneurial power. It suggests fixed resource thinking.

The following phrase attributed to Adam Smith is worth repeating many times, "resources are fixed only in as much as our imaginations are fixed." Creative ideas in trade create expansion and more business. Those people I got into a first home will likely have equity when they sell it and buy a bigger one later. If they didn't purchase the first one, they might never own a home or put it off to only acquire a small one later. Buying now created a lot of economic activity and more potential future activity.

Many potential buyers never act and rent their whole lives. The consistent difference between people having something or nothing in their old age in the USA is whether they bought real estate or not. When they own young, there is usually more potential for future buying. Of course, even with the trend of increasing values over time, everyone should be aware and careful enough not to buy at the peak of asset bubbles.

Buying at a fair price creates possibilities. They could purchase a retirement home or have gift money for their children from an increase in equity because they owned the first property. Gift money from relatives is often the difference between young couples buying a home or not.

There is a significant potential for increased economic activity in the exchange of valuable commodities, real estate in this case, with human employment through the process and wealth creation, all because they purchased the first property.

By activity, I don't mean spending, but the productive action in making it all happen. If you automatically equate "activity" with spending, it might be time to check your Keynesian mentality. An owner or his employee buys something with the proceeds from their contribution to the value they add in facilitating the transaction.

I buy my lunch with a small piece of what I create when I sell someone's home or broker a loan for them; I transfer it for food through a medium of exchange or money. Whoever receives it can then use it for something else. They add value to it by expanding or reinvesting their profit. They make an exchange of value and increase it from their work and creative action.

Spending doesn't create jobs, but profits and paychecks allow for more investment and additional consumption. We enhance value in what we receive in exchange with others as we produce and trade productively. When we grow, money represents what we have improved. If we spend productively on our businesses or our investments, we receive a return. Unproductive consumption doesn't create anything. We won't replace what we've destroyed. Remember this the next time you buy something. You will appreciate your and everyone else's efforts more, and money will have nobility. Understanding this will make us better citizens. I'm not saying some well-deserved recreational activity has no personal value, but that we should recognize when and how we destroy the worth of our previous output and if and how we're sufficiently replacing it and growing.

It's unfortunate when the government overregulates and tries to control or increase the economy by redirecting wealth and income. It is nonsensical, attempting to control which businesses get money with the ideals of any politician's social engineering, and it's precisely the wrong way to create demand, supply, or economic prosperity.

The government can't jump-start the economy. It can contribute to an attractive business environment through sound policies, competence, business-friendly rhetoric, and infrastructure, then watch dream fulfillment and enforce rules of the road type laws. Government meddling and attempting to control only hurts general prosperity and hinders dream realization.

Entrepreneurs create demand in what and how they supply. Supply produces the product or service, the mindset to buy, and the consumer's previous production value in hand to trade. It's true if you create and sell to a neighbor for reciprocal value or someone in another country, whether you are one person or part of a huge corporation.

Efficient production and trade between more and less affluent societies make all wealthier and creates the most demand. Economist Thomas Sowell shows that if one country produces everything more efficiently than other countries, it's still worthwhile to import some things from them. Why? If they are ten times better at producing valuable products but only twice as good at making cheaper ones, they'll become wealthier overall, focusing on what they do best. By creating more of, and trading the expensive items, than trying to do everything themselves, they can import more cheap items than if they made them. A less efficient country gets work, and although less affluent than the more productive societies, they all receive more overall (Sowell, 2001, 28-31).

Supply creates demand in many ways. Multipliers happen from productivity: from building and multiplying entrepreneurial activity, reinvesting profits, banking, leveraging, and capital investment, but not from demand.

Demand doesn't create its own supply in the aggregate or on the ground in the real world. It does nothing of itself. Without a supply of something valuable, it doesn't even exist because it doesn't create anything and can't fulfill needs or make wants as something valued can.

9

Supply Destruction

"...a product is no sooner created, than it, from that instant, affords a market for other products to the full extent of its own value."

Jean-Baptiste Say

I F SAY'S LAW is correct (and it undoubtedly is), isn't the opposite true? If the government hinders entrepreneurs from creating valuable products and services, won't it impede supply creation? If an ongoing profitable business now must comply with multiple times the regulatory burden at much more cost, doesn't it destroy a percentage of future production? If it becomes cost-prohibitive to start a business or enter a market, what does that supply others? If companies quit in the face of the excessive burden, what do they contribute to humanity?

Small and medium-sized businesses have always been significant job creators in the U.S.A., and many huge companies began very small and on shoe-string budgets. The little guy struggles to cope with many thousands of pages of new laws and regulations, telling him what he can and cannot do, especially when they assault him by trying to micromanage his daily operations. In this kind of environment, wouldn't you expect less job creation from smaller shops than historically? Wouldn't it hurt general productivity and our overall standard of living?

On the one hand, fewer productive people mean those supplying valuable goods and services have fewer trading partners. Supply, or production, becomes more challenging as demand, or consumption, falls because there's less production from the other side of a potential transaction. These burdens cause cautiousness among creators, as exemplified in the Obama years. Suppliers from both sides of any possible deal generate and acquire less, and they have less to trade with others.

If it takes a mortgage broker an hour to put together a customer application package, or if he completes the same task but in eight hours, does it matter for prosperity? It matters for mine. It matters for all the other small mortgage brokers in the country too. All that time for all the mortgage brokers and the loan officers combined turns into extremely reduced output with disheartening pain and suffering.

There were twelve pages to a mortgage application package with the federal and state disclosures before the Mortgage Safe Act, Dodd-Frank, and all the new massive regulatory power given the Federal Reserve Bank to implement and oversee so much additional bureaucracy. Now, the first pile of papers a mortgage applicant must sign has about fifty-five pages. That's right, over four times the paperwork the first time you sit down, with many more pages to sign along the way at each stage in the loan process. For now, the application is only four pages (twelve or so pages soon, they say), but many additional, often repetitive pages of disclosures confuse people.

After the initial application, per the laws, the wholesale bank had to do all the same disclosure paperwork again as administered under the Obama administration. You heard that right. The government required the whole confusing pile done a second time, so the mortgage applicant got the same things in a slightly different confusing format twice. The wholesale bank also had to examine everything the broker did and send it back to us to correct any jot and tittle we may not have dotted or crossed per their judgment. John and Mary Homeowner may have started reading it, but they flipped pages and signed at some point. I saw it every time.

To begin with, I'd apologize for all the paperwork to follow; there is nothing we could do about it; it's the law! I'd tell my clients the path of least resistance is to keep smiling and do what they ask. It wasn't only human sympathy on my part, but an immunization against all of us becoming too disheartened—which could cause them to stop cooperating and then, along with all the pain of going through it, I wouldn't get paid.

A lawyer for the State of California told me they found in a study, the more disclosures there are, the fewer people read. I asked him how much taxpayer money they spent to discover this. He didn't know. I asked him why he didn't just ask any loan officer in the state or even in the whole country because everyone knows it. He seemed surprised. We talked further, but his leftist bent hindered the conversation. He continued attempting to defend the new laws any way he could with no common sense or business acumen. It must have been like talking to Chuck Schumer, Nancy Pelosi, Elizabeth Warren, Bernie Sanders, or Barak Obama.

Mortgage applicants don't have time to read it all. Even if someone were a speed reader and a genius, they couldn't get through something so confusing the regulators often don't understand it. If people don't read all these disclosures when the broker gives them a copy, do you think they read it when the bank sends them an almost identical pile to sign again? Mortgage applicants often become bitter after the pain of refinancing or getting a purchase loan. It could be why so many are not refinancing when they should.

Wholesale banks used to copy the broker-supplied disclosures and file them for compliance. They now use a computer-generated click-through system for the disclosures; in other words, they make it easy for the applicants not to read it. Before these new laws, they were fewer but more understandable.

The Good Faith Estimate for the State of California was much more explicit and straightforward before these laws. Now, all the states must use the same confusing form the geniuses made up at the federal level. Before the federal government intruded into all this with thousands of pages of new laws with all the new regulations, both the federal and state disclosures were easier to understand.

The smallest brokers are under the most pressure from the new regulations. Larger companies can take compliance expenses better. They can streamline systems and afford to hire compliance and processing staff in-house. These laws hurt the big guy and kill the small guy. A small owner-run brokerage must take his time dealing with all the compliance instead of spending his precious time trying to get business.

Recently, a wholesale bank demanded, probably based on their lawyer's interpretation, I use a new disclosure form they do not supply that was not in my mortgage underwriting software. The software company, which stays on top of the stream of new regulations, insisted the software was up to date and legally compliant; they are the most popular mortgage underwriting software provider in the country. The bank wouldn't process the loan any further unless I got a form signed with specific dates to meet compliance, but no one had it anywhere.

The loan was locked with the clock ticking. If it expired, I would lose the applicant's rate, my client, and prices had gone up. If a locked rate expires before funding/closing, the disclosures become useless with my many work hours down the drain. If a deal no longer makes sense because it becomes too expensive, the client won't go through with it. The client had already paid $625 for an appraisal on the investment property refinance.

If it didn't go through, they'd expect their appraisal money back, and I'd never get business from them again. This government caused pain and suffering, unnecessary risk, additional expense, and limitation on my income is brutal. If you were a small mortgage broker, would you think the federal government is trying to drive you out of business? It's entirely unnecessary and wholly government-caused. Think of all the unpaid hours, the needless work, and the stress involved.

Finally, I drafted a form on my computer, sending it back and forth with someone helpful at the wholesale lender who helped me work it to their understanding of compliance. It took me several hours. More money lost. The client never knew what I went through, but if I didn't figure it out behind the scenes and the rate lock expired, that customer and any future business with them would surely be gone. Future money lost.

Sometimes, I ask regulators about regulations they can't figure out, and different compliance officers at wholesale banks tell me different things. The government prosecutors or regulators could say we did something wrong because of the different interpretations. The government could legally destroy us or fine us out of business by construing the law one way instead of another.

The thousands of pages in new laws have created more application and disclosure paperwork and more underwriting compliance checklists and paperwork, more escrow compliance and paperwork, more appraisal compliance and paperwork, more funding compliance and paperwork, and on and on.

There used to be a funding checklist. Now, there is a much more arduous funding audit. Someone must go through every file with a fine-tooth comb before wiring the money, and the bank may demand new things from me at the last minute, or they can't fund the loan.

A massive amount of extra unpaid work hurts the industry in many ways. It could produce a justifiably angry borrower. They could sue if they couldn't buy a house or were out an appraisal fee, inspection fee, or for a deposit that a seller kept after the buyer has waived his loan contingency but can't close on time or not at all.

The law now requires the underwriter to review all the credit information again and re-pull the applicant's credit report a second time before funding—before they can do the pre-funding audit with each loan, every time. All of this can become disconcerting as loan locks reach expiration, especially with many closings on the same day or at month's end.

More and more government-caused unpaid work means I now must make quarterly and annual reports to the government no one reads. With the federal rules on top of the state rules, I had to pass an additional state and national test on top of the state test I took when I was licensed years ago in California. That is three tests for my one license. With the new laws implemented, all mortgage salespeople now had three different tests, not only brokers; recently, the bureaucrats combined the state mortgage test and the national test into a longer but single test. Someone getting into the business now must pass two tests for the one license in California.

But Congress exempted the big banks. More testing for the little guys, but still none required for the big guys. It all has courses beforehand that take time, and with the quarterly and annual reports, the yearly class, and test, to keep my license active—all of it costs money, and who pays for it? You guessed it. Adding insult to injury, they charge us for it all.

The big banks convinced the politicians that they only hire respectable people or something, so no tests for them and more tests for us. Did you know that when you walk into a national bank and work with one of their loan officers, their "mortgage experts" have no licensing? The government gives them a license number when the bank asks for it!

The government now controls how brokers make money, but once again, it exempts the big banks from the rule! Can you imagine the government dictating your pay, especially when they exempt your competition? They don't tell us what we make overall, but each of our clients with any particular wholesale lender must pay the same percentage. It puts us at a competitive disadvantage because we can't lower our pay to compete unless the borrower pays commissions out of pocket; the bank isn't allowed to pay us if our percentage is different. If we can't increase our percentage on small loans, we can't make enough money, and on large ones, we must lower our percentage, or it's a waste of time. We won't get the loan.

Even worse, if there is enough rebate from the loan, it can't go to our compensation if the government formula for costs says we're beyond compliance. The disclosers must state that the borrower pays our commission like an added cost (even though structured with a significantly reduced interest rate). Suppose there is any extra rebate over allowable covered charges. In that case, it can only go to principal reduction after the loan begins, so it doesn't help to lower someone's interest rate with no out-of-pocket costs. And we have to charge the customer our full commission in upfront points to do it! Are micromanaging laws good for borrowers? No, but they are for our competitors, the retail banks when they're exempt.

It's a fact that these laws and regulations attack small business and favor big business. If you're looking to stereotype Republicans here, the Democrats controlled both houses of Congress when they passed. Who's all for the rich? Who is in the big banks' pockets? The Dems are for the little guy? Sure.

Once again, every year, brokers and their salespeople must now take a course and pass a test to keep their licenses active, but, like the rest of it, the big national bank's loan officers and reps are exempt. One year, the instructor asked how many people had been in the business for more than a decade. In a room of about one hundred brokers and their loan officers, the vast majority raised their hands. He then asked how many had been in the business seven years or more, and a few others raised their hands. No one raised their hand when he asked about less than seven years.

The instructor then tried to tell us how all the new laws help those still in the business because of less competition! I raised my hand, and he called on me. I said it sure seems the government is trying to destroy the industry as no one is coming into it. You could have heard a pin drop just before the room erupted in applause.

The law now requires us to verify all deposits on an applicant's bank statements over a couple of hundred dollars. We must document where the money came from with a check or receipt or a withdrawal slip from a bank and a deposit receipt matching the bank statement, with a signed explanation letter. Do you always save these things from a couple of months back? Could you find them?

People make small deposits for various reasons. It could be parents reimbursing other parents for little league expenses, someone paying you back for something, or a personal item you sold. If you can't prove where it came from with a paper trail, the deal is dead—no mortgage for you.

Everyone loses their time and effort—all are angry, frustrated, and disheartened, with all of it unnecessarily caused by the government. It used to be you proved their income, and if they had additional small deposits that they didn't claim, they couldn't use it to qualify. Sound reasonable? If the government doesn't precisely understand each deposit of a couple of hundred dollars or more with documentation layers, the bank must cancel the deal.

Tracking proof of small deposits may not sound like much to you, but on top of hundreds of other pages you must go through and sign in the process, it can just be too much—the straw to break the camel's back for an applicant. If we didn't do the disclosures precisely right, the broker or bank must keep going back to the applicant getting things resigned.

Any escrow company handling a refinance loan or a purchase transaction has lots of new compliance with much more paperwork; they now have exact "tolerances" for escrow disclosures. Some escrow disclosures require zero tolerance; what I put on the initial disclosures must match the bank "estimate" and what escrow balances out on the closing statement. A senior escrow officer, a woman who had been in the business many years, began sobbing, telling me how hard it all was for her when the bulk of these laws came down on all of us.

The lawyers say the Good Faith Estimate is now legally considered a contract. It's not a good faith "estimate" anymore. It's why many hard money lenders left the industry. After the deal closes, a lawyer can find a slight discrepancy and sue a mortgage broker with much better odds of winning than before. Even if the broker might win the suit because he did the paperwork correctly, who wants lawyers threatening them?

There are many other reasons the real estate industry suffers when the mortgage industry suffers. Draconian mortgage laws affect Realtors with everything from getting a client's loan approved for buying a home to the timing of closing escrow because of so many regulations and hoops banks must go through in funding each loan.

One Harvard Study from February 2015 points to the effects of draconian regulations favoring big businesses over medium and small shops. It documents how community banks lost market share at nearly double the rate after Dodd-Frank than they did during the financial crisis.

"...community banks' share of U.S. banking assets and lending markets has fallen from over 40 percent in 1994 to around 20 percent today. Interestingly, we find that community banks emerged from the financial crisis with a market share 6 percent lower, but since the second quarter of 2010 – around the time of the passage of the Dodd-Frank Act – their share of U.S. commercial banking assets has declined at a rate almost double that between the second quarters of 2006 and 2010. Particularly troubling is community banks' declining market share in several key lending markets, their decline in small business lending volume, and the disproportionate losses being realized by particularly small community banks (Lux & Greene, 2015, 1)."

The study concludes:

"We find that while community banks weathered the crisis with greater resilience than many mid-size counterparts, since the passage of the Dodd-Frank Act, the pace at which community banks have lost market share is nearly double what it was during the crisis (Ibid, 31)."

Is it any coincidence the national banks, some of whom needed bailing out a few years ago, have taken over so much more market share and have grown significantly more dominant in the last few years? Could this crony capitalism be at least partly congressionally caused?

I've seen many small to medium-sized mortgage companies go out of business since the implementation of Dodd-Frank and the Mortgage Safe Act. Wholesale lenders I knew from years ago call me, and the first thing they do is congratulate me for still being in business. It's the first thing they say. Why? So many brokers they try to contact are gone. Do you think the massive new regulatory pressure isn't a significant cause? I can tell you firsthand it is.

I told an appraiser this story, and she said the same thing is happening in the appraisal industry. According to her, the average age of an appraiser now is over fifty. I Googled "the average age of a real estate appraiser" and found many articles on how their numbers are shrinking and the average age continues rising.

An article about how a quickening shortage of appraisers now hurts the real estate industry from Inman online gives several reasons, among them the following:

"While stricter regulations were meant to protect the consumer, it has kept new appraisers away and caused the industry to stagnate (Sheckler, 2018)."

An article from Working RE called "The Decline of Real Estate Appraisers" reinforces the story:

"Every year, for the past eight years, the number of active real estate appraisers has declined. The Appraisal Institute (AI) estimates that the number of appraisal professionals is currently shrinking at three percent a year and warns that sharper declines may be on the horizon as appraisers begin retiring en masse (Peck, 2016)."

The ridiculous licensing requirements and regulations massively increased paperwork but also enforced government-controlled lower pay. Many appraisers continue giving up their businesses in the face of it, with fewer choosing this career. The government made operations much harder, but their bureaucratic assault continues with the draconian laws still in place.

Appraisals cost more now, the government sets the price, but the appraisers make less because a big chunk goes to an "Appraisal Management Company." The federal government created a new and unnecessary industry between appraisers and loan officers who now need to order appraisals through intermediaries.

On top of the enormous amount of control-oriented regulations, the government took all past clients away from them. If you were an appraiser who built your business over many years, providing excellent service and building relationships with mortgage brokers and lenders, they took it all away from you.

Appraisers now must go on a list to get jobs. It's illegal for mortgage brokers or loan officers to talk to the appraiser during a transaction, and we can't order the appraisals from those we know and trust. I used to order appraisals directly from competent appraisers I knew from the past. It was less expensive for the mortgage applicant, more reliable, and faster before the government took over the process.

Sometimes we get incompetent appraisers as they come randomly off the list or don't know the area. We have no control over who we get, and values can vary wildly. It can blow a deal, slow down closing, or force us to appeal through a government-enforced process through the appraisal management company that the new laws mandated into existence.

It takes time to gather all the documentation to write up a case against an inaccurate valuation. The go-between companies are interested in siding with the appraisers against the buyers and brokers. They want a good relationship with the appraisers, but it also makes them look better to regulators if they are too low rather than too high. More damage to productivity. More money lost and more entrepreneurial and consumer suffering.

I used to call the appraiser directly to make complaints. They would say to e-mail comps that support my position, and they would either agree or disagree, but it was a quick process of direct communication. The laws in place now assume we are all criminals, so they control the process inefficiently. The politicians hysterically blamed appraisers and brokers, justifying their horrible laws. We caused the housing overvaluation!

In my firsthand experience, during the refi boom, appraisers made so much money their first concern was to avoid recklessness, and they were very protective of their licenses. I can honestly only think of one or two times I felt they went too high, and I didn't push them to do it. The high valuations were government-driven, mainly from excessively liberal lending guidelines through Fannie Mae and Freddie Mac. Comparable homes supported the prices as people were paying that much. With the system in place now, appraisals are more expensive, less reliable, and less accurate—big surprise. The government control-oriented solutions made matters worse.

Can you understand my frustration at the election when President Obama ran on how superb the new banking and mortgage laws were? He boasted about them, owned them, and was proud to defend them. He demonized Mitt Romney because he wanted to repeal many of them. I thought, how can the voters support these policies? Do they know how harmful and inhumane they are?

They were a trophy for Mr. Obama. He sold the illusion of how the government had fixed our mortgage problems. Did Obama not understand economics? Did he want to destroy the system? How could he support these laws if he knew the economic basics the giants defined so long ago? The truth is, these draconian laws do far more harm than good.

The following statement attributed to Adam Smith, I'll continue repeating: "The only way we increase our standard of living over time is through increased productivity due to two things that are often interrelated, new technology and new methods."

After Obama implemented his "progressive" vision, the only thing we used new technology and new methods for under his administration was to try to survive under so much new compliance paperwork that drained out our productivity gains. Each year computer technology increased, but regulations always seem to grow more. Because this is true in many economic sectors, it's one main reason he oversaw such a weak, flat recovery. His full two terms averaged only 1.525% economic growth (U.S. Department of Commerce, 2017). How could he not understand why?

Government control produces stagnation, and Obama's terrible record shows it. Many left-leaning news sources report only flattering propaganda pieces about his time in office. If Keynesians ever admit to his minimal growth rate, they argue it's from the government not creating enough aggregate demand in the economy. Their remedy? You guessed it, like a broken record, they push for more deficit spending; our national debt then gets so many zeros on it even these academic geniuses can't count that high.

Given how many industries went through a tough time with draconian regulations under Obama's first term, either the American people didn't know or didn't care. Obama won reelection easily. With a vote like that, one could say America's business isn't business anymore. Bureaucratic government is now America's business! Obama's campaign slogan should have been something like, "your business is my business," or "keep quiet while we drive you out of business," or "the administration to shift all business to large businesses while we drive mom and pop out of business."

At least the voters understood the administration's controlling mentality enough to put Congress in the opposing party's hands early in Obama's Presidency, but the Republicans seemed confused too. Why does the awful junk remain in place? Because some Republicans and most Democrats are ignorant or self-concerned—they use Keynesian rhetoric for votes.

Electing Donald Trump, a very colorful, spicily speaking, and straight-talking real estate developer and reality TV star, must be directly attributable to Obama's total lack of understanding of business and economics. At least there is someone in place now with business acumen and proven talent.

A lobbyist for an association of mortgage professionals told me the Trump administration's attitude is far more business-friendly than the previous administration: they ask how they can make it easier for us to operate. The Obama Administration's demeanor was harsh and generally skeptical of any suggestions for streamlining policy. As our treatment under the new laws, business people were all criminals in their minds.

Alarmingly, he also said the Trump Administration doesn't support repealing the awful laws entirely because it took such pains and time to get used to them. They believe the Democrats will put them back when they gain power and disrupt things again. They think we must learn to live with and streamline them. I don't know if it's true or he was just talking, but if it is, it's a huge disappointment and a horrible mistake. Still, even with the laws remaining in place, the Trump administration has applied them in a much friendlier way. The application process is now more streamlined and virtually all electronic, and there are improvements with regulatory implementation.

Much improvement is a herculean and almost miraculous application of technology and streamlining from the wholesale lenders, a real testament to American grit and innovation. But why does the government have to be our enemy? What happens when a more hostile administration gains power? You can count on stricter interpretations and added laws to satisfy their hostilities towards commerce.

Shouldn't enough Republicans and Democrats in Congress and those in the Executive Branch, including the President, understand how constricting all these oppressive laws are to businesses across the economy? How about how unfair and inhumane they are for those struggling to grow their businesses? They should repeal the legislative assault going back years, but definitely, signed into place against the American people by Obama and G. W. Bush if they want us to reach anywhere near our growth potential.

10

Demand Destruction

"...production, the true source of individual influence, as well as national power."

Jean-Baptiste Say

GEORGE W. BUSH and Barak H. Obama signed several massive and destructive laws thousands of pages long into place. They set up economic hindrances from the smallest to the largest companies in different industries in different ways.

Especially under Obama, excessive regulations became incredibly destructive. The result was a stifled economy growing far below its potential; small and medium-sized businesses, very significant job creators historically, were not so under Obama. The most connected crony capitalist largest corporations had an unfair advantage. From advertising and sales to operations, competing against the larger companies became more arduous.

More even than Dodd-Frank does, one law mainly attacks small companies, but the general public doesn't think twice about supporting it without concern for the little guy. Bush signed it, and it came out of a Republican-controlled Congress, but most people consider it uncontroversial.

There are still many people who haven't refinanced their mortgages even though interest rates remain excellent, and they could go up at any time. As I write this, they just jumped up a bit more and are no longer at the lowest point in recent history.

The Federal Reserve Bank keeps hinting they'll raise short-term rates more this year if not at their next meeting. Government bond yields, which mortgage rates typically follow, could go up from historic lows for multiple reasons, excessive public debt not being the least of them. All those people who haven't yet refinanced into much better interest rates should now.

Even though the Federal Reserve Bank's actions and influence have kept mortgage rates unnaturally low, the public record shows enormous numbers of people with relatively high rates who won't respond to advertising; I wish I knew why. I can see recording dates in the public record by title company data. By comparing these with rates at that time, many people could refinance now and lower their monthly payments by hundreds of dollars. Even though they could save thousands each year and many thousands over the years, they aren't taking action.

Legally contacting past clients is now a problem too. I wish I could call all these people on the phone, but the government won't let me; I'd have to break the law. If they knew they could refinance at no cost to them, why wouldn't they? I doubt most of them are waiting for rates to go down further, and I'm sure they don't all have bad credit or income problems.

Historically, I've mailed letters explaining how I'll lower their monthly payments at no cost to them. They can get a new loan with all the costs covered, and I'll do the application work for them. They'll need to supply me information and sign with some clicks on their computer, there will be paperwork along the way, but I'll try to make it as easy as possible.

Many of my letters go to investors with multiple properties, and I can see that they live in expensive neighborhoods by the public record. I mail to their homes referencing their investment properties; they get the letters because I receive very few Post Office returns. I know these investors typically don't have cash flow problems from my years of experience, and they would almost all have excellent credit, but they rarely call, and the government won't let me call them.

I have historically gotten a better response than other mortgage companies and real estate companies with letters and advertising. I write briefly but directly with creative imagination, using word pictures, vivid descriptions, emotional points about their kids and families, etc. My numbers have usually been respectable.

When writing this type of advertising, the goal is to reach the prospects' creative imaginations, not sell them anything with the marketing piece but to compel them to call me. Sometimes mailings alone work, but most often, they don't. I used telemarketing companies specializing in contacting these slow-to-respond homeowners; there is nothing like a prescreening appointment setter approaching them first.

Sometimes I mail letters or postcards to homeowners all around the state, but each mailing costs thousands of dollars. If this doesn't result in business, it can put you out of business quickly. Printing costs add up, mailing lists with targeted data are relatively expensive, but the postage adds up the most. Business is riskier than it used to be, with responses much lower, but now with all kinds of new laws and regulations the government continues piling on, we have even more pressure.

List companies compile data from the public record and sell the name, mailing address, and available phone numbers for a fee. I say "available" phone numbers because the government effectively outlawed the way we successfully contacted homeowners.

Combining mailing and then telemarketing, which followed letters or postcards, was a cost-effective strategy. The loan officer or the mortgage salesperson would have a warm call appointment set up by the telemarketer instead of a much less efficient and more difficult cold call. It was a numbers game, but a small mortgage company could spend a few thousand dollars in advertising and get a percentage more back over that from closed deals consistently. Telemarketing, the customer contact machine, worked. Enter the government.

It seems those of you at home didn't like being on the receiving end of those telemarking calls, so you got your politicians to destroy the marketing machine small mortgage companies used most efficiently. People may have thought telemarketing calls were annoying, but it was how the business worked, and it got hard to contact people refinanced, saving them vast amounts of money.

Think of all the additional disposable income across the economy for investment, savings, and buying goods and services, all that saved money would represent. What could you do with an extra $3,000 per year? What about an additional $5,000? Could you put it in your retirement account or savings plan every year and watch it grow and become much more in twenty or thirty years?

You could have $100,000 more at retirement virtually for free in 15 or 20 years. Could you pay off debts? Could you get your kids braces or send them to private school? Could you pay the daycare bill with it? If it didn't cost you anything, wouldn't you do it to make your life or your children's lives better?

Refinancing these people was good for them and good for the economy.

They could get a lower payment at a much-reduced interest rate or get a shorter term with the same or a similar monthly outlay. They could take ten or twelve years off the loan, potentially letting them retire years earlier. Would that be good? Maybe they could help others in their retirement, spend more time volunteering at church or do something with their family they always wanted to do before they were too old.

These days, when I order marketing lists, and they ask if I want phone numbers with the mailing addresses, there is a big wrinkle. We must scrub the names against the Do Not Call List; the result is very few phone numbers with mailing addresses.

Many people reading this may have no sympathy because they hated getting those phone calls at dinner time. An emotional reaction is understandable. Out of principle, I didn't go on The DNC List. I'd indeed be a hypocrite if I did, but I also knew what a restraint of trade it is for small businesses across the country in my industry and many others.

In many ways, I don't recall ever seeing more anti-small business legislation than the Do Not Call List. When President George W. Bush signed it, he babbled something about generally being a "pro-business kinda guy," but people are getting too many phone calls at dinner time or something.

How would I describe this? Is it fair to call him a pro-consumer but anti-business President at that moment? I can't say he was pro-consumer. No, he was a restraint of trade President at that moment. The economy is trading value with each other. If I were President and they brought me a bill like that, I'd laugh at them and give them a speech about how America's business is business. I might tell them to move to Cuba if they want freedom from any commercial solicitation in my less subtle moments.

It exemplifies a new American mentality through sweeping anti-small business legislation; it forces those bothering you to stop it. It's thoughtless to use a sledgehammer to kill a gnat. Is it mean-spirited? Why not look at the phone display before you answer? If it's the kids, a friend, or your mom, and you want to pick it up, go ahead. Why can't people unplug or turn off their phones at dinner time if they desire quiet? No, we turn to the government to solve our problems, and we get a sweeping, comprehensive, punitive law that attacks commerce, especially small businesses.

Solving this annoyance with technology, entrepreneurially, organically instead of using toxic pesticides on the economy, if you will, would've been far healthier for us all. If the phone display shows my business name when I call, you'll know it's me, and you can answer or not. The new phones could just lightly beep to whatever setting you choose, and you could look at the display and ignore what you don't want to answer. We should all probably shut our phones off at dinner time anyway and then look through the phone log after spending this valuable family time, but technology can make it easy for you if you are expecting a call.

If I want to be proactive with those lackadaisical homeowners now, I could always follow up by old-fashioned door knocking. Just mail them a letter or a postcard or two, then go out and say hello. How can the government stop me from tapping on peoples' doors? How else can the government restrain trade for small entrepreneurs and hinder the economy?

Although the Supreme Court has upheld commercial freedom of speech generally (Court, 1976), residents can post a sign on their property, saying, "No Solicitation," making it illegal to be there. Fair enough. Why not enforce the law? Consistently applied reasonably stiff fines could protect peoples' domiciles from rapacious door knocking. If it became too obnoxious, the free market profit motive could provide the answer. Small-time camera installers could supply the solution, and you wouldn't even have to go outside; a motion sensor could snap a picture.

Why not provide a simple, signed complaint with photos to the police if people trespass after you've posted signs? The authorities would most likely tell you they're too busy to bother with enforcement. How do our local governments control the situation? Many have set up a draconian political apparatus to solve the problem.

Increasingly, cities and towns make it virtually impossible to knock on peoples' doors for commercial reasons lawfully. Some municipalities allow it only after a background check, getting fingerprinted, paying a significant fee, and going through and signing a bunch of paperwork with personal supporting information. You then wait for the approval.

Many articles online report municipal laws requiring picture I.D. placards you must wear, among other things. If they okay you after jumping through many hoops, you'll have to wear a badge that says SOLICITOR (Minneapolis, 2018).

How's that for a business-friendly government? Each little regulation may seem reasonable, but it's death by a thousand cuts. Their goal, it seems, is stopping this entry-level business activity. They should call these badges "scarlet letter signs." Direct sales now has the stigma adultery once did.

Do you remember when companies hired kids as door-to-door encyclopedia salesmen for their first sales job? People would door knock selling many things, even pots and pans, not anymore. All the hindrance stops this beginner-level commerce. It sure isn't Mayberry in America anymore.

Have you seen the TV News reports with the Police breaking up little children's lemonade stands? I'm not kidding; I saw this on the local TV news!

Are you thinking only in California? What about other "blue" states or even "red" states? What about everywhere in the U.S.A? Forbes reports police shutting down lemonade stands in Georgia and Iowa and saying it's not rare that government "officials" call the cops on kids selling cupcakes in many places across the country with their parents getting fined hundreds of dollars (Kain, 2011).

CNN reports Texas' police shutting down a lemonade stand because the two little girls didn't have a $150 "peddler's permit." They were trying to raise $100 to take their dad out for his birthday. The city agreed to waive the permit fee, but the report continues:

"A Texas law prohibits the sale of any food items that could spoil without proper temperature control, and lemonade is included. In addition to a permit, a health inspection must take place before a permit is granted (Zaru, 2015)."

The police shut them down. It continues:

"Other states have similar laws." In 2011 a group of kids who set up a lemonade stand outside the Congressional Country Club in Montgomery County, Maryland, were fined $500 for not having a vendor's permit." (Ibid)

Of course, if the kids followed all the rules, the authorities would probably stop them with zoning or child labor laws. What's the main lesson for the children these days? The government won't let you! No entrepreneurial dreaming for you! The government is the boss! Or is the first lesson that you are a slave to government decree? Politicians could call these "conditioning laws" or "designed to form children into obedient citizens through government control." How about "laws to break children's commercial spirit?" It's just a guess, but the Police in Cuba probably wouldn't care if little kids were to sell lemonade on the corner.

We must ask ourselves which way we're going, towards freedom and prosperity or government-controlled mediocrity, or worse? Where are we going? "Where there is no vision, the people perish (Proverbs, 1987)..." Are we caught between competing visions? Is one winning over time? What if the radical one leads us the wrong way? Have we forgotten who we are as our youth receive social indoctrination?

Without more productivity than we've had in the last few years, we won't be able to pay the public debt we've chained to ourselves and our children. What happens in the future if we train our kids out of entrepreneurship? Once you submit to government control, how bad will it get? How much power will an ever-hungrier monstrosity demand?

They hurt my ability to obtain and service clients, make money, and create demand in the economy by converting stubborn potential customers into trade transactions. They hinder my profits, they impede the betterment of those stubborn consumers by stopping them from saving a lot of money, and they ended the work their saved money could do in the economy before it began. They also lowered the income of Title Companies, Escrow Companies, Appraisers, and Banks and erased what they could have done with the profits from lost transactions. All the related employees made less.

Instead of allowing technology to solve the annoyance problem with telemarketing, the government created enormous difficulty for me and others. They destroyed a massive amount of business with one sweeping draconian law. If new phone apps made this kind of marketing obsolete, it would be part of a natural technological advancement. The drastic anti-business DNC List legislation has many more consequences.

According to the Federal Trade Commission website, part of the Do Not Call penalties work like this:

"A company with which a consumer has an established business relationship may call for up to 18 months after the consumer's last purchase or last delivery, or last payment unless the consumer asks the company not to call again. In that case, the company must honor the request not to call. If the company calls again, it may be subject to a fine of up to $40,654.

If a consumer makes an inquiry or submits an application to a company, the company can call for three months. Once again, if the consumer makes a specific request to that company not to call, the company may not call, even if it has an established business relationship with the consumer (Federal Trade Commission, 2016)."

I may get an over forty thousand dollar fine each time I try to stay in contact with a past client. We may not call unless it's within "18 months after the consumer's last purchase or last delivery, or last payment..." So much for the best way to do business. The government made it so much harder for the little guy that it's almost unbelievable. What small business person can afford this fine each time they call if someone complains?

Mortgage rates can drop to historic lows for brief periods, but I can't pick up the phone and call past clients I haven't had "an established business relationship" with within the last eighteen months, so I'm stuck. They know me if I call, they'll hopefully rely on me, but the law has a draconian fine over my head if I try to do business. I could perhaps call them at work, but some people can't take calls; at some jobs, people can't, or they may have changed employers. Trying to build a new client list by telemarketing people's workplaces is nearly impossible.

Past clients are usually the best prospects because they trust me and probably would say yes after I make the case. I can mail them a letter or e-mail them, but the odds of it working are minuscule compared to calling them on the phone. There are also do not mail lists now, and you need permission to send e-mails. Oh well, the government has that covered too. It seems they want to make customer contact illegal, except for TV and radio ads, which only the big guys can afford.

Recently, a company tried to sell me a marketing plan for listings with a few other Realtors on a conference call. They supposedly had a great list company that provided prospect follow-up phone numbers. Merely mail two or three times and call them a day or two after they received the letters. It was foolproof; only if you bought it, you were a fool!

Without thinking it through, I bought the list and did a mailing. I guess I was tired that day, but I hadn't tried telemarketing for such a long time, and anyone can make a mistake. Following the law, I began the task of scrubbing the numbers against the DNC List. Most companies do this for you before you receive the information.

So I paid for prospect phone numbers I found were illegal to call with over ninety percent on the DNC List. When I brought this up on their next weekly conference call, the guy admonished everyone to follow the law, changed the subject, and answered someone else's question. They were selling a program the law precludes from working. I canceled, but other people kept buying the program even after I exposed it. Desperate for leads, these Realtors lined up to break the law.

These DNC List rules apply to all businesses and industries. Wait, not for charities. You know, the firemen or the policemen widows' fund that gives a few bucks to some charity and keeps the "profit" for themselves? They can still operate. The politicians also left themselves off the list. That would interfere with free speech, right? Free enterprise? Our political leaders don't know what it is, or they don't care. They make up any reduced tax revenue by printing and borrowing currency anyway! They spend it into existence!

Many businesses used to call past clients every few years, like roofing companies, interior decorators, house painters, and many others. Not anymore, not without breaking the law. I suspect these small businesses often ignore it all, take the risk, and call anyway. The honest, law-abiding ones may go out of business.

If you are an interior decorator and business is slow, what would you do historically? Just go through past client files, call them, have a friendly conversation, and get some business if it made sense for them, right? Only these days, after you go through all the time and trouble to sign up for the DNC List, then take all the time to scrub the numbers you want to call, you probably can't legally call any of them. You'll find you had to go through all kinds of government bureaucracy, but you can't use this bread and butter sure-fire way to get business. These things psychologically wear on small business people and hurt productivity.

Draconian laws hurt people and hurt their families; they are inhumane. What happens if you decorated some homes a few years ago, but now business is slow? What do you do if you put a roof on someone's house fifteen years ago, and you think it's time to call for repeat business? How does a house painter feel as he realizes when going through past client files that he can't call them without breaking the law?

I was talking to a boatyard owner a while ago, and I asked him how business was. He said it was good, but he never worries about it. I replied, really, recession-proof? He said, well, years ago, I was in sales, and I learned that if things get slow, I have so many past customers' files, I can make calls to get some boats in the yard.

He had a false sense of security because it's illegal to call most of his past customers. I can't tell you what a sickening feeling it is when you realize this and that there is no other reason than a bullying, overbearing, and heartless government in the way of you making a living. The congressmen responsible for these laws still fly, even to other countries, on our dime. The Presidents who sign these bills live very well for the rest of their lives after they throw massive logs in small business peoples' paths.

In the mortgage industry, the competitive advantage is to the large banks and mortgage companies by running expensive TV ads in my past clients' faces all night, commercials I can't afford. Depending on how much TV my former clients watch, they may see offers sounding too good to be true five or ten times a night, maybe more.

They can simply pick up the phone and make a free call to get their questions answered or go online for a free quote. The fantastic offer often doesn't apply to them, but now a salesperson has them on the phone. They get their information and get the application going before the homeowner understands what's happening. The bank has a business contact now with my past client, and they can call them back to close the deal, but it's illegal for me to call them.

It was sad seeing telemarketing companies I knew for years go out of business. Hey, thanks, Mr. Bush! Many of those company owners probably voted for you. I remember talking to the proprietor of one and listening to him describe how it would be positive, now having a better closing ratio talking to people who didn't go on the DNC List. His voice was shaking as he was trying to sound confident. He was a human being, Mr. Bush, and so were all his employees.

Those people who didn't initially go on the DNC List got hammered with telemarketing calls because they were the only ones left they could legally call. The gasps of a dying industry struck down by the government. Eventually, most everyone went on the DNC List, and those telemarketing companies are now no more. What tragedies befell that owner and his jobless, incomeless, former employees? One law virtually wiped out the whole industry.

You may have no sympathy because you hate telemarketing calls. This is understandable. My point is to show how sweeping draconian laws hurt us all. If we used technology or innovated to solve the problem, there could be a specific law making it mandatory business names and numbers come up with incoming calls. Instead of the proverbial sledgehammer to kill a gnat, we'd all do better.

Instead of running to our politicians who "want to do more," we should accept competition and enjoy our freedoms! Freedom-killing cumbersome legislation packages with thousands of pages fuel the administrative state. How many ways does the "the government knows best" mentality the Keynesian era reinforces affect us?

Be wary of intrusive laws and draconian government regulations. The next time they may put you or your employer out of business.

11

Just Let the Government Do It!

"...every prodigal (unproductive consumer) appears to be a public enemy, and every frugal man a public benefactor."

Adam Smith

W HY SHOULDN'T THE government spend and control more? Because the people pay for it: the people support the government, it doesn't provide for them. If the government gives out more than it receives over time, the public debt will grow, escalate, the country will weaken, and eventually fail by fiscal implosion. Then it won't be able to provide handouts anyway.

It's possible, for a considerable number of years, economic activity can increase quickly enough, even with added debt each year, that the overall debt becomes a smaller percentage of the economy. It's reckless and risks inflation while a controlling government hurts growth. The piper will eventually extract payment because the spending and control achieve the opposite of driving growth. Any culture with many able-bodied dependent people will decline ethically and morally too. We need more productive people to pay down our debt, not fewer. I am not making a case against helping those caught in a terrible place or against charity, but against theories that claim spending drives the economy: creation and exchange do.

We use a Keynesian formula to calculate our Gross Domestic Product. By adding government spending to the equation as economic activity, Keynes increased the amount the people had to carry instead of driving the economy. With an activist government controlling the economy, Keynes hindered growth, and, consequently, we add debt nearly every year. These concepts are anathema to the political left because they've had first-rate Keynesian brainwashing. They celebrate activist government as they conflate it with a better economy.

Their equation is simple: more government equals a bigger economy. It's basic math: count government activity as economic activity. When public spending increases, Gross Domestic Product does too. How convenient.

If Keynesianism is correct, it should all be quite easy! Since consumer and government spending drives the economy, why not create consumers by giving more and more people government jobs? It could put a lot of spending money in their pockets with paychecks to meet their needs plus a bit more, adjust their disposable income to maximize the marginal propensity to consume, and fill everyone's wants and needs. We could publicly produce great things many people will want, besides all they need, through government planning. We only must do it right this time!

We don't have to be like the Soviet Union about it. Our officials wouldn't necessarily be so austere in a politically "free" society: just put the word "Democratic" before Socialism, and we'll all feel good about it! Our leaders only must convince everyone they're right, produce valuable things, and convince everyone else to obey. They could even hand out money to jump-start the economy with things like forgivable loans and Obama phones!

So why not produce great things like new Corvettes and put one in every driveway? Start with mine! The government would pay their Corvette manufacturing employees well because it can just print money anyway, and people will spend their paychecks to drive the economy while they produce. It's a win-win! Many other well-paid government employees can buy Corvettes with the printed money representing their paychecks, as the government creates prosperity in an imaginary Keynesian world!

Am I thinking Keynesianism through too much? Is it wrong to imagine where it may lead? How silly can I be? You may say this is not what Keynes meant, but controlling or eventually taking over the large industries, whether by government ownership or by "controlling the instruments of production," as Keynes put it, would eventually include car companies, would it not? Under the more developed "progressive" thinking, the car companies would do what the government bureaucrats wanted, or they'd force them into it, take them over, or shut them down. The government knows best, right?

Of course, left-wing ideologues, ardent extreme environmentalists, and even eugenicists would run things in Keynes' world, so they'd probably find Corvette production offensive. It wouldn't be socially acceptable to drive one, not only because people might see them in an American car, but primarily because Corvettes use gasoline.

They might say this makes the concept immoral! Although, of course, they wouldn't use the word "immoral" because that itself would be offensive. There would be nothing wrong with the government producing electric cars; on the contrary, they would jump for joy at the great idea! Any Keynesian economists and their political friends reading this might only think the government producing electric cars is evil because they didn't think of it first!

In this "progressive" fantasy, the government could produce electric cars for everyone, providing high-paying jobs, which means a higher standard of living for others. The workers would spend their fat paychecks to drive the economy, helping save the planet! They could then progressively force all gas stations to put in electric charging stations until they could force them to phase out the gasoline pumps altogether.

They could orchestrate this through strict executive orders and mandates, and they could pass "progressive" legislation using fines, forcing the gas station owners out of business if they didn't comply. Or they could make compliance with draconian regulations so cumbersome and expensive, with so much paperwork, it would push those greedy business people out of the way gradually. They could "help" those undesirable businesses fail.

All of this, of course, leads to the government distributing electricity and cars. They could control fairness and create jobs in a state, consumer, environmental, win, win, win. They might even think of punishment and reward-based incentives for the subjects, um, citizens, to have fewer children and achieve equilibrium in population growth.

Reality tells us it won't drive the economy because the government doesn't produce things within the real economy. How do inspiration and efficiency propel the process without freedom, competition, market-driven price signals, and profit motive? You'll get prices the government decides above their inefficient production costs, and the consumer will buy with the amount the government allots to them. The masses end up without much money and with few products and services after waiting in line.

Obama tried feeding start-up electric car companies with printed and borrowed money, but they failed. Big surprise. Remember, it wasn't government ownership, except General Motors for a time because of the bailout, but managing the instruments of production through a socialization of investment with his electric car company debacle.

Like other big car companies, today's General Motors operate with so many environmental mandates, mileage standards, workplace regulations, insurance regulations, union rules, and with the government's many other terms, it's sort of like a quasi-governmental relationship.

What's next? Congress charterers them, the President appoints the top executives, the Senate confirms them, and Congress has hearings and oversite over their business operations and financial condition? The only reason "progressives" don't push for this now is probably because our politicians are dysfunctional. If we can get our leaders to work better together, why not merge car companies into formal government control? The politicians can then force them to do their politically correct bidding more directly or close them down if they want.

Of course, reality doesn't work this way. The government hinders production by enforced controls, but they'll create many more inefficiencies if they try outright ownership. If they attempt to control the "market," they'll take away resources from freely creating people in the real economy and suffocate it, but there is a slim chance they'll make good cars. The government works on a very different paradigm by its nature. Do you remember the state-produced vehicles in the Soviet Union? Families went on a waiting list for years for a primitive and austere little box with wheels.

For revenue, government bureaucrats take resources away from producers through taxes and fees. They create money out of thin air by adding numbers to computer accounts through the central bank, print it, or borrow in the citizen's names. The government then redistributes it all away from the producers in sort of a reverse procurement process. Government agencies don't try to run efficiently but spend their whole allocation each year to *get* as much or more next year! Keynesianism takes from profits and paychecks and hands to others. It hinders but calls it growth.

In a Keynesian world, the government usually controls business owners through excessive rules and regulations to make them behave in ways politically pleasing to the politicians. Time is money, and if I spend too long and waste so much money complying, you are hurting me. You harm my customers too because they get worse service at higher prices. An oppressive government also psychologically harms people and may drive them out of business by hindrances. When you realize you don't have the power to fight back, and you must comply with such unfair laws, your drive for prosperity may slip away. A societal malaise can set in.

If the government tries to force prosperity by printing money and paying additional government employees, will it improve or drag down the economy? Will it create asset bubbles from all the printed money, then inflation, and then deflation when the bubbles burst? It develops imbalances and instability in Keynesian crony capitalist markets. Does it provide a more productive society or produce ungrateful, lazy workers?

Will it lead to or exacerbate low self-esteem, crime, imprisonment, fatherless homes, poor performance, especially among boys who go to prison emulating the father they never knew, and generational poverty? Maybe morality with a traditional family structure holding to sound religious principles is healthier for individuals, families, and society? Is an overbearing secularist government the answer or the problem?

Will more rules and regulations make the government employees do their jobs well or hurt worker esteem? Will people appreciate their jobs if they're guaranteed? Don't government monopolies create a lack of competition, hurt independent producers, lower product quality and improvement? Would we have all our smartphone technology if there was still one government monopoly phone company like we had just a few decades ago? Would airfare be as inexpensive as it is without airline deregulation? Would fuel prices be as low as they are without deregulation?

When the government controls and manipulates interest rates by making them unnaturally low, won't it create imbalances? Will the government borrow too much? What happens if interest rates go up suddenly, and the only way the government can pay its debt obligations is massive money printing and more borrowing? Do unnaturally low interest rates correspond to insufficient savings? Doesn't this represent the government playing favorites by punishing savers and rewarding spenders?

More natural, less manipulated interest rates create savings and investment capital or working capital, especially for small businesses that borrow from local banks. Large firms benefit when people buy stocks with their savings, and anyone who owns them profits if the value goes up.

Citizens now have a disincentive to save with unnaturally low interest rates caused by government manipulation—so they spend it now as Keynes wanted them to. The result? They often become government-dependent in old age with no future nest egg, and small businesses don't have sufficient investment capital. Does all the excessive money printing we've had over the last years flowing into the stock and bond markets portent future inflation? The government creates disequilibrium, or bubbles and imbalances, when they print and borrow money and inject it into the system to make up for the lack of savings and investment.

When President Obama came into office, he had his White House staff read *Animal Spirits* by Akerlof & Shiller. He wanted them to know how economics works. These men, Professors from Berkley and Yale, describe themselves as Keynesians and behavioral economists, but they contradict foundational Keynesianism when they proclaim personal savings benefits. They admit countries with higher savings rates have higher growth rates than countries where citizens spend more of their incomes.

"Indeed, both of these countries (Singapore and China) have made very high levels of saving a major vehicle in achieving spectacular economic growth (Akerlof & Shiller, 2009)."

"As we have seen, savings policy can also be one of the keys to a nation's economic growth (Ibid)."

They then say "animal spirits" can help explain the "arbitrariness and variability of savings (Ibid)." Gentlemen, the reason our people don't save, and this mentality has sunk into our culture, is because Keynesian economists and politicians have extolled Keynes' theories of spending to drive the economy for over eighty years. It's the same underlying reason our politicians can't get off their deficit spending addiction. Do you want to fix the problem? We must abandon Keynes altogether. Remember, he didn't say his theories were for cyclical dips to get things going as many today claim, but for "the general case (Keynes, The General Theory of Employment Interest and Money, 1936, 3)."

Doesn't the truth that people who save and invest create faster economic growth than those who spend almost all they make throw a wrench in the whole Keynesian program, if we're honest? Doesn't this directly discredit "demand creating its own supply?"

How many aspects of Keynesian economics must fail before we finally give it up? Personal savings also gives people purchasing power to buy higher-priced goods and services when they do spend. They may put a down payment on a home, remodel or add square footage, acquire higher-priced items outright, the manufacturing and distribution of which tends to create higher-paying jobs. Investing in stocks creates business working capital.

Personal savings is good for the economy! When banks loan a multiple of deposits to local businesses, in effect, several times the number of their reserves, higher savings help multiply business expansion. The money goes to work when savings are productive for others who leverage it and again when the depositor withdraws and uses it, primarily when they buy more expensive items or invest it in an enterprise.

Savings, instead of creating a drag on the economy, creates investment, multipliers, and jobs. The problem with our economy is Keynes' "measures of socialization (ibid, 378m)" and his "central controls (ibid, 379)."

When the politicians and the government bureaucrats cause imbalances by manipulating and attempting to control the economy, they'll then try to manage the housing bubble, stock market bubble, government bond bubble, and any other asset bubble they caused. Do you know what this usually means? Watch out below!

The Obama administration exemplified using Keynesian economic strategies with excessively low interest rates, massive money printing, the government playing favorites with social engineering, and spending far more than it took in tax receipts. These things never jump-started or drove the economy. The only excuse they had was they saved it from being worse. Sure. Obama's Keynesian policies became a heroine feed that we couldn't seem to get off while the economy underperformed for years on end.

The federal debt rose to nearly $20,000,000,000,000 by the time Obama left office and has now passed that figure. The Federal Reserve Bank used its "tools" for years, but much of it looked like pushing a string. Can we admit deficit spending doesn't drive or even "jump-start" the economy? If we stopped this foolishness, the Keynesianism that causes our uncontrolled and unbalanced budgets, the Federal Reserve Bank wouldn't have to employ crazy money printing in response. We must stop putting Keynesians in positions of power, like the Fed, immediately.

The politicians caused this mess with John Maynard Keynes as their excuse. You would even hear financial news commentators excitedly report it was working, under Obama, when they saw a few isolated positive numbers or the results of one reasonably good quarter. We have turned the corner now! Unimpressive numbers ensued in the following months. When they said it was working, the "it" meant Keynesian economics. When Einstein said the definition of insanity is repeatedly trying the same thing and expecting a different result, he could have referenced stimulus packages.

The U.S.A. is now fat with debt; under George W. Bush, we were pretty chubby, on the verge of fatness; Barack H. Obama fed us until we approached morbid obesity. The Keynesians say we should eat more, much more, and not worry about the weight because it doesn't matter. They say we must eat more all at once to get thin because borrowing massively and running up the national debt—spending all that money we don't have is good for us.

With Keynesian thinking, we create a fizzle in economic activity with money we borrow and print, and there is nothing substantial in it because there's no produced value behind it. It's like getting drunk to feel good; it creates the pleasures of short-term activity with a hangover of debt and pain to follow.

How does it work out in life when you keep getting drunk in the face of obstacles? Do your problems go away? When we avoid the pain of cutting government spending, are we like a drunk who can't push himself away from the bar? When will our creditors throw us out on the street?

Will we become so fat with debt we'll be like the person who can't leave their house? How productive will we be then? So big, we can't function? Has our spending addiction blinded us to the possibility of our economy becoming more balanced and productive? Do the politicians' promises for votes spoil us with unsustainable expectations that get our citizenry fat, lazy, and stupid? Can we finally admit Keynesianism is a distortion tax on us all? Vote in more Keynesian politicians, and it will only get worse.

Economics is producing and trading valuable goods and services with each other; it's not the government. All demand-pull theory is ridiculous.

People's dreams employed by knowledge and skill in action drive the economy. It fires along with reciprocal trade like an incalculably vast internal combustion engine, all cylinders firing, with the valves opening and closing, all the parts humming along hopefully in harmonious balance. Bureaucratic oppressive controls cut off its oxygen; they suffocate it.

We must come to the full realization that John Maynard Keynes was wrong. This awareness must then bring a business-friendly government. Today, our politicians with the right mentality get blocked and obstructed by those who only want to tax, redistribute, borrow, print, and spend more. They justify it, and their partisan groupthink, by Keynes.

The way we count GDP, if economic output goes up a little, but government spending goes down a reasonable amount, the government data could report the economy shrinking. If the economy shrinks but government outlays dramatically increase, GDP could show positive. If there is growth but massive spending, GDP could look better than it should as debt piles high. If we eliminate bureaucracies that hinder entrepreneurs, the cutbacks on unnecessary spending shrink stated GDP. Can you see the Keynesian bias in this? Isn't this deceptive, "fake" data?

During the depression, both Hoover and Roosevelt, with Congress, ramped up government spending into the disaster. However, the economic implosion was so bad in the trough that the outlay didn't make the data look good, and employment never improved appreciably through the thirties despite such spending and massive added debt.

In 1932, Hoover's last year, GDP shank 12.9%, but the unemployment rate was 23.6%. Things bounced back in 1933, FDR's first year. GDP shrank only 1.2.%, but annual unemployment hit 24.9%. In 1934, the economy reportedly grew at 10.8%, with joblessness at 21.7%. In 1935, growth became 8.9%, with joblessness averaging 20.1% (Amadeo, 2018). Include discouraged workers, the many not counted who quit looking for work, and unemployment may not have improved. FDR spent more than Hoover, but what happened? GDP seemed tremendous, and there was real growth when the economy naturally bounced off the bottom but was the spending a driving force with such an ongoing unemployment problem?

The jobless rate dropped into the mid-teens with healthy-looking GDP in 1936 & 1937, but it went back up to 19% in 1938 (Ibid) after they raised taxes again, trying to cover gaping deficits with so much added debt. The high tax burden shrunk output with more lost jobs. The economy couldn't hit a sustainable stride under the tax, spend, and controlling government policies. How can we address the problem unless we have clarity in how we compute and classify the data to see it for what it is? Spending is not the economy!

We must change our statistical calculations to reflect reality, bring clarity, and cure confusion. GDP must represent only production and trade, exchanging value from both sides of transactions. We must expand free enterprise within our country and with those in other nations to solve our debt problems. Delineation and clarity are crucial. With increased business activity and overall higher value, we have a more substantial economy. Government spending isn't a business activity.

Although the government classifies "entitlements," like Social Security, Medicare, and Medicaid, as "transfer payments" and doesn't count them in GDP, their growth increasingly threatens to swallow up our budget. We have a sacred trust to people who've paid into them and the disabled and needy among us, but is an ever-increasing government take-over the answer, or is responsible reform? Does "Medicare for all" really pay the bills or sink us?

We shouldn't spend government money, increase public workers, or increase the government's size and control as if it's part of the economy. We must stop deceiving ourselves; budget-busting leads to disaster. Increased business, not government transactions, sustainably pay our bills.

How should we count public expenditures on independent contractors? Separately! Putting government spending to contractors and private landlords in distinct categories, and expenses like public employee salaries into another, and accounting for costs separate from economic activity brings clarity. Economic activity is creation and exchange; when the government trades tax money with free producers, it is value redirected from its original producer, not government created. Handling tax money should be a sacred trust but never a supposed way to drive the economy through spending.

Part IV

History

"Fellow citizens, we cannot escape history."

Abraham Lincoln

12

History, Debt, and Income Tax Politics

"I cannot undertake to lay my finger on that article of the Constitution which granted a right to Congress of expending, on objects of benevolence, the money of their constituents."

James Madison (Who wrote the Constitution)

BEFORE THE PROGRESSIVE era, except in war, government spending never increased without a roughly equivalent revenue stream. Increases went along with increased tax receipts as the economy grew, and we paid down or fully paid off the debt from significant wars over time. Usually, there were surpluses and sometimes deficits, but government debt stayed relatively small, and budgets continually approximated balance (Office of Management and Budget, 2018, Table 1.1).

Then came a Constitutional Amendment allowing the federal income tax. During 1909, a Republican-controlled Congress, both houses, voted with more than the required two-thirds majority sending a potential constitutional amendment to the state legislatures for consideration. If approved, Congress could make laws instituting a federal income tax for personal and business incomes directly, without apportionment to the states and not based on census numbers.

Instituting a direct federal income tax was very popular; most people and politicians considered it progress. The Democrats were almost entirely for it, too, and many of them championed it years earlier. The states approved it with more than the three-fourths required to amend the Constitution, and Congress, then entirely in the Democrat's control, ratified it shortly afterward in 1913. They then passed, and President Woodrow Wilson, a Democrat, quickly signed a federal income tax bill into law.

Before this, tariffs, excise taxes, and businesses' fees were the chief federal government revenue, but most people considered them regressive. Although on production and trade, they hurt the poor the most because they were passed along with mark-ups on staple items and simple imports like a bottle of whiskey that a worker might want. There were even some political arguments that if the rich paid more with an income tax, they, having more clout with the politicians than the working man, would help reign in frivolous government spending. No one made a case for a behemoth federal government but a more efficient and fairer tax system by substituting government revenue from the other sources with an income tax. The progressive income tax would make the rich pay their fair share through a higher marginal percentage at higher incomes, but with rates relatively low for everybody (Jensen, The Taxing Power, the Sixteenth Amendment, and the Meaning of 'Incomes' 2002).

The following income levels and their corresponding personal income tax rates show what happened quite quickly after implementation. What the politicians sold the citizens was far different from what they got. Were intentions honest initially? Maybe for some, but not for others? Once the progressives got hold of things, it all changed quickly. John Maynard Keynes then gave them the economic theory to support and accelerate it all.

The Tax Foundation supplied the following data, it's adjusted to 2013 dollars (Tax Foundation, 2018), rounded, and I don't consider deductions and their effects. Notice the trends, patterns, and abrupt changes.

In 1913, the first year of federal income taxes, rates started at only 1% up to almost $455,000 personal income, but they went up gradually to the top level of 7% at over 11.6 million dollars. With the new lower tariffs, lower excise taxes, and more modest fees on businesses, along with a new minimal corporate income tax, it brought in about the same revenue to the federal government as before (Office of Management and Budget, 2018, Table 1.1). Not a large percentage of people paid over 1%, and very many people paid nothing.

Corporate tax rates were 1% in 1913, but this new business income tax would theoretically come from profits and not be passed along directly in higher-cost staple items to the poor. Although not discussed here, corporate tax rates went up somewhat similarly to personal income taxes in the ensuing years. They are arguably worse for the economy because they remove producers' investment capital and move it to economically unproductive government spending.

Government spending remained about the same in 1913 as the year before, with a nearly balanced budget. This was true for the years 1914 and 1915 (Ibid). In 1916, the lowest federal income tax of 1% doubled to 2% up to $421,273. Tax rates went up gradually for higher incomes, but now the top level was 15% at just over 42 million, more than twice the initial maximum rate but starting at a higher number. The politicians wanted more money in the coffers anticipating WW I, and this was the first move.

Not too bad compared to today's income tax rates. On the other hand, what would such a quick increase only three years after implementation portend? Right here, we can say goodbye forever to that first low level of taxation and sensible government spending. There is an expression, "war changes things," but why would it change future tax policy and government spending in peacetime? It is the twenty trillion-dollar-plus, Keynesian question.

The constitutional amendment allowing the federal income tax didn't put any limits on Congress. And as the war raged in Europe, we can say the U.S.A. prepared for it in 1916, when rates roughly doubled. The United States entered the war in 1917. Instead of the civil war era's income tax of 3% to 5%, increasing to 10% for the very wealthy, things were very different after the Constitutional Amendment.

It was questionable whether the Civil War income tax was constitutional or only allowed as a temporary war tax. The federal government was skating on thin ice when it was not so clear-cut. The Supreme Court decided they could do it during the war, but even a tiny straight federal income tax after the war wasn't constitutional.

Watch what happened to tax rates in the fourth year after the new constitutional amendment. In 1917, the lowest tax rate was still only 2%, but for income up to $35,874. Did you notice that? Now, the graduated increase started at a figure of about thirteen times less than the year before. Remember, these are all in 2013 dollars. The last starting rate was 2% to $421,273, but after the increase, and in one year, the tax rate became 12% at $421,273, six times more at that level.

The top rate went from 7% in 1913 through 1915 to 15% in 1916. In 1917 it became 67%, at almost 35.9 million dollars, at a lower threshold than just over 42 million the year before. In 1916, with an income roughly equivalent in today's dollars to $35,900,000 taxable, a citizen paid a 14% top marginal rate. In the following year, 1917, the same person got hit with 67% at that level! The government went from taxing to pay expenses to taxation for redistribution. It's funny, but I don't remember the constitutional amendment saying anything about that. I do remember Karl Marx demanding a steeply progressive income tax from his list of first steps to dismantle capitalism. "A heavy progressive or graduated income tax." (Marx & Engels, The Communist Manifesto, 1998 [1848], 75).

It was wartime, but that is one confiscatory tax! The poor rich? The unbelievable gall of government? The fact is the law didn't limit the "progressive" politicians, and the pattern of taxation in the U.S.A. changed permanently; the sky was now the limit. They could use the tax code after the war for a socialist government philosophy. Is that too strong a description? Under the post-war Keynesian theory, the top marginal rate was 92% in peacetime! Would you call that progress or a socialist progression? The truth is, for political progressives, it's the same thing.

The ever-increasing government's voracious appetite required more than just confiscation from the rich. Middle and low-income Americans eventually paid more, too, because the wealthy's astronomical tax rates couldn't feed the beast. It seems the well-heeled don't wield all the power people say they do. Now see the rich get soaked even more while the politicians throw the poor and middle class progressively further under the bus.

In 1918, the top income tax rate went up 10% to 77% at a much lower amount of over $15,204,901. Now that's some quick progress! President Wilson asked for this increase because of war costs, and he appealed to the American people to consider his leadership in the midterm elections. He argued they'd be happy to pay more out of patriotism. The people voted and handed both houses of Congress back to the Republicans (Wolfensberger, 2004, 12-13).

In lame-duck status after the election, the Democrats voted for the increase before the Republicans took over. It was sort of a parting gift for the President and for the voters who'd have to pay for it. Wilson, of course, even though the people didn't want it, signed it into law. The lowest rate tripled to 6%, up to $60,820. The initial starting rate of 1% to roughly $455,000 in 1913 became 24% at that level in 1918. World War I ended in November of 1918, but the United States still ran enormous deficits in the two years of war, even with the enormously high-income tax rates.

Although I'm exposing the pattern with personal income tax rates, it's notable how President Wilson and Congress raised other taxes. Once again, they laid into businesses and consumers by raising tariffs, taxes on business operations, and fees even higher than they were before, along with new higher business income taxes (Wolfensberger, 2004, 9). So much for what they told the American people before they amended the Constitution.

The year after the war ended, 1919 saw a slight adjustment downward to a starting income tax rate of 4% up to $53,085. At the top, it became 73% at about 13.3 million and over. With minor modifications, this stayed in place after the war until 1922, when Warren Harding, a Republican, was President. For the rest of the 1920s, the Presidency and both houses of Congress remained in Republican control.

Harding signed into law a sizable change down for very high-income earners, with other modifications mostly a bit lower for everyone else. The top rate went down to 58% at 2.7 million and over; at the bottom, it became 4%, up to $54,665.

If someone were to say the Republicans were all for the rich, how much were they when they still took 58% of the top bracket's income? The Democrats indeed raised tax rates immensely, and the Republicans adjusted them down, but they were still so many times higher than initially. The difference between what the American people supported in the constitutional amendment and what they got is obscene.

President Warren Harding died in office, August 2, 1923, and his Vice President, Calvin Coolidge, became President. In 1925, the bottom rate went down to 1.5%, up to $52,479. The top went down to 25% at about 1.3 million and over. The economy had just come out of a horrible dip, was doing well, and was about to do even better.

The brackets changed gradually for the dollar amounts in all these years. For example: In 1925 it was 1.5% to $53,706, 3% to $107,412, 5% to $134,265, 6% to $187,972, 7% to $214,825, etc., up to 25% at $1,342,655 and above. I only referenced the top and the bottom rates in all the examples to show how the political mentality changed. I think typing out all the brackets would tend to confuse rather than clarify.

Until the 1950s, there were no distinctions for married or head of household, and in the 1970s, filing single became an option. Through those years, I reference rates and dollar amounts for married filing jointly. My goal is not to belabor minor points, but again, only to show the trends and the patterns in dollars adjusted to the year 2013 so you can relate more easily.

Income tax rates in 1925 and through the next few years with minor adjustments were the lowest they would be again. The economy boomed and brought surplus tax receipts with relatively modest government spending through the 1920s (Office of Management and Budget, 2018, Table 1.1). The combination of a growing economy and payments to the national debt lowered the debt to GDP ratio to a respectable figure on the eve of the Great Depression.

The stock market crashed in October 1929 after rampant speculation near a softening of the business cycle. Whenever the prevailing belief is things will keep going up, watch out below! Couldn't a correction of inflated stock prices be healthy? Isn't the economy slowing after almost a decade of such incredible growth, usual? Interestingly, in the next year, 1930, the first year of economic slowing, then thought to be only a recession, the government had a surplus at the 1920s era tax rates (Ibid)!

Protectionism was politically popular, and Mr. Hoover ran for office, saying he'd protect the farmers. However, when the tariff bill came out of Congress, it was so laden with protectionist measures from special interest groups trying to get a good deal, he couldn't support it. Although he said he was against the Smoot-Hawley trade tariff bill because it went too far, under political pressure, President Hoover signed it on June 17, 1930, massively increasing tariffs across the economy. The result? The whole world retaliated, and with the international trade war and a horrifying drop in trade, global commerce came to a trickle (Gordon, 2017).

Hoover and Congress began deficit spending on "government works projects" to get the economy going. He also called business leaders to ask them to spend more money and agree they wouldn't lower wages (hindering natural adjustments during a sharply deflationary time). His policies were an attempt to "maintain consumer spending" and "stimulate employment (Herbert Hoover Presidential Library and Museum, 2018)." President Hoover and many Republicans embraced the newly prevalent "progressive," "demand-side" ideas with the Democrats, and they did all the wrong things.

They spent so much into the slowing economy it created an enormous budget deficit, and they then tried to achieve balance with tax increases. They raised taxes back to 4% to a $67,035 starting rate, and at the top, 63% at about 16.8 million, and the lousy economy collapsed.

Today, many economists believe terrible central banking by the Federal Reserve exacerbated deflation, further crushing the economy. "The money supply in the United States declined by one third from 1929 to 1932 (Sowell, 2001, 22)..." The thing Keynes put so much faith in, a large, powerful central bank that would save the day, didn't. The Fed shrank the money supply in a sharp downturn!

Franklin Delano Roosevelt became President in March 1933, just as the economy hit bottom, and the Democrats swept disproportionate control of Congress. They kept the same rates until 1936 when they increased the top bracket to 79% at 82.6M. The year 1936 is when John Maynard Keynes published *The General Theory,* attacking Say's Law to support the progressive ideas with his detailed mathematical tome on demand-pull spending-based theories.

In 1941, the top income tax rate went to 81% at just over 78M. Aid to Britain and military spending was ramping up in anticipation of war. Not only were the rich going to get it, but everyone was going to get it. The bottom rate was 4% up to $65,598 in 1940; this was true since the 1932 Hoover increase from 1.5% with a similar dollar amount. In 1941, the bottom bracket became 10% to $31,237.

Not being satisfied, in 1942, the bottom rate almost doubled to 19%, up to $28,171. The top went to 88%, at a much lower number of about 2.8M. In 1944, the bottom rate went up to 23% to $26,090. The highest bracket went to 94% at just over 2.6M. Remember, these are in 2013 dollars, and there were also social security taxes starting in the 1930s.

The war was over in 1946, and the bottom bracket became 20%, to $23,548. The top bracket was 91% at about 2.35M. Notice how the rates went up during the war even more than they did in WW I, but similarly, they didn't come down much after it.

In 1952, under Democrat President Harry Truman and a Democrat-controlled Congress, the bottom rate went up to 22.2%, to $17,328. What was the political slogan for that, "tax the poor?" "Make the poor pay their fair share?" How do you define private wealth confiscation? In the low-income peoples' case, it was stripping them of their subsistence! Is this how the Democrats were for the poor? Take it from them and maybe give some back in government aid? The politicians were just not able to tax enough out of the rich to feed the beast. The top bracket became 92%, just over 1.7M.

Besides the top adjusting slightly to 91% in 1954 under Republican President Dwight D. Eisenhower, the rates stayed the same with little movement in the dollar amounts until 1964. In fulfilling President John F. Kennedy's wishes for tax cuts, after his assassination when Vice President Lyndon Johnson became President, the top rate went down to 77% at just over 2.9M. At the bottom, 16% to $7,406. In 1965, they lowered the highest to 70% at 1.45M, and the lowest to 14% to $7,289.

Except for small changes in the dollar amounts and deductions, generally lowering taxes for lower incomes and raising them for higher ones, the brackets remained about the same until 1977, during Jimmy Carter's Presidency. The bottom rate then became 0% to $12,124, instead of starting at 14% up to $4,035.

Income tax rates didn't change much until President Ronald Reagan's time. In 1982, the top bracket came down to 50%, starting at $203,661. The bottom rate didn't change; the poorest still paid $0, except for Social

Security, Medicare, Medicaid, and unemployment taxes that everyone must pay on earned income. Each year through the '80s, the amount applied to the 50% bracket went up a bit. If you made a little over $200,000 in 1982, you paid 50%. Except for the very top earners, taxpayers got a little break as the dollar figures applying to specific rates went up each year. By 1986, those earning about $200,000 paid 45% but the 50% rate applied to $367,120 and above. In 1987, the top rate dropped to 38.5%, but now the lowest income earners didn't get a free ride on federal income taxes. Starting at over $0, they paid 11%.

A very significant change happened in 1988, Reagan's last year in office. The top rate fell to 28%, and the bottom was 15%, but these were the only two brackets. Anything over $0, and you paid 15% up to $57,738. Over that, 28% on additional income. Interestingly, with the simplified structure, lower tax rates, and reform in deductions, government tax receipts continued increasing in 1988, 1989, and 1990 (Office of Management and Budget, 2018, Table I).

In 1991, Congress and President George H. W. Bush added another bracket of 31% over $138,481 when the economy had already gone into recession: they also added the "luxury tax" of 10% to combat the deficit with an extra charge on expensive consumer products. Government tax receipts came in for 1991 and 1992 with less increase than in the years before these added taxes (Ibid), and the deficit widened. Expensive manufactured goods suffered as consumers protested and stopped buying luxury items. For example, yacht sales fell, many workers lost jobs, and some well-known and established boat builders went out of business.

On top of the extra bracket, the luxury tax was an additional insult to the American people. The Republican President broke his "no new taxes" campaign pledge under pressure from the Democrat-controlled Congress, and they used it against him in the next election. They repealed it only after about two years because it didn't bring in projected tax receipts. In reality, instead, it hindered production and exchange, and things improved after its repeal. Although 1992, President Bush's last year in office, had a much improved annual growth rate of 3.6% (U.S. Department of Commerce, 2017), he lost re-election.

In 1993, President Bill Clinton and a Democrat-controlled Congress added two additional brackets. There was a 36% bracket over $222,444, and a 39.6% bracket over $397,221. Clinton came into a good economy, but growth continued at a little slower pace than Bush's last year, averaging 3.3% over his first four years (Ibid). Instead of the economy accelerating after coming out of recession, his added taxes reduced economic potential.

Deficit spending continued through Clinton's first term. He always had a long spending wish list in his State of the Union Addresses he called "investments," which, of course, exposes Keynesian thinking. In his first midterm election, the Republicans winning both houses of Congress frustrated his government grandeur ideas and held him to fiscal restraint.

His second term had considerable economic growth and debt reduction. Still, in the last year, a technology stock bubble burst, and then the general stock market began sliding down in his final months in office. He left the next President a relatively mild recession. There was no causal effect of higher taxes starting in Clinton's first term and considerable economic growth in his second.

Clinton's second term's growth resulted from colossal technology gains and a related speculative stock market bubble. His rhetoric of a pro-business "new Democrat" was likely helpful. His flexibility in going along with the

Republican-controlled Congress and Speaker Newt Gingrich's "Contract with America" brought relatively conservative policies, balanced budgets, and debt reduction. Increased tax receipts from a good economy paid down debt instead of going to his State of the Union spending wish lists.

President George W. Bush and a Republican Congress implemented very modest tax rate reductions. In 2001 the top bracket went from 39.6% to 39.1%. In 2002, it went to 38.6%, and a new bottom bracket of 10% replaced 15%. What, in 2001 was 15% from $0 to $58,598 in the bottom bracket, was now 10% from $0 to $15,315 and 15% above that to $59,600. In 2003, they eliminated the top bracket; it was 35% for the rest of his Presidency.

Dennis Hastert, the Republican House Speaker, and Congress spent liberally. President Bush wasn't fiscally conservative either, even beyond required September 11th spending. Their rhetoric and actions exposed their Keynesianism. The debt grew, and modest economic growth and much wealth vanished with a collapsing real estate bubble and an imploding stock market as his second term ended. The next President received a mess.

President Barak Obama and Congress left the Bush-era tax rates in place for much of his Presidency; they believed money in consumers' hands would improve the weak economy. In 2013, they added back the top bracket of 39.6% over $440,876. The trend of building government debt without a large-scale war accelerated under Obama.

The economy improved with some negotiated fiscal restraint with the Republican-controlled Congress. Raising taxes into a moderately growing economy may have helped lower the massive deficit initially but didn't come close to balancing the budget and likely slowed growth. Historically, increasing tax receipts from a quickly growing economy and fiscal restraint close budget gaps and bring debt reduction. Blinded by their Keynesian beliefs, by taking working capital out of producers' hands from their tax increases, draconian regulations, and overly restrictive laws, higher growth eluded them.

Obama had record deficits throughout his presidency. Although they were relatively large toward the end of his administration, they were not as enormous as they had been in his first few years during the severe recession he inherited (Office of Management and Budget, 2018, Table 1.1). The top bracket wasn't close to the Keynesian heyday. Still, when you add in Social Security, Medicare, Unemployment, Obamacare taxes, with State and local taxes, the story begins to fill out.

All of Obama's supposedly stimulative deficit spending and control-oriented Keynesian policies never jump-started the economy or drove anything close to healthy growth. His best annual growth rate was 2.9%, the worst best calendar year performance for any President since Herbert Hoover (Bureau of Labor Statistics, 2018).

Obama's first term average growth rate was only .875%, his next four-year average was just 2.175%, and his entire two terms averaged only 1.525% (U.S. Department of Commerce, 2017). Given that he inherited a severe recession in his first year, it's still no excuse for never having a decent economic performance for any calendar year after that over two terms or as an overall average. Draconian regulatory policies and overly encumbering laws with deficit spending and tax increases have consequences.

After the Republicans controlled Congress and stopped him from doing stimulus packages, and held the government to some fiscal restraint, Obama had his best two years in his second term. When Congress restrained the Keynesian remedies, the economy improved.

13

Debt to GDP Ratio Politics

"And to preserve their independence, we must not let our rulers load us with perpetual debt."

Thomas Jefferson

O UR NATIONAL DEBT is the amount the federal government currently owes in accumulated debt. We, the citizens, owe it, but the politicians we elect continue amassing it in our names.

"Gross domestic product (GDP) is the monetary value of all the finished goods and services produced within a country's borders in a specific time period (Investopedia, 2018)."

The Gross Domestic Product is a way we measure the size of the economy. When a country has a large economy proportional to its national debt, it has a low debt to GDP ratio. To come up with the Debt to GDP ratio, simply divide our debt by our GDP. It gauges our ability to pay off our debt.

When our politicians spend more than we collect in taxes annually, we

171

have deficits, and our national debt increases. The government borrows by issuing bonds; they are promises to repay the loan with interest. The government may also create excess money out of thin air by adding digits to computer balances or print it to pay our bills, but this tends to lower our money's value, creating inflation. Our fiat money system enables Keynesians' printing and spending policies that the gold standard once restricted.

Our founding fathers didn't give us a system designed to fail, but things began changing in the "Progressive Era." The Peter G. Peterson Foundation website reminds us of our country's original approach this way:

"Prior to the Great Depression, deficits were unusual in the U.S. Budget. Surpluses occurred in over two-thirds of the years between 1800 and 1930 (Peter G. Peterson Foundation, 2018)."

History doesn't lie. After Keynes published his book in 1936, the progressives had the "general theory" to persistently push higher taxes. And his spending driving the economy theory increased the national debt nearly every year. We now have a dangerously high debt to GDP ratio with the astronomical national debt. I've rounded the following information in a quick historical run-through for simplicity (Phillips, 2012).

After the American Revolution, the newly born United States of America had a debt of about 30% of its Gross Domestic Product, or a 30% debt to GDP ratio. Our forebears paid it down steadily except for a blip-up for a couple of years during the War of 1812. The U.S.A. continued paying down its debt while the economy grew until the middle 1830s when we paid it off. We paid off our national debt! Until 1861, on the eve of the Civil War, the U.S. national debt was never more than tiny compared to our GDP; like a credit card, you could pay off anytime without thinking much about it.

The Civil War drove up our national debt to about the same percentage of GDP as the American Revolution. At the end of the Civil War, in 1865, the debt to GDP ratio was about 30%. In the years after the war, as the economy grew, the U.S. government spent relatively responsibly proportionate to the size of the growing economy. With many surplus years and some in deficit, the national debt to GDP ratio went down from debt reduction and economic growth until it was about 5% on the eve of WW I.

Just after WW I, peaking near the end of 1919, it was back up to about 30%. Do you see a pattern? Our federal obligations went up from significant wars to about the same level of GDP, but we paid it down to little or even to nothing sometime afterward. Do you see the underlying story? Any national debt building up to significant levels was only war debt we paid off later.

There was no upward spiraling debt in peacetime. No monetizing debt—no borrowing by the Treasury Department in our names only to have the Federal Reserve Bank print money to acquire it—covering massive deficit spending by Congress. No deficit spending to theoretically get the economy going. No tax and spend policy.

No shell game where the Congress spends money we don't have as the Fed's balance sheet continues growing secretly to infinity. No one knows how much we really owe. We probably don't have numbers to count that high anyway. No inflation strategies to devalue our currency and thereby effectively reduce our debt while simultaneously, the value of our bank accounts. No Keynesian economics. Not yet.

Through the 1920s, the debt to GDP ratio improved steadily. Strong economic growth and budget surpluses brought actual debt reduction. It seems the old pattern of paying down war debt still had some political sway with the Republicans who held Congress and the White House. The booming economy produced copious tax revenue even with several tax rate reductions through those years.

Get that, progressively lower tax rates with a booming economy and increasing tax receipts while paying down the national debt! On the eve of the Great Depression, in late 1929, the debt to GDP ratio was about 17%. Down from about 30% to about 17% in a decade.

Applying progressive policies into the sharp economic contraction following the stock market crash at the end of the roaring '20s, President Hoover and Congress increased government spending as the economy drastically shrank going into the 1930s. They thought they could drive the economy from the "demand side." Tax receipts sharply dropped too, but with the spending increases, much higher trade tariffs, and severe income tax rate hikes, economic activity plummeted to its lowest depression-era level as FDR took office in 1933. Congress was now firmly controlled by the Democrats. The Republicans joined with Democrats implementing progressive economic policies making a dangerous situation a disaster. FDR walked into a financial catastrophe, but he and an entirely Democrat-controlled Congress doubled down on the "progressive" remedies, especially with many more controlling laws and policies that hinder production and exchange. FDR also took the first steps in removing the U.S.A. from the gold standard to allow for more money printing. He made it illegal for U.S. citizens to redeem dollars in gold, although foreign governments still could.

Today Keynesians wouldn't implement tax increases in bad times, but for the wrong reasons. They think it takes consumption out of the economy when the reality is it restricts capital investment, production, and resulting trade, the value we exchange from both sides of a transaction. They call for higher taxes in good times, as we've seen, to redistribute wealth and supposedly drive and control the economy by the government managing demand and resulting production. Although Keynes was a protectionist, his followers today typically don't recommend tariffs in slow times either.

With the combination of declining production and more government spending into the economic contraction, the debt to GDP ratio ran past any previous wartime level to about 33% by the end of 1932. It went from about 17% to about 33% in three years without a war. By the end of FDR's first year, 1933, with most spending already in place by Hoover and a "progressive" Congress, the debt to GDP ratio was about 39%. The economy bottomed as FDR stepped in, but it bounced off the bottom until 1938 when it contracted into what economists sometimes call the Roosevelt recession.

Many people don't realize the economy grew after 1933; they tend to think it bounced along the bottom through the 1930s. Counting government spending as GDP falsely improves the numbers while adding additional debt, but the economy grew despite the expense. Although activity bounced back from the very bottom as it always does after a steep decline, restrictive government policies designed to help, instead, hindered growth.

Economic output didn't reach sustained 1929 levels for more than a decade; not until war production drove it much higher. The awful unemployment improved but was never better annually than the mid-teens before it worsened again and went back up near 20% in the late '30s. Low single-digit 1929 levels returned in 1942 from war production (Steindl, 2008).

The debt to GDP ratio didn't seem to rise so fast because the economy grew in relation. It was about 43% at the end of 1939, but it had gone up in one decade from 17% to 43% in peacetime! Piling on debt like this without a major war was a new phenomenon and the beginning of a new pattern.

John Maynard Keynes wrote an open letter to President Roosevelt, published in the New York Times, December 31, 1933. He outlined the "progressive" remedies more than two years before he published *The General Theory*. Instead of being entrepreneurially driven, increasing output is always by government orchestrated consumer spending. His thinking is consistently backward. Instead of creating value for exchange, it's continually spending more to cause consumption to increase output, demand driving the economy through government interventions and spending.

"...the volume of output depends on the amount of purchasing power (Keynes, An Open Letter to President Roosevelt, 1933)."

"Individuals must be induced to spend more out of their existing incomes; or the business world must be induced...to create additional current incomes in the hands of their employees...or public authority must be called in to aid to create additional current incomes through the expenditure of borrowed or printed money (Ibid)."

Do you think mass production can't lower prices? If the entrepreneur creates efficiencies with faster assembly line production, won't he produce more in less time? Can't he then sell it for less to gain more market share, and even, potentially at a higher profit margin per unit? Like his error that there can't be inflation in a recession (stagflation), Keynes, the consummate left-wing professor with no business experience, assumed there couldn't be rising output without rising prices.

"Since there cannot be rising output without rising prices (Ibid),"

He expressed his political bias and controlling mentality while supposedly teaching FDR about economics:

"I do not mean to impugn the social justice and social expediency of the redistribution of incomes aimed at by N.I.R.A. (National Industrial Recovery Act of 1933) and by the various schemes for agricultural restriction (Ibid)."

Keynes expresses religiosity: "faith in the wisdom and the power of government!" His faith, of course, is in the wisdom and power of men!

"...in comfort to men's minds through a restoration of their faith in the wisdom and the power of Government (Ibid)!"

Just over four years after his open letter, he wrote personally to FDR, telling him how much he admired his economic policies. In addressing "the present recession," he said the recovery (from the depths of the depression) was "mainly due" to several factors. Of course, they were his earlier suggestions: Government orchestrated easy credit, adequate unemployment benefits, public works projects, and government investment in "instrumental goods" to supply the increased demand (materialized through his progressive remedies).

He describes each remedy, but it's standard Keynesianism. One interesting note is how he comes right out and claims that adequate unemployment benefits "carry the economic system" in slow times. It's easy to Google and read his letters online. I took out his tortuously wordy explanations and abbreviated with ellipses for clarity:

"...an adequate system of relief for the unemployed... (will) carry the economic system (Keynes, Private Personal Letter, 1938)."

Henry Morgenthau Jr. was FDR's Treasury Secretary and close confidant and friend. He helped design and ardently supported the new deal. After years of promoting it, his comments in a private meeting with Democrat members of the House Ways and Means Committee, May 9, 1939, recorded in his diary, expose the stark reality.

"Now gentlemen, we have tried spending money. We are spending more than we have ever spent before and it does not work (Morgenthau, 1939)."

"I want to see this country prosperous. I want to see people get a job. I want to see people get enough to eat. We have never made good on our promises (Ibid)."

"I say after eight years of this Administration we have just as much unemployment as when we started. And an enormous debt to boot (Ibid)!"

Do you get the idea they didn't know what they were doing? On the other hand, he said it quite well. Keynesian economics doesn't work. Although the unemployment rate was better than at the very bottom of 1933, it was, in fact, higher in 1939 than in 1931, a year and a few months before FDR took over from Hoover (United States History, 2018).

After a decade of Keynesian-style government spending, specifically designed to "create something approximating full employment," including

Hoover's massive increases with FDRs, the left-leaning Treasury Secretary believed we had nothing to show for it but enormous debt. It's nice to hear a politician tell the truth, even if behind closed doors.

World War II ended in 1945, but the debt to GDP ratio peaked in 1946 at about 120%. The U.S.A.'s liabilities were now more than its annual economy. The accumulation resulting from such an expensive war on top of about ten years of tax, spend, and government control policies.

The U.S.A. now had a mixed economy with too much government intrusion, but with much more efficient business production from wartime inventions applied productively in business applications. We were getting more done in any given period creating much more value for trade because of new technologies and new production methods.

Although tax rates remained very high after the war, an excruciatingly high unemployment rate before the war became an effectively fully employed economy. The increased efficiencies created tremendous value for producers to trade with each other. There was a production and building boom across the U.S.A. Government spending came down from the wartime high. With some government budget surpluses and a quickly growing economy, the debt to GDP ratio began coming down rapidly; by 1949, it was about 93%. Down from 120% to 93% in three years.

There was a brief fall in GDP, reflecting the drop in wartime spending, influenced by the way we count government spending as economic growth under our Keynesian GDP construct. Despite "progressive" prognosticators predicting another depression without enough government spending to drive the economy, as military expenditures dropped, instead, the economy showed underlying strength.

There were peaks and valleys, not a straight line up, but the economy was much stronger and more productive than before the war. Through the 1950s, even with President Eisenhower in office, a Republican, the draconian marginal tax rates implemented during the depression and increased during World War II, dropped just a little after the war. We see the same pattern as during and after WWI, but more drastically in the full-blown Keynesian era, as the last chapter details.

The General Theory, Keynes' final book, swept academia, and college professors were falling all over themselves to explain further and clarify his teaching. Keynes believed the government could control and spend enormous amounts of printed and borrowed money to create prosperity in wartime, but it could do the same in peacetime. Economists shifted their thinking to the "demand side," which gave the political left their economic theory for the ever more extensive, more controlling government.

The western world became thoroughly Keynesian, but do you think the top post-war 92% marginal income tax rate helped prosperity? Did the government inspire anyone to succeed by confiscating $.92 out of every additional $1.00 people earned? Isn't it an oppressive government that takes over 90% of another person's pay over a certain amount? If you like taxing others this much, you must have totalitarian tendencies!

By the end of 1959, the debt to GDP ratio was down to about 54%. This drop was not primarily due to debt reduction, although Congress paid the debt down in some surplus years through the 1950s. Nor was it due to responsible government spending, as most years had deficits. It was mainly from a growing economy. The post-war boom didn't eliminate our massive obligation but made it a smaller percentage of a much larger economy.

The debt increased every year through the 1960s, but the debt to GDP ratio improved each year as the economy grew. Inflation now also improved the ratio because our obligations become less in real terms as our money lost value. It's important to remember that it becomes much harder to outgrow continually amassing debt when it's a more significant percentage of the overall economy as it is today—as the Keynesian debt trap threatens to overwhelm us. By 1969, the debt to GDP ratio was down to about 35%.

The pattern of ever-higher inflation and reckless government spending into a growing economy continued through the 1970s. President Nixon attacked Keynesianism while running for office but declared himself a Keynesian once he acquired power. He implemented compulsory wage and price controls on the American people, attempting to curb inflation. Why couldn't Nixon cut government spending? Was it that the Keynesian President and a fully Democrat-controlled Congress thought it would slow the economy? He finished the job FDR started regarding the gold standard by abandoning it altogether and freeing up the printing presses for a Keynesian inflationary spiral! Some say he had no choice because foreign governments were now demanding gold for the US dollars they held. We'd printed to the point where we didn't have gold to back our currency, and paying gold for it would bleed us dry quickly. We were bankrupt because of Keynesianism, so we doubled down to kick the can down the road, and the problem has only grown worse since.

If you are a Keynesian, as many in the Republican Party seem to be and virtually everyone in the Democrat party is, why care about efficient government spending? Why not lose track of a million dollars here or there? Like John Maynard Keynes said, in a slow economy, you can print money and drop it from the sky to get things going.

Nixon turned to a Keynesian answer caused by a Keynesian problem, inflation. He doubled down and made things worse. The strict control of oil prices in the face of geopolitical oil politics resulted in spiraling higher costs and long gas lines. Couldn't we have done better under the Arab Oil Embargo if we produced and sold freely? Would it not have been our best weapon against it?

The national debt increased each year in the 1970s, but the debt to GDP ratio fluctuated as the economy sped up or slowed down. Overall, it ended down, and by 1979, it was about 31%. Ever-increasing inflation through the 1970s was now getting much worse.

For President Jimmy Carter's last year in office, 1980, the debt to GDP ratio was 32%, but the inflation rate peaked in June at 13.6% (Bureau of Labor Statistics, 2018). There was now a condition John Maynard Keynes said was impossible: rampant inflation with a recession.

When I was in college, I had a dumbfounded-looking professor explaining the resulting new term "stagflation." He was a convinced Keynesian, and he described how they thought it was impossible—until now. When the government tries to control the economy, will it lead to equilibrium or imbalances?

Jimmy Carter made some moves in the right direction. He deregulated banking to some degree and altered monetary policy by appointing the Federal Reserve Chairman Reagan retained through most of his presidency. Still, like most politicians of his day, Carter was confused by Keynesianism. President Ford dropped Nixon's forced wage and price controls, and Carter continued the policy with government panels and boards (International Encyclopedia of the Social Sciences, 2018). They suggested, or, you could say, coerced but didn't compel businesses to control wages and prices. Remember what Keynes said, "If the government can control the instruments of production, it will be enough."

The economy came out of recession and rebounded moderately in President Ronald Reagan's first year in office, 1981. With a budget mainly in place from Carter, the debt to GDP ratio bumped down to 31% because of modest economic growth. Reagan outright rejected the notion of wage and price controls on principle to combat the terrible inflation problem; he believed it only worsened matters. What Nixon proclaimed when running for office but didn't practice, Reagan understood and practiced. Economics meant the free market to Reagan, not the government.

Reagan's policies were growth-oriented: lower tax rates with less, more reasonable government regulation. Under Reagan, curbing out of control spiraling inflation wouldn't be by the government forcing or coercing wages and prices but by monetary policy.

With Reagan's support, the Fed drastically increased interest rates to stop the economy in its tracks because of the inflationary spiral. It worked; economic activity dropped as interest rates soared. Inflation came down, the economy then turned back into an even deeper recession in 1982. It's often called the "double-dip recession," which was terrible for many people.

The Debt to GDP ratio was 34% by the end of 1982. The economy slowed, and tax receipts were less than they would've been, but government spending didn't slow overall. In 1983 the debt to GDP ratio hit 37%.

Annual inflation was 9.8% in 1979, 12.4% in 1980, and 10.4% in 1981. By 1982 it was 7.4%, and by 1983, 4% (Bureau of Labor Statistics, 2018). Inflation came down to more reasonable levels, and the economy took off. Reagan's approach worked. The six years of the Reagan recovery following the double-dip recession saw remarkable growth with more moderate inflation. The economy grew an average of 4.55% for the rest of his presidency, and at its fastest pace, in 1984, it grew at 7.3% annually (U.S.

Department of Commerce, 2017). Inflation hasn't been a problem since.

Even with tax rate reductions, receipts to the government only fell one year, 1983, they then hit the highest they had ever been the following year, 1984, and continued climbing through Reagan's Presidency. The deficits were related to spending, not decreased tax receipts, but even with incredible economic growth, the debt to GDP ratio was nearing 50% in Reagan's last year in office, 1988. Massive military spending increases drove the deficits.

Some economists criticize Reagan for so much government spending. Many Keynesians claim the 1980s economic growth was because of government spending, but they didn't print and borrow to put money in poor people's pockets to spend it to drive the economy; the significant increases were not economic theory related but for the military.

Domestic spending increases slowed under Reagan in some areas but not others, but with such economic growth, many more people gained employment, and overall incomes increased. Reagan said he wanted additional domestic spending cuts, but the Democrats controlled the House of Representatives through his presidency. Remarkably, he got the military spending increases in negotiations with Speaker Tip O'Neil, but he had to agree to high domestic outlays in the deal. The government spending didn't create a Keynesian consumer-driven economy but a cold war victory.

Inflation remained reasonable, going forward, with less government control, not more. Lifting regulations on energy production brought down energy prices allowing energy producers to produce and trade more freely. Competition and trade lead to technological advancement, more jobs, better-paying jobs, and ever more creativity and dream fulfillment, and there was a peace dividend.

Reagan never espoused government spending as good for the economy, and he never believed it was. The excessive government spending under Reagan was political; he negotiated with a Democrat-controlled House of Representatives, he didn't get the cuts he wanted, and the increases were mainly military. If considered rightly, as war spending, we won the cold war and should have paid down the debt afterward.

The economy went into recession in George H.W. Bush's third year as President; after such a substantial expansion under Reagan, a cyclical slowing is usual. Bush navigated the Savings and Loan crisis and cut military spending after the cold war victory. Still, general government spending continued increasing, the Democrats controlled both houses of Congress, and there were Gulf War expenses. The Debt to GDP ratio continued swelling in his four years, and at the end of his Presidency, in 1992, it was about 61%.

President Bill Clinton received an economy already out of recession and growing reasonably well. He supported cutting military spending, but the short-lived peace dividend from winning the Cold War occurred while Clinton regularly used the military internationally to keep the peace. In 1993, in his first year in office, with a Budget mainly left from George H.W. Bush and the Democrat Congress, the debt to GDP ratio ended at about 63%.

Government debt increased each year in Clinton's first term, but the economy continued growing moderately, and in the last year of it, 1996, the debt to GDP ratio reached about 64%. In his next year in office, beginning his second term, 1997, the debt to GDP ratio was down to around 62%. In 1998, it was roughly 60%, in 1999, 58%, and in 2000 the debt to GDP ratio was down to about 54%!

Economic growth and debt reduction delivered consistently good results. The fiscal restraint Newt Gingrich and a Republican-controlled Congress with their "Contract with America" held Clinton to in his second term brought balanced budgets and debt reduction into a growing economy. President Clinton was very eloquent in taking credit for the fiscal restraint he rejected before losing Congress. Still, he was flexible enough to accept the political winds and work with the Republicans. President Obama was incredibly inflexible in comparison.

Much of the late '90s growth was tech bubble related; tech stock issues sometimes traded for hundreds of dollars a share on a futuristic idea before the business produced anything. Bad fundamentals always portend problems. The tech bubble burst, and the general stock market began faltering near the end of Clinton's Presidency. George W. Bush inherited a relatively mild recession.

Newt Gingrich, as Speaker of the House, apparently believed what he said when campaigning for office. He did what he said he would do, and we got balanced budgets, debt reduction, and an improvement in the Debt to GDP ratio in the late 1990s. A growing economy makes this easier to do.

Notice how there was a growing economy with conservative fiscal restraint? Also, notice how the Keynesian principles don't ever get the economy doing well in bad times? Keynesians can only conveniently claim things would've been worse had we not racked up the debt.

Especially rhetorically, we somewhat pulled away from Keynesian economics in the '80s and the '90s. President Clinton called himself "a New Democrat" and even acted a bit like one after losing Congress to the Republicans. It was then he proclaimed, "The era of big government is over!" Realistically, the enormous government spending and control apparatus didn't shrink much in those years.

President George W. Bush had Keynesian advisors around him. I almost crashed my car when I heard on the radio that they were mailing everyone

$400 to jump-start the economy! Doesn't it sound stupid? He also signed the Patriot Act with all its intrusive financial tentacles after 9/11, the Do Not Call List with its sweeping commerce killing effect on small businesses, and the Mortgage Safe Act. The last of these came out of a Pelosi-Reed controlled Congress during the bank meltdown.

Bush believed in more central control, or he wouldn't have signed such egregious over-regulation. He could have made sure the Patriot Act was about terrorism and not about making all kinds of financial transactions so much more bureaucratic. Why not do the right thing and veto the Mortgage Safe Act? Was it just political optics during the crisis, or did he not know what he was doing? I don't know which is worse.

Obama was coming into office, and he would have done it, but Bush should have let him. When he signed the Do Not Call List, which came out of a Republican-controlled Speaker Dennis Hastert led Congress, and when he allied with Sen. Ted Kennedy to take an amount of local control away from schools, Bush defined himself. By his actions, he is a big government "kinda guy." These are not the acts of a free enterprise President.

Bush spent more and agreed to federal control of local curriculum through the Department of Education; he pushed through a massive increase in Medicare Benefits. Even left-wing political pundits accused him of being a big spender. Vice President Cheney told us, "deficits don't matter." There was no fiscal restraint to help balance the Bush tax cuts. When the economy improved, government spending continued increasing, so we never saw a surplus.

It's true September 11, 2001, called for more security and military spending, but do you remember when Bush told everyone to do their patriotic duty and go shopping? If you are a patriot, go to the mall and spend money?

If he had not had the Keynesian mentality, he might have said, let's get to work and produce more than we ever have before! Or, let's get out tomorrow and build things for each other or create valuable products and services for trade with each other! "American's business is business," President Calvin Coolidge said, who was a free-market kind of guy. The revealing thing in Bush's statement was spending money so it will draw production, or "demand creates its own supply." Keynes! The correct answer is to produce valuable goods and services for trade domestically and internationally. In 2008, President George W. Bush's last year in office, the debt to GDP ratio reached 67%, but the economy was in free-fall as he walked off the stage.

After President Obama's first year in office, 2009, the debt to GDP ratio was 83%. The economy contracted sharply from the real estate bubble bursting and the subsequent bank panic, and combined with his reckless and ridiculous "stimulus package," the deficit soared. He inherited the crash, but he made matters markedly worse from spending so wastefully.

Although the budget his first year was mainly in place from Bush, Obama added to the deficit that year with his infamous Keynesianism—his roughly $800,000,000,000 stimulus package. The Democrat-controlled Congress passed it without needing his urging, and he signed and began implementing it quickly; it rolled out over 2009, 2010, and 2011. It was like Professor Keynes himself occupied the White House.

The next year under Obama, 2010, the debt to GDP ratio hit about 90%. It reached 95% in 2011; in 2012, 99%; in 2013, 100%; in 2014, 102%; in 2015, 101%, because the economy grew a little faster compared to the added debt. His last year in office, 2016, as the economy slowed, it hit 105%!

Losing Congress to the Republicans in his first midterm election saved Obama's presidency from an even worse fiasco. If he had kept Congress, he would have done stimulus package after stimulus package, and who knows how high our debt to GDP ratio would be. Obama campaigned for re-election, blaming the Republicans for not letting him do more stimulus packages—and the American people voted for him!

Marked by extreme over-regulation and excessive government spending, Obama's economic results were lackluster growth and almost as much additional national debt as all the Presidents before him combined (Office of Management and Budget, 2018, Table 1.1).

With an economy sliding sideways if barely growing after accounting for population growth and inflation, we got an enormous increase in debt with a tepid recovery. Do Roosevelt's Treasury Secretary's comments echo down the decades at us? "We have tried spending; it does not work…?"

Obama wanted government spending to put money in consumers' pockets to drive the economy while military cuts during a long-drawn-out war on terror left our military infrastructure depleted. He followed the exact opposite of Reagan's policies. Look at the different results both economically and militarily.

Our aged and worn military aircraft needed repair or replacement while we used them day in and day out in bombing raids overseas that couldn't seem to take out the enemy. Tie the military's hands with restrictive, politically correct engagement policies while wearing out the equipment with inefficient operations?

After years of budget constraints, he left our Army, Navy, Airforce, and Marines dying in an excessive number of non-combat crashes while flying our "aged" equipment; these problems persisted into Trump's Presidency.

(Tomlinson & Griffin, 2018).

It not only takes money but considerable time to turn these problems around. Many of our planes sat idle, needing repair without enough funds allocated for replacement parts, and with training hours and personnel cut significantly (Copp, 2018).

Entitlements are only becoming a more significant demand on our budget over time because of our aging demographics. Instead of a realistic and sustainable view of them, the left is continually pushing for more "generosity" and expansion. We've had Keynesian spending and stimulus packages with nothing to show for it. Going forward, as President Trump wrestles with Congress over funding, so far, the only compromise they've found includes Keynesian style budget-busting.

As our national debt worsens, we must spend more on the military and entitlement obligations. The awful reality is, with so much accumulated government debt, meeting our general needs becomes increasingly difficult as our debt payments, exacerbated by rising interest rates, eat up a higher percentage of our budget.

Obama ushered in the only time in history besides after WW II that our national debt became bigger than our economy. This time we ran it up without a major war, and he left us in a dangerous place without a post-war boom to pay it down.

The most Keynesian President we've had in some time bequeathed us a stagnated and decelerating economy. In the last quarter of 2016, it grew at under 2%, and in the first quarter of 2017, which he handed off to Trump, it grew at just over 1% annually. Obama took us from 67% to 105% debt to GDP ratio in eight years and without a major war.

14

Bouncing Back Historically

"In this present crisis, government is not the solution to our problem; government is the problem."

Ronald Reagan

THE U.S.A HAS had many economic slowdowns from before the Great Depression and since. The countless articles, papers, and books about it all agree; there was no downturn comparable in length to the 1930s. How can we say the enormous government spending under the new "progressive" theories caused economic growth? Can we say it hindered it? It redirected money from producers to government expenditures and consumers, but was it a net positive or negative? Did it prolong the pain?

If we had Keynesian policies and positive numbers with a growing economy, couldn't it occur for other reasons despite Keynesianism? It's natural for the economy to bounce and recover off the bottom. When people are alive and doing something, economic activity can't go to zero.

Before the Great Depression, all the downturns have some other things in common besides being much shorter. The government didn't try to spend its way out of them, it didn't go deep into debt because of them, and better times ensued much more quickly than in the terrible malaise of the 1930s.

The lengthiest estimates from earlier depressions are five or six years; the other slowdowns were shorter than these, some a year or two, but any historical debt to GDP ratio chart shows it went up little even in the longest or sharpest of them (Phillips, 2012).

The 1920-1921 depression had a worse deflation rate for 1921 (McMahon, Inflation, and CPI Consumer Price Index 1920-1929, 2018) than 1932 had, the worst year of the Great Depression (McMahon, Inflation, and CPI Consumer Price Index 1930-1939, 2018).

Republican President Warren Harding and a Republican Congress were so fiscally conservative in response that they lowered taxes considerably when he came in during the mess, especially for higher incomes (Tax Foundation, 2018) and cut spending substantially (Office of Management and Budget, 2018, Table 1.1). Even with the drop-off in tax receipts from the depressed economy and the tax cuts, they ran surpluses (Ibid)!

Can you imagine our government running surpluses during a recession or a depression instead of deficit spending? The policies worked, the economy reset and took off; the pain was over in less than two years with a decade of boom following. Both decades, the 1920s and 1930s, started in economic catastrophe, but one of them we call the roaring twenties, the other, the Great Depression of the thirties.

The U.S. Office of Management and Budget shows an average government surplus for the years 1789-1849 and barely an average deficit for 1850-1900 (Ibid). These, our country's first one hundred plus years, seem to have had relatively frequent recessions, depressions, and bank panics.

There were no actual debt consequences in all eighteenth and nineteenth-century recessions or depressions. On the other hand, the explosion in government liabilities during the Great Depression is quite historically consequential; it was the inception of a destructive mentality fueling an ever-increasing burden into the future.

Can we say Keynesian economics stabilized the business cycle? The Great Depression happened after the progressive era began, and we can see FDR implemented the ideas Keynes encouraged in his letters. Hoover did too. The evidence is the "progressive" economic policies exacerbating the Depression, and post-WWII, we've also had several severe recessions but with much-added seemingly perpetual debt. I think all the ramifications of a much more primitive economy are a better explanation for less stability in earlier times.

The U.S.A. didn't even have a central bank through most of the nineteenth century, thanks to Andrew Jackson destroying it in the 1830s. Such a lack of interconnection creates instability, making bank panics much more likely. Infrastructure is critical for stability and prosperity.

Without communication technology, you could invest in something and not know for months what was happening. Lack of communication and knowledge can lead to panic. Modern instant interface lends itself to better decisions and better understanding.

Rumors create panic, good communication staves off fear, and defuses rumors. Back then, travel was slow and often hazardous; now, it is safe and swift. We can video conference, call, text, or e-mail messages, and send contracts and other documents in seconds. Modern communication supports growth and stability.

The government could have even spent more on direct relief for humanitarian reasons as 1930s popular opinion demanded, which would have added to the debt. Still, without so much control on businesses with draconian taxation and excessive regulation, the economy would have moved faster and without so much debt piling up.

If helping those in need is moral, why isn't telling a free American how they must run their own business immoral? John Maynard Keynes believed capitalism was intrinsically corrupt. Our politicians and, therefore, our laws today reflect this mentality. Did Keynes help cause this thinking? Can we say our left-leaning politicians are his theoretical children? It seems some are Marx's descendants too. The decent thing to do is to control until they can replace our fundamentally corrupt system. I say their edicts are immoral because they deny human freedom.

The bureaucrats decide people must do it the way the academics say, but their approach may limit opportunities and drive entrepreneurs out of business. Isn't recognizing a God-given right to achieve one's life vocation a moral imperative too? If Capitalism is corrupt, it's because of human nature. Should we destroy human freedom because there are dishonest people? Your controlled system will have crooked people controlling honest but hindered business people.

FDR implemented control of production policies and quotas that frustrated entrepreneurs, and although he comforted consumers with his rhetoric and a soothing voice, he slowed employment by hindering entrepreneurs. How does a government increase consumer spending while inhibiting business freedom? Which comes first, the paycheck or the consumer spending?

If the government provides the paychecks, does that inspire or free up entrepreneurs? It's important to delineate what the economy is and is not to see what drives it and not hinder production and trade. It's not government spending nor control; it's a trade amongst people free to exchange value.

Do we want regulation? Smart rules of the road type laws enforced consistently are indispensable, or else we have anarchy, instability, and wide-ranging poverty. What is too much? Why is control wrong in a practical as well as a moral sense? Shouldn't we elect those running the government realizing that they work for us and remove them if they act as if we work for them? Our income tax system, for example, treats us as slaves! The more productive we are, the more they take away, and the faster we must run on the politicians' gerbil wheel to make ends meet.

The "Progressive Era" began an ever-expanding bureaucratic state, with unelected lawmakers in life-long administrative jobs ruling over, especially our business lives. They run the government, and Congress continues giving this beast more power with each two-thousand-page law they pass, handing over rule-making and enforcement control. A two-thousand-page act becomes ten or twelve thousand pages of rules we must obey as law!

See the following quote from Barak Obama's White House website, the Office of Management and Budget, on May 23, 2016. Consider if it celebrates what began this controlling mentality.

"The History of Major Regulatory Programs"

"… Federal regulation is usually dated from the creation in the late 19th century of the Interstate Commerce Commission (ICC), which was charged with protecting the public against excessive and discriminatory railroad rates. The regulation was economic in nature, setting rates and regulating the provision of railroad services. Having achieved some success, this administrative model of an independent, bipartisan commission, reaching decisions through an adjudicatory approach, was used for the Federal Trade Commission (FTC) (1914), the Water Power Commission (1920) (later the Federal Power Commission), and the Federal Radio Commission (1927) (later the Federal Communications Commission). In addition, during the early 20th century, Congress created several other agencies to regulate commercial and financial systems -- including the Federal Reserve Board (1913), the Tariff Commission (1916), the Packers and Stockyards Administration (1916), and the Commodities Exchange Authority (1922) -- and to ensure the purity of certain foods and drugs, the Food and Drug Administration (1931).

Federal regulation began in earnest in the 1930s with the implementation of wide-ranging New Deal programs. Some of the New Deal economic regulatory programs were implemented by the Federal Home Loan Bank Board (1932), the Federal Deposit Insurance Corporation (FDIC) (1933), the Commodity Credit Corporation (1933), the Farm Credit Administration (1933), the Securities and Exchange Commission (SEC) (1934), and the National Labor Relations Board (1935). In addition, the jurisdiction of both the Federal Communications Commission (FCC) and the Interstate Commerce Commission was expanded to regulate other forms of communications (e.g., telephone and telegraph) and other forms of transport (e.g., trucking). In 1938, the role of the Food and Drug Administration (FDA) was expanded to include prevention of harm to consumers in addition to corrective action. The New Deal also called for the establishment of an agency to enforce the Fair Labor Standards Act of 1938 in the Department of Labor, which is now called the Employment Standards Administration."

Obama's White House website goes on, but it's not fun to read. New agencies and additional regulations piled on through the 1940s, 1950s, 1960s, 1970s, and into his Presidency, empowering the administrative state. They seemed proud of it.

Notice these words from the second sentence, "The regulation was economic in nature, setting rates and regulating the provision of..." It goes on, "this administrative model was used for..." Examples of government agencies follow. The Obama administration is here making an argument for "setting rates," or prices, as an example of "regulation." They believe government control of how much you charge your customers is the model? If you're a business owner, my guess is you're horrified by this mentality.

For individual and general prosperity, free people must live, build, and trade freely, without all these big brother agencies looking over our shoulders. Much of this massive government is Keynesian economics at work. It's not only an excuse to control but to hire more government workers. You know, so they can spend their paychecks to drive the economy.

There's nothing wrong with working for the government. There are critical and necessary public employees, but hiring more than we need or giving away enormous salaries and pensions doesn't drive the economy. It's theft! The massive number of government employees we currently have isn't for economic stability; it hinders, not creates, prosperity. It's a redistributive jobs program. Read in his own words what Keynes said he wanted and then look at what we have! What kind of system has political "commissions" controlling production? Setting prices (and wages) is not free enterprise!

According to John Maynard Keynes, our leaders supposedly create "something approximating full employment" by hiring additional government employees. Keynesians believe they control society in fairness and drive the economy simultaneously, but government jobs programs most often help elect left-leaning politicians. They get enormous political funding from public employee unions, the behemoth grows, and we get deeper into debt.

The people paying the government employees, the taxpayers, pay to elect one party: the confiscated public employee union dues buy votes for the Democrats. To show how far gone we are, because he understood the conflict of interest, even FDR opposed broadly giving public employees the power of collective bargaining (FDR Presidential Library & Museum, 2016 [1937]). But President John F. Kennedy made federal public employee unions legal by executive order (U.S. Federal Labor Relations Authority, 2018), and the ensuing political corruption favors one side.

FDR tried to pack the Supreme Court by adding more justices of his choosing after they struck down so much of his control-oriented New Deal legislation as unconstitutional. In the power struggle that ensued, with the President so popular and Congress so overwhelmingly on his side, one Justice switched his vote, and the court approved most of what FDR wanted. Congress, realizing they had gotten their way, and the government paradigm had changed to the "progressive" constitutional interpretation, didn't need to vote to add additional justices (Leuchtenburg, 2005).

The court began legislating from the bench by interpreting away traditional moral beliefs through "the living, breathing document" approach. The federal government now has the authority to control the economy.

So why did such a severe economic malaise last through the 1930s? Politically driven government hindrances. Free people couldn't produce and trade efficiently. It exemplifies why third-world countries stay poor, although they are usually a much more extreme example.

When does so much power lead to over-regulation? Every day in America today. The depression era changed our economy and social structure in many ways. "Progressive" economic theory became installed structurally: the idea that we should drive the economy with massive government spending increases. Keynesian economists clamored for more when they said Obama's stimulus packages didn't work; they said it needed to be at least twice as large as it was. In this case, the more, the better, is bankrupt. We would become such if we tried this craziness.

World War II also changed the economy in many ways, but this kind of government spending funneled to private companies on war research and production would bankrupt any country in a few years if the war didn't end. The only reason we survived the WWII debt build-up is our enormous increases in production capabilities learned in the race for survival. The victory allowed us to produce and grow enough to avoid default from incredibly improved efficiency. We still haven't paid off the debt, though. Countries destroyed by war will usually need help from the victor or others or default on their obligations. Check history.

If the government tries to improve the economy with such silly things as solar energy startups through political favoritism, the waste and debt will multiply. Solar energy is not bad. It can be an excellent thing, but relying on jobs paid for by government spending in solar power companies is part of the "progressive" foolishness contributing to the national debt trap.

Did the "Great Society Programs," pushed through by President Lyndon Johnson, create more prosperity? Were they a sound public investment like the interstate freeway system was? Freeways allow for more human productivity, while welfare sometimes pays the able-bodied to be unproductive. If Keynesianism is correct, and demand creates its own supply, consumer spending drives the economy. Therefore, welfare, disability, unemployment benefits, and food stamps stimulate the economy, as Nancy

Pelosi and Paul Krugman tell us.

Since the 1960s, the poverty rate among the elderly is down. Social Security and Medicare eased much pain and heartache. Still, data shows poverty up in working-age adults, even higher for people in their productive years than older folks (United States Census Bureau, 2017, Table 3).

Why didn't getting money in the elderly's pockets make working-age people more prosperous because older folks spent more? Government money spent on the needy aged makes sense for moral reasons, but if Keynesian economics works, why wouldn't it work for economic reasons? Why wouldn't it create more prosperity for working-age groups as demand would create its own supply?

Shouldn't the elderly with much more disposable income drive the economy with their consumer spending? Don't the old need consumer goods for immediate consumption? Aren't these the high numbers of marginally poor Keynes said would spend what was in their pockets quickly? Older folks are an ever-increasing percentage of our society. Still, they aren't bringing us a vibrant economy when the poverty rate among working people is higher than among the elderly. Why isn't the poverty rate lower now than in 1960?

You can say there are other reasons for the higher poverty rate among working-age people, but there is no evidence unproductive spending creates a net gain. Older folks spend more now than fifty years ago, but if they don't produce and replace the value destroyed by their consumption, how can it be a net positive? It's those basics in classical theory proving Keynesianism wrong again.

Which is the moral position, requiring work if welfare recipients can, or giving them money? Helping those in a terrible place is good for us all, but is feeding human degradation healthy for anyone? How about fraud and theft?

Isn't it best to consider how we do it? At the community level, those closest to the people is usually the best place to start with aid. Church, neighbor, family giving is voluntary and good for the soul. Big government is confiscatory and forcibly redistributive. If welfare rolls drop drastically with work requirements, it seems we can filter out much fraud.

Maine implemented such reforms as requiring work or time volunteering, setting limits, etc. They significantly reduced fraud, and many people stopped requesting it. The State became more efficient and helped the genuinely needy while simultaneously getting their State budget in order (Adolphsen, 2017). The average income went up statewide, once again showing us that production (supply) creates consumption (demand), not the other way around.

During World War II, Americans accepted marginal income taxation at over 90%, but it continued this way until the 1960s; we complied with 70% or more through the 1970s. The government enforced business controls, and excessive taxation formed us into more obedience in our personal and professional lives as freedom wained.

Instead of our political leaders espousing free trade by deregulating oil in the face of the Arab oil embargo, we settled for the government telling us we could line up for gas, what days of the week we could get some and how much we could put in our tanks. Remember, during President Carter's term, the $5.00 minimum and maximum at the pump? We could only get gas on certain days when our license plate ended in an odd or even number. How much commerce did it impede, especially in those days before computers, when we had to go out to sell and service clients?

We took them telling our car companies to reduce performance in our vehicles. American production quality collapsed with our national pride by the late 1970s. Government control hurts us spiritually as it negatively affects our humanity. We settled into malaise. There is something to be said for the spirit of freedom. Reagan knew this and injected some of it back into a psychologically starving populace.

How can we know what promotes economic recovery and prosperity in general? In understanding what the economy is, we can identify how it operates most efficiently. It is production value exchanged freely within a stable society. Whether it's Marxian, Keynesian, or any other, we should doubt theories that ignore or deny time-tested foundational truths.

The economy isn't 70% consumer spending, as they report. How could the remaining 30%, in a Keynesian biased formulation, be part government spending, say 17%, business spending (investment), say 18%, with net exports, say -5%? Is it possible so much less business investment, 18%, can make so much more consumer and government spending, 88% combined? Isn't it just another way to suggest demand creates its own supply?

The truth is, business activity is the economy. Entrepreneurialism drives the economy. Consumer spending is only an indication of successful business activity. It can't increase without putting us deeper in debt or running down our wealth without rising profits and paychecks coming first.

If we understand the basic economic principles and how we need our freedom to thrive, we'll see we must stop the career politicians by sending them home through term limits. The system is now too rigged; they've designed it for themselves to stay in power for life to control us and spend our money. We must also dismantle the unaccountable deep administrative state bureaucracy and streamline government with simple, enforceable laws.

Ultimately, bouncing back means adhering to our Constitution; the American experiment is too important, too precious to let fail.

Part V

Today

"America will never be destroyed by the outside. If we falter and lose our freedoms, it will be because we destroyed ourselves."

Abraham Lincoln

15

Riding Down the Keynesian Road

"It is impossible to avoid a precipice when one follows a road that leads nowhere else."

Jean-Baptiste Say

WE NOW HAVE over twenty trillion dollars in national debt, not including ever-increasing government entitlement obligations of much more. What happens if we continue deficit spending? How many more stimulus packages and ongoing deficits can our national budget endure? When does guaranteeing government pensions higher than working people earn while in comparable jobs in the real economy overwhelm us? How can we let such recklessness proceed with a clear conscience? Not only for the U.S.A. but isn't this dangerous for all Western Civilization? Are we whistling past the graveyard already? How do we get out of this?

What should we say to politicians proposing "jobs bills" or "stimulus packages?" Can we stop the collusion between government employee unions and the corrupt politicians they continually reelect? We must speak and vote, no! The better we understand basic concepts, the better we can speak out. We need more rock-solid, resilient, knowledgable, and honest politicians in both major political parties with Presidents who will veto stimulus packages. Cutting taxes intelligently allows free people to produce more, but we must account for the initial drop in tax receipts strategically and very mindfully.

Unless it happens inadvertently, when the economy slows, briefly, or in an emergency like a major war, deficits matter very much. The government must never increase spending attempting to get the economy going!

We can climb out of this with a better economy while simultaneously paying down our debt, but expanding government spending is not growth. It is a Keynesian deception to say the GDP increases by counting government spending as growth. We must stop including it as part of our GDP. It is time to come up with a more honest calculation.

Taxpayer money spent intelligently for infrastructure allows for real growth if commerce speeds up and becomes more efficient, but government spending itself is not growth; forcibly redistributing wealth hurts efficiencies and productivity while putting us all deeper in debt. We must replace the Keynesian sham. We can't spend our way out of trouble; we must create and produce valuable things and exchange them so that tax receipts increase naturally. History shows us it works. We can grow and pay down the debt!

Slowing economies often produce government budget deficits, but during the peak and even the flat part of the business cycle, we should have surpluses and debt reduction like we did before the 1930s. It doesn't hurt and is, in fact, helpful if we run the government lean and efficiently.

Productive private expenditures, apart from government spending, are intrinsic to the growth process. Production costs build products and services more valuable than the value destroyed in creating them.

Spending destroys value when it doesn't replace itself. Put money in unproductive peoples' pockets, so they consume, and the utility is gone. Increased production and trading of valuable goods and services between ourselves worth more than the cost of making them is economic growth.

The following truth that some attribute to Adam Smith is worth repeating many times: "the only way we increase our standard of living over time is through increased productivity due to two things that are often interrelated: new technologies and new methods." We do not increase our standard of living over time by pushing the Keynesian proverbial spending to consumption string. The answer is spending on profitable production, creating things valuable to each other, and trading. It is how we get out of the debt trap. Creation on the one hand and fiscal restraint on the other solves it. We have to get this straight before catastrophe strikes!

Have you looked at the big debt picture around Western Civilization, honestly? In the U.S.A., what does a national debt over twenty trillion dollars, besides entitlement obligations multiple times that guaranteed by the federal, state, and local governments, mean for us? What about our children and grandchildren? Why don't we care about posterity anymore? Isn't not caring about our posterity immoral? Why can't we agree that it's wrong?

Can you see how logical and straightforward fundamental economic theory is? What about how Keynesianism breaks from immutable truths? Is common sense something to be shunned? What about survival? Isn't only thinking of our present consumption, or just regarding the short run, corrupt and decadent? If we understand economics, we learn to build and promote building, not that all consumption is helpful. We will have profits and paychecks and the resources to help others and teach our children by example. We can have the strength, clout, and resources to defend ourselves and others, not on borrowed money.

When necessary, borrowing happens in an emergency or for leverage, but thoughtfully, strategically, and responsibly, with a plan to pay it back. Just like profit must, government tax receipts must cover financing costs, or we're heading toward disaster; financing debt payments should come from cash flow and not from more borrowing. Imagine our politicians ran the government with business acumen?

To some degree, hopefully, President Trump and enough Republicans see this now, but more Democrats must get it too. What happens when the Keynesians take over again? We can't go in the right direction until enough in the other major party come to the truth.

Why can't the Democrats deal with reality? Socialist theory is their problem. Keynesianism gives them a perpetual excuse for more government spending, which equals a larger government with more design and control from elitists, so we have continually reckless budgets.

Building up the national debt by unproductive spending is analogous to filling up your credit cards from excessive drinking, eating out, and vacationing. On the other hand, debt against a productive real estate asset, like a commercial or apartment building, not only allows for income over the debt costs but is relative to the asset's market value that it facilitates. The government issues bonds against freeways that enable more economic productivity to pay for themselves through more business activity and tax receipts, analogous to how tenants pay down an apartment building mortgage.

Once we pay off the bonds, the freeway remains, and with maintenance, it continues augmenting productivity as the apartment building remains productive with proper upkeep. Unnecessary government workers with the pain in added bureaucracy against producers, solar energy debacles, and wasteful spending, increase the debt with no production paying for it and no asset to show.

Would you feel good leaving your children *each* a $1,000,000 unsecured debt or more? Do you want to inherit massive debt from your parents? Could your kids build a life for themselves, starting with that kind of debt hanging around their necks? Would they declare bankruptcy? What if they couldn't claim bankruptcy? What if no one was behind them supporting them if they got stuck and couldn't make it? Remember, this is a problem we're causing!

Who'll bail out the USA if our interest rates soar and we can't make our debt payments? It could happen fast if we keep massively adding to our debt, and something sets off a financial panic or an inflationary spiral that increases interest rates and our debt payments. It could continue happening slowly over time by following deficit spending policies until the trigger when it all slides off a cliff quickly.

It has happened to large countries before, yet there is no one big enough to help us. If it happens to us, it will occur worldwide because so many others play the same reckless game, and so many depend on us. Who will help them with us on our knees? Which country will fail first to set off the chain reaction?

Should we leave our children and grandchildren a national debt that, even if they can pay it off, will negatively affect their standard of living, with such high taxes and a government so short on money? Can you imagine how this would adversely affect their country's standing in the world?

Instead of massive debt, wouldn't you prefer to leave your children, say, at least a paid-off house, bank accounts with some money in them, and maybe some other things of material value? You could prosper and leave them much more than this. You could bequeath them a stable financial situation, or you could hand them a mess. What about our country—what about our political situation? It doesn't seem hard, a country as wealthy as the U.S.A., to imagine leaving our fiscal house secure for future generations. An objective observer should say it's easy.

America's founders wrote in the Preamble to the Constitution "for ourselves and our posterity." What kind of moral breakdown have we had if we don't care about our children and grandchildren anymore? To what level has our culture sunk? How self-indulgent are we? Here kids, take our twenty trillion in debt. You're welcome! It's all happening because of an economic theory that tells us to be concerned only with the short run.

Today, especially our left-wing politicians, keep pushing for more government spending even when we are running enormous deficits, so we keep moving toward the cliff. We all must admit John Maynard Keynes' theories do not work to turn in the right direction. He was wrong. He did not respect the entrepreneur, and he did not recognize applied creative business freedom as the driving force in economics. We could all look at economics realistically and spend accordingly; our tax receipts are undoubtedly high enough for the government to do many things responsibly.

We could be an example for the rest of the world by leading what is left of a confused Western Civilization back in the right direction instead of driving it toward the cliff. We can produce and manage our way out of this by effectuating our dreams. We can do it by thinking about short-run and long-run growth as we seriously account for our debt obligations.

Honest politicians must repeal many controlling, intrusive hindering laws, pass simple, straightforward, clear ones against fraudulent behavior, judiciously cut spending, and understand a business-friendly mentality.

"America's business is business" brings prosperity within the parameters of a stable business-friendly government. When we cut taxes, we should reduce spending too. We need citizen politicians with business acumen who love their country to rise, serve, and go home—the way the founding fathers did.

We all must understand *how,* at its very foundation, Keynesian economics is wrong: demand does not create its supply, and the fiscal multiplier is a fantasy. Then responsible politicians won't have to negotiate for tax cuts against spending crazed, irrational Keynesian ones. We depleted our military during the Obama years without enough money allocated to fix or replace aging planes and other equipment. With the right mentality, responsible politicians won't have to agree to higher spending on many other things, compromising with those espousing Keynesian tomfoolery because of desperately needed military money, busting the budget.

Structurally and operationally basing government on the original Constitutional model will take the courage of our convictions. We must streamline many government agencies and conclude that less is more and end many altogether. We'll be more inspired to do it when we realize they are Keynesian jobs programs designed to control private industry and shift the economy into a public endeavor. Giving people jobs so they'll spend their paychecks doesn't drive the economy. The ultimate Keynesian goal is to take the free out of free enterprise.

The Department of Education website as of, December 19, 2017, claims the following:

"4,400 employees and $68 billion budget," and "in 1980 (it came into being) by combining offices from several federal agencies... (U.S.Department of Education, 2017)."

Did they mention how many more employees and how much more bureaucracy they've propagated since their inception? Has this helped test scores at all? No, Google it yourself and read all kinds of data. Test scores haven't improved since the Department of Education began. It has made educating more cumbersome for the State and local people who teach the children, but without overall improvement.

Is the Department of Education a financial and bureaucratic swamp kept in place through favoritism and political corruption? Canada doesn't have a comparable federal education department. They handle things locally and from the provinces, but they report better test scores than the U.S.A.

Our politicians say it's all for the kids, and they may even throw out the truth that an educated citizenry is more productive economically, but is all this bureaucracy an investment in our kids? Similarly, are the teachers' unions for the kids or the teachers? Are they mainly for the control-oriented politicians receiving the forced union dues that re-elect them? If the return on investment is negative, with lots of expenses with no results, what becomes the intelligent decision? Getting rid of this bureaucracy shouldn't be a difficult decision for fair-minded and honest people.

An efficient government is a local government in many ways. It usually better addresses people's needs, including schools. The top-heavy federal government model is a Keynesian jobs program setting us up in the long run for a government employee pension implosion. States, counties, and city politicians are also confused by the Keynesian spend your way to prosperity lie. Their budgetary and pension nightmares give evidence. Many want the federal government to bail them out with printed and borrowed money, extending and perpetuating the Keynesian shell game.

We can follow our left-leaning politician's advice and continue a weak growth path with government hindrances that won't keep up with our growing debt or pension obligations. We can cut taxes and increase spending, so the debt explodes upward as we've done before. We can let professional politicians who never leave office but only get rich, somehow, while "working for us," destroy our children's and grandchildren's future. Or we can vote in business-friendly politicians but insist they balance budgets and reduce so much overregulation and repeal such draconian laws as we suffer under today. How does a politician become a multimillionaire on a roughly $175,000 salary? Corruption, that's how. If they don't act responsibly, send them home!

The truth is, we won't send them packing; we would give the other political party an advantage because they won't send their corrupt politicians home. The side with the long-standing politicians remains entrenched with lobbyists, and they know the manipulation game to stay in power better. We need constitutional amendments, one for congressional term limits. If the founding fathers saw our position today, I think they'd do this first; they'd then set up safeguards against the administrative state, dismantling it.

Or we can stay on course toward the cliff. Eventually, those at the bottom of the economic scale will see benefit cuts, with Social Security, Medicare, Medicaid, and everything else squeezed. If your children can't work for some reason, or if they become old without having enough assets, they could be excruciatingly poor, with a government unable to keep its promises.

Keynesians believe government spending creates multipliers. They say we should have fewer children by exercising population control and increase deficit spending with more largess toward our retirees to get out of trouble. Once again, the truth is the opposite. We need more prosperous kids to support the growing number of retirees. Elitists ignore common sense.

Suppose we don't increase our productive workforce. In that case, those who work will have to pay higher taxes as people retire, which will hurt growth, while knowing they will not receive much if any retirement benefits because earlier generations spent too much on themselves. As time goes on, on the wrong path, the correction becomes tougher. An extreme uncertainty, lack of confidence, malaise, and eventually instability ensues as the Keynesians tell us to print, borrow, and spend more.

Inflation may devalue our currency, destabilizing society, and make an unsure life even more painful. The rampant late 1970s inflation could look tame. The feeling back then was, how high will it go? Interest rates could soar, and although home prices may shoot up, they may lose value in real terms as everything else rises faster. Very high mortgage rates could cause home inflation to be less, perhaps, than consumer staples, fuel/gasoline, clothing, and food.

Did you notice how Keynesian driven politicians always seem to want higher taxes? Wait until things unravel if we keep following their advice. Get ready for much higher taxes if you make a good living; you will not have much of your paycheck for yourself. You could be paying much higher taxes on money that quickly loses its value while it all causes further economic upheaval. When our military becomes smaller, weaker, and less of a force for peace globally, will the bad guys become trustworthy? Wait until the bully dictators in this world see us weakened. Do you think they test us now?

Can we rely on China to keep the peace? Under what terms? How many people have they executed this week for smuggling cigarettes? Historically, they arrested women and had forced abortions performed by government "doctors" because they already had a child or a girl and not a boy in the womb. Recent reports say this officially ended, but can we rely on a country with atheistic Communist policies? Is morality relative, or is there such a thing as right and wrong? What is good and evil in an entirely relativistic, arbitrarily moral world?

Have you considered the importance of love is in all this? If you left material things behind but did not love your children, how would it affect them? Is the love parents have for their children overrated—or the love children have for their parents?

We all know, at least most of us, I believe, that love is far more valuable than money or material things, but shouldn't you leave them well trained as good citizens and good stewards of their county's assets? Is it our ignorance or laziness that allowed Keynesian economics to become so prevalent?

Does recklessly leaving your children debt instead of assets represent love, abuse, neglect? What do you think? How would you feel going out knowing you saddled your kids with *your* virtually insurmountable debt? Would you want your parents or anyone else to do that to you? Why are we doing it? Is it a good thing, raising your children to believe in elitist theories like Keynesian economics? What kind of lesson is it for our children that we can spend our way out of financial trouble?

What kind of person are you if you let your kids go off to college and become convinced these disastrous notions work? Where do you send your kids to school? It's hard to find an economics department that is not Keynesian infiltrated today. Have you watched some of the political focus groups with recent college graduates? It seems the upcoming generation is already mostly Keynesian brainwashed, especially from the "best schools." You should ask your kids how they feel about paying off the enormous national debt.

The politicians, the college professors, and the news media are all setting us up for disaster. John Maynard Keynes and his control-oriented ideas are setting us up for catastrophe through his modern-day acolytes. Why aren't enough people talking about this? How have these foolish ideas become infused into so many of the most "intelligent" people?

John Maynard Keynes taught us not to worry as he quipped, "In the long run, we are all dead." These phrases, the long run and the short run, are common economic jargon. He believed the long run would take care of itself by deficit spending in the short run.

Keynes's theories emphasize the short run. He postulated that government spending and the full employment it would produce would create enough prosperity so the debt wouldn't matter; a growing economy through deficit spending would give us more power to pay it off if we wanted to. So why does our debt and debt to GDP ratio continue getting worse? Keynesians will say it's because we haven't spent enough to improve things.

How often do the smartest people make the biggest mistakes? The powerful have a great responsibility. It should be first not to harm; do not set the people and their children up for disaster. Let the people prosper, do not try to make them prosperous. If they are not thriving, you can't make them so. The government can only foster an environment, but successful individuals set an excellent example for others by honestly producing and trading with other productive people.

The government can be business-friendly, but it can't give non-producing people money and achieve good economic results. Ideological pet government spending projects do not operate on fundamental economic principles; it's crony capitalism.

We must stop government schemes to redistribute wealth and always reject socialist systems: resources aren't like a fixed pie that the rich hog, but "resources are only fixed in as much as our imaginations are fixed!" Personal and economic growth and interaction in trade is the answer. Opportunity for all must become our common motto. Didn't it use to be?

The citizens' wealth comes from chasing their dreams. Even if you give them something, they will likely lose it because they didn't earn it and won't know how to keep it. A moral, loving, disciplined home produces productive and responsible citizens. Government babysitting doesn't. The politicians must stop "doing more" because they so often do more damage.

Trouble begins when those in power disregard the common man's dreams; they see people as widgets in a Keynesian formula. They delude themselves with their "demand-side" arguments, i.e., "we simply need to inject more demand into the economy to create more production." They miss the truth: economics begins and thrives by entrepreneurial dreams in action. Their left-wing beliefs represent a lack of humanity from people who say they care. The economy is people striving, producing, and trading.

Ever since he came up with them, government leaders went headlong implementing John Maynard Keynes' theories. In a personal conversation, Keynes told Hayek if his ideas didn't work, if they created inflation as Hayek warned him, he'd be the first to call for their reversal (Malthus0, 2012).

Keynes knew his "ideas" were experimental. He wrote in the final chapter of *The General Theory* that their being correct was "an hypothesis:"

"But if the ideas are correct—an hypothesis on which the author must base what he writes (Keynes, The General Theory of Employment Interest and Money, 1936, 383) ..."

After so many years of watching his contrarian ideas argued for, expanded, defended, and explained by politicians and their economist friends since he first postulated them, can't we say we've tried them exhaustively? We've even tried to correct their flaws. They don't work at the very foundation; the hypothesis has failed; they contradict the time-tested theoretical giants. Keynes has proponents beyond common sense.

His followers from left-wing schools of thought who embrace his ideas have no potential reversal in mind. Why? They use him for politics. Karl Marx's name won't sell politically, but they still have Keynes. The Democratic Socialists of America use Marxist theory warmed over, stealthily, with sweeter-sounding words. Mainstream Democrat Party politicians guide society in the wrong direction with Keynes; they'll use anything that gets them elected and steer us to a government-managed economy.

Just listen to almost everything that comes from them regarding economics; their words and actions prove it. Too many of our politicians want more deficit spending when we have over twenty trillion dollars in national debt. They scream about tax cuts unless we're in a severe slowdown because they think deficit spending pays for itself through their fanciful "fiscal multiplier."

President Trump took a similar deal from Chuck Schumer, as Ronald Reagan accepted from Tip O'Neil. Both Presidents believed military spending was an urgent priority because of the very left-wing President before them who neglected to fund our troops and their equipment. It was a national security question, so the Keynesian politicians forced each man's hand in the bargain. What a deal? Our politicians look like the Keystone Cops!

The Democrats controlled the House in Reagan's time, and Trump couldn't get past the sixty vote margin in the Senate; Speaker of the House

Paul Ryan supported the deal because he thought it was the best they could get. So we got another run-up in Keynesian caused debt from all kinds of additional wasteful spending as a tradeoff. The only way to stop the crazy debt spiral is to understand what is right, what works, economics, and live by it. We must get clarity on both sides of the political aisle.

You can use your imagination regarding how bad the disaster could eventually become if we keep trying to spend our way out of trouble. Imagine not enough food, violence in the streets, no heat, no healthcare, a violent struggle for survival? I don't want to write a science fiction story for you. If society breaks down morally and people become so deprived of necessities, let's call it a people both depraved and deprived, quite a dangerous combination, it could get worse than you or I could imagine. Did you see the rioters and the looters all over the news for various causes in President Obama's last couple of years and after President Trump's election? Think of that on a massive scale. Think of worse than Venezuela if we don't change our ways.

Who organized all those riots? How else could they all come out in ten different cities across the country on the same day, holding the same signs, chanting the same slogans, and using the same tactics? It's eerie how this all seems to work together, the moral and the financial breakdown, then "the resistance" that fights against intelligent decisions.

Sometimes life is stranger than fiction, but remaining confused or in denial won't help us. Clarity and courage will. Follow politics. It leads directly to the opposing economic schools of thought, and it may expose radicals. Stay on the road toward the cliff, and you will eventually go off it. Who then comes into power to install order?

16

Who Supports the Scandal?

"...liberty is the heritage of all men. Destroy this spirit, and you have planted the seeds of despotism around your own doors."

Abraham Lincoln

MANY ECONOMISTS CLAIM no political leanings, but they support the scandal. They talk confidently about the goodness of government spending and advise confused politicians. What happens when the economists leave the room and the puzzled politicians contemplate and discuss all this counter-intuitive Keynesian preaching with their advisors?

Their speechwriters must be very careful when telling them what to say about economics. If they say too much, they could look crazy at the podium like Nancy Pelosi regularly does. Her Keynesian words embody the scandal. The following quotes from youtube videos are all too telling. Why don't more people cry foul when she says things like this:

"It's the biggest (economic) bang for the buck when you do food stamps and unemployment insurance (Your World with Neil Cavuto-Stuart Varney,

2011)."

"Unemployment insurance extension is not only good for individuals; it has a macroeconomic impact. As the macroeconomic advisors have stated, it will make a difference of 600,000 jobs to our economy (Pelosi, 2011)."

"Unemployment insurance, the economists tell us, returns two dollars for every dollar that is put out there for unemployment insurance. People need the money; they spend it immediately for necessities; it injects demand into the economy; it creates jobs to reduce the deficit (Ibid)."

"If you want to create jobs, the quickest way to do it is to provide more funding for food stamps (Ibid)."

"...unemployment insurance...this is one of the biggest stimulus to our economy (Ibid)."

Check online, and you'll see Ms. Pelosi say many similar things. She's selling it, and she leads the House Democrats! John Maynard Keynes would be proud of her. The damage this woman does is incredible. She is tremendously powerful, especially when the Democrats have a majority, and she always pushes for more spending. Her speeches are the consummate left-wing Keynesian propaganda. Being from San Francisco, Nancy doesn't appear to worry about looking nuts; she must seem reasonable to her constituents. They probably think she sounds sophisticated! She says these things with passion and honesty, and it defines delusion.

Our education system is a scandal. College professors teach Keynesian economics like it is factual, real gospel. They give Keynes much more than equal time than classical economists like Richard Cantillon, Adam Smith, Jean-Baptiste Say, or modern level-headed writers. Some college graduates with economics degrees I've talked with have never heard of the three giants; although they have often heard of Smith, most don't recognize Say, and very few know of Cantillon. They all know of John Maynard Keynes.

Keynesian college professors lecture glowingly about demand creating its own supply, the fiscal multiplier, and the marginal propensity to consume, sometimes using textbooks they write and require their students to buy. If not their own, they use ones written by one of the many economists who "furthered" Keynesian ideas and became the left's scholastic champions. The computations, arithmetic, formulas, and neat-looking graphs train their students through leftist political indoctrination by faux economic theory.

The farther along students go into their costly Keynesian Economics educations, the more they put numbers into equations that don't work in the real world. Higher education's academic laboratory creates the most confusion because students believe professors with no practical business experience. Once they graduate, they have the power, the credentials, and the societal positions to confuse the masses. If they do well enough, maybe they'll become professors and pass the theories right along.

Erroneous inputs equal corrupted outputs. Assumptions that don't account for real-life variables or consider our humanity apart from "animal spirits," ideas that don't contemplate the business person's decision-making behavior, mislead. It's the foundational economic truths that most easily expose Keynesianism. If the consumer doesn't drive the economy, their arithmetic is worse than worthless; it's deeply deceptive.

The truth our kids must know is that entrepreneurs drive the economy;

consumer spending is only a gauge to measure successful entrepreneurial activity. Economics is trade between two or more capable parties with the value that gives them the power to exchange. Commerce comes from production—unless someone else provides for another, or they borrow or steal, so they have something in hand for consummation, they can't trade for what they need or want. The consumer must first produce value for a transfer between parties unless they're a bane on society, as Adam Smith described with "prodigals" that don't replace what they destroy.

If demand equals consumption, and supply production, as all Economics 101 textbooks tell us, we must realize production must come first to have the value to trade. Then how can demand be the driving force? The Giants were right, and Keynes was wrong. Supply (production) is the economic engine!

The value of, or the proceeds of previous business production, in other words, the paycheck or profit from trading your labor and skills represented in a medium of exchange, or money, buys a loaf of bread with the proceeds of that business production. Both sides of the trade first come from a business transaction; the buyer previously exchanged value and then had it on hand for consummation.

A Realtor buys his dinner with a small piece of the home he sold. The carpenter buys his food and pays his rent with a bit of the framing he did the week before. The builder, or the entrepreneur, advanced him money from the future home sale, the value he'll receive in exchange.

Since the supply of valuable goods and services produces the value to trade, to buy and sell through profits and paychecks, can you imagine if college professors taught economics is the value of supply exchanged on both sides of any transaction? If they still used, *A Treatise on Political Economy,* by Jean-Baptiste Say as the standard textbook, couldn't we have avoided all the Keynesian confusion? We wouldn't have such massive debt.

Would we still hear the slanderous strategic political attack phrase, "we've tried trickle-down economics before, and it doesn't work?" Suppose we understood that easy taxes help small, medium, and large businesses to create more value for others. Would politicians continue using the false political slander, "supply-side economics doesn't work?"

Leftist politicians first erroneously define economics. They use a partisan pejorative strawman to describe their political opponents' beliefs before knocking down the phony descriptions. They say the economy is 70% consumer spending when it is not. They confidently espouse Keynesian economics by promoting wealth redistribution, more massive controlling government, higher taxes, and more regulation. When they use terms like "supply-side economics" pejoratively, it implicitly gives credibility to supposed "demand-side" economics, which doesn't exist. It's all a scandal. No one produces or causes production from "the demand side." There really is no "supply-side" economics either, just economics—supply and supply, production value exchanged, or trade.

If a private party buys a car from another private party, they made a deal; they exchanged value from their business profit or paycheck on the one side for ownership of a valuable earned asset. If the buyer uses a loan, he is merely getting an advance on the value he creates over time, makes another exchange with the bank, and pays it down with interest. Borrowing the money facilitated the transfer, as using money as a medium of exchange does, both tools for added productivity. The parties engaged in trade for the perceived worth. Each supplied the other, supply, and supply. The buyer uses the car to drive to work, and the seller uses the proceeds in another exchange.

When paychecks come from the government, profitable businesses or their employees ultimately paid the government salaries through their taxed valuable activity. No consumer can buy anything in the big picture unless with the value of some industrious business action. Consumers don't drive the economy; business activity comes first.

Keynesian-loving college professors often have no real-world business experience; as I said above, their boots have never been on the ground. The better they are at the Keynesian arithmetic, the more they adore the ideological beliefs, the better chance they go right into the ivory tower as direct hires out of graduate school. These are the best and the brightest in a Keynesian world. With so much prestige involved for these technical geniuses, other powerful options may open beyond their vaunted professorial positions — more scandal.

They may go into a left-wing think tank furthering their Keynesian beliefs, solidifying their partisan politics. After some time teaching in the ivory tower or padding their resume' at the think tank, they may go to Washington as economic advisors to the most "progressive" politicians. To call them political advisors is more accurate than calling them economists because they often justify "progressive" or socialist ideas through more government spending couched in economic theory. After serving in politics, they usually go back to the ivory tower to teach the next generation.

There are many examples of this, but former President Bill Clinton's Labor Secretary is a good one. Robert Reich became a Harvard professor and then a Berkley professor after his Labor Secretary tenure. He previously served in the Jimmy Carter and Gerald Ford administrations. Before that, a Rhodes Scholar at Oxford in England, a Dartmouth graduate, and has a Yale law degree (University of California Berkeley, 2018). He writes books and speaks on economics in many venues.

He and former House Speaker Newt Gingrich got into it on the ABC News Sunday Program Roundtable discussion. They were talking about the new Pope, but Reich couldn't help steering the conversation into economics when he chimed in derisively, attacking, saying the Pope was against,

"...supply-side, trickle-down economics (ABC News, 2013)."

Notice his mixing the derogatory phrases "supply-side economics" and "trickle-down economics" into a new, "more inclusive" disparaging compound phrase?

We see here a left-wing intellectual using "supply-side economics" as a classic straw man. In truth, supply creating demand is established in theory and practice every day; it is tried and true. Jean-Baptiste Say defined this more than 200 years ago. It works every time someone produces a product or service someone else wants. It proves itself every time you buy one product in the supermarket instead of another, or work harder, making more at your job so you can save to buy something you want. Supply creates demand. Entrepreneurs creating value drive the economy. And the term "trickle-down economics" is a strategic political attack phrase. No respectable economics department teaches this political slander.

The left's false working definition, their strawman, is this: cut taxes for the rich, and in this way the government *gives* them enormous piles of money, then, as they spend it, some of it will eventually "trickle-down" to the poor. It works well with their other slander, "Republicans are all for the rich."

Their answer? Don't *give* the money to the rich. Take it from them in the name of justice, and give it to the poor so they can spend it to drive the economy. More prosperity follows when the unfortunate consume quickly, causing and multiplying activity because (they think) demand creates its own supply, and the fiscal multiplier will kick in! They proudly proclaim, "the rich should pay their fair share," so the government can "redistribute wealth" and "give others a break." We can then have a "more equitable society," meaning more controlled outcomes.

Did you notice Reich's fixed resources thinking? He argues Keynesianism grows the economy, but first, it's confiscatory and redistributive. As if there is only so much money, and the rich hog it. Implicit in his reasoning is the government owns what you have and gives you your money. He controls you.

When the host asked Reich why the separation between rich and poor has gotten worse under Obama, Reich blamed Republicans for obstructing spending more federal money. He responded:

"It has something to do with the intransigence of the speaker's party, because every time there was a jobs bill, every time there was an effort to expand, ah, low-income housing, every time there was an effort to provide more opportunities to young people (Ibid)..."

Newt Gingrich aggressively stopped him, saying,

"baloney...every major city that is a center of poverty is run by Democrats...and their policies have failed, they're not willing to admit it, and the fact is it's the poor who suffer from them (Ibid)..."

Gingrich used reality to follow up on his earlier point that the war on poverty has failed, and we shouldn't deny facts. Earlier, Reich claimed it worked for a time, but there wasn't enough political will to embrace it, in other words, to spend more. Keynesian economics, with some Marxist political philosophy sprinkled in, is the foundation for these failed policies.

Reich complained about how wages (under Obama) were stagnant, but rents kept going up, and he dared to end the heated exchange saying:

"Newt, I'm surprised you're not taking responsibility for any of this (Ibid)."

Ladies and gentlemen, this epitomizes the intersection of economics and our modern political scandal: blaming the other side for what you're doing or what you've done.

While loudly talking over one another, trying to make their points, Reich's position was the government needed to spend more to solve our economic problems. Imagine if Newt Gingrich said, Robert, demand does not create its own supply! Economics is value exchanged! How can Keynesian economics work in practice when it fails in theory? My guess is Reich would have changed the subject with another attack or obfuscation.

Reich argued for increased government spending and control because Keynesian theory tells him to and because he can use it to expand government control. His rationale is always on the demand side, which, in reality, doesn't exist.

Reich might agree new freeways can improve overall productivity. He could also accept or uphold more infrastructure repair spending for safety, but he wants the outlay to redistribute wealth forcibly. Putting tax money in workers' pockets jump-starts and pushes the economy forward when they spend their paychecks in his Keynesian mind. In other words, take from you and give it to them to drive the economy.

He thinks demand creates its own supply. Keynes believed in slow economic times, the government could print money and "throw it up in the air." Reich and all the political left embrace this. At least, this is the theory behind their intellectually vacuous and irrational arguments. The truth is money without production value behind it waters down everyone's money. It robs the wealthy least because their assets protect them from inflation as they rise in value or hold their value in real terms against it. Inflation profoundly hurts the middle class, but it steals most from the poor.

The left argues that not putting money in needy peoples' pockets is immoral despite the immorality resulting from their policies. Look at our cities, at people who live generation after generating having gotten something for nothing. The truth is they pay for it with their dignity. What is the leftist solution? Easier access to food stamps, free utility payments, free or nearly free government housing. If helping the unfortunate is morally required of us, is it perpetuating their degradation?

Government-sponsored affordable housing becomes necessary when the government creates too many barriers to development. Prices go higher and higher because of government bureaucracy. There becomes so high a cost in time spent from jumping through bureaucratic hoops, with code compliance, fees, taxes, over-regulation, and land control. What the citizens can afford and house construction costs and home prices generally go out of equilibrium. Building spec properties is risky enough without the government making it so much more arduous and expensive, hindering development, resulting in a housing shortage with sky-high prices.

The government causes the problem, and Reich and his allies give a bureaucratic state solution, creating more imbalances and unaffordability.

When fewer people can buy a home and rely on government assistance for their housing, moral decay tends to set in.

Professor Reich might also notice he can't directly tie any implemented Keynesian policy to resultant prosperity. The economy may have done well in times of excessive Keynesianism, like during the post-war period, but this doesn't prove the Keynesianism caused it.

It's taking credit by association while ignoring our incredible competitive advantage after WWII over the other industrial economies damaged by the war. With so many things in our favor, especially technological advances and production methods learned during the war applied throughout the economy, and we should've done better without "progressive" hindrances.

What would Robert Reich do if he finally admitted Keynesian economics doesn't work? Would he ever admit it? What excuse could he then use for more government? Reich is a true believer, it seems, judging from his seemingly honest, even raw caring emotions. Either that or he is a great actor. You can count on this: he will drop Keynesian economics as soon as he can use anything sounding better to argue for more government spending and central control.

Do his emotions cloud his thinking? The left seems to have an, us against them mentality. They feel for the have-nots and think they can help by fighting those they see as their oppressors, even though they typically live in the most well-healed segregated neighborhoods.

The reality is, free and fair dealing among people, rich, poor, and everyone in-between brings the most prosperity and opportunity for all. An, us against them mindset is detrimental to all. You will always have the rich and the poor with you, but the freest economies have a large middle class.

Is it that intellectual liberals think themselves above reality, above common sense? Reich *wants* Keynesian economics to work so much he'll go to any length to persuade himself it does. It must be those emotions overriding objectivity again.

Those with Keynesian-focused economics degrees may also go to Wall Street and hire into a left-wing trading house instead of choosing academia. Here, they make connections, and if successful, get rich gambling with mathematical systems and programs that don't reflect real-world economics or business decision-making.

The central bankers, who worked at the same trading houses and first learned from Keynesian economics professors from the same prestigious universities, may inadvertently help them by continually creating and pumping more fiat currency into the system as stock and bond prices rise. They thereby inflate values and commissions in this special place with unique positions and select information for gambling with the odds in their favor.

Short-term Wall Street trading does not teach how real-world business works. In his day, Keynes fervently traded stocks. He gambled himself a small fortune within his portfolio, then lost it, then gambled it back again; he knew fear and greed firsthand. Did he confuse what short-term stock market gamblers do every day with what business people do in producing value?

Isn't it interesting how Keynes saw demand as the driving force in economics when supply is the engine as he seemed to confuse the fear and greed of short-term stock market trading for the businessman's creating value? Why else would someone claim the economy runs on "animal spirits?" The actual economy consists of people taking measured risks and following through to provide value or utility for others for compensation in return, not on reactive emotions or gambling.

Producing quality products and services requires human dignity. If someone thinks all morality is relative, that there is no objective right and wrong, or merely as one individual may define it, wouldn't it follow they could see erratic and emotional behavior as ordinary? They might even develop an economic theory that says "animal spirits" drives human behavior or that businessmen reflexively react to government-created demand.

Isn't it disrespectful to humanity? When one sees himself as intellectually superior, with his judgments defining morality, will he then think of the world as filled with emotional and irrational human widgets? He becomes the higher being as he disrespects the common man.

Keynes associated, in his personal life, and as a Cambridge professor, in the most secular, anti-religious, socially radical elitist circles of his day. What kind of man leads the Eugenics Society in England? His "progressive" thinking is at the heart of the scandal.

Could elitists who imagined an economic theory that redistributes wealth to the poor to spend money to drive the economy strip those same human beings of their dignity? Did Keynes fail to understand the economic foundations because he lacked a moral footing?

Doesn't handing people money and telling them they are oppressed strip them of their humanity? Isn't this scandalous? The self-fulfilling prophecy may be this: Treating people as dependent animals, and providing for them, expecting them to spend all the money they have, causes them to behave with animal spirits. Has it contributed to strengthening the family or to societal breakdown? It hasn't brought prosperity to our inner cities, has it? Isn't there more violence in these neighborhoods since they received the forcible redistribution of wealth through Keynesian economics?

Do you want more scandal? The more prestigious the university your child attends, the higher the odds he will receive Keynesian indoctrination.

How is it, affluent suburbs around the country provide overwhelming votes for Keynesian indoctrinated politicians each election? Could it be upper-middle-class brainwashing? It can't mean they're unintelligent. Do the policies somehow favor the well-healed, at least to assuage their guilt? College professors and administrators benefit, and anyone in a government bureaucracy rides the gravy train, so it's understandable that college towns, state capitals, and the suburbs around Washington D.C. champion Keynesianism when they vote.

But who is the electorate living comfortably in affluent suburbs around Boston, New York, Philadelphia, Washington DC, San Francisco, Seattle, or any upscale suburbs around the USA? Why do they vote this way reliably? Where did they get their beliefs? Do they feel proud of their economic situations but guilty about others in different neighborhoods? I don't have anything against rich, poor, or in-between, but why is there so much erroneous economic thinking amongst the highly salaried? Generally speaking, entrepreneurs, whether rich or poor, know better even if they don't have formal training because they have common sense. The top pay scale employees, it seems, mostly don't. Do you think it's our scandalous education system?

Who do you think sits in TV news anchor chairs and works in the newsrooms? Who do you think writes in the most prestigious newspapers? The products of the "best schools" and their left-wing "progressive" professors. They don't bat an eye when the sound of Keynesian economics hits their ears. They think it sounds "intelligent." How is there so much misunderstanding about basic economics among them?

We know Adam Smith described "A system of natural liberty" and of "free enterprise." The left finds this offensive because their designs are always for more government intervention and control. It's why they cynically use the term "capitalism" in the way Karl Marx did as if it's about the greedy rich capitalizing on or "exploiting" the poor. Did a poor person ever give them their high-paying job? Do they hate the guy who owns their company?

You'll never hear them use the much more accurate and pleasing terms of "free enterprise" and "natural liberty." Using the phrase "laissez-faire" is out of the question unless they demonize it; they may use the word "entrepreneur," but only in a politically correct "energy start-up" or "organic farming" context.

They don't trust our rights are "natural rights" that come from "nature's God," as our founding fathers expressed in The Declaration of Independence. They believe our rights come from the government, which means politicians and courts' decisions apart from God. But if the government gives, it can take away.

Embracing "entrepreneurship," "natural liberty," "free enterprise," and "laissez-faire" creates more flourishing small and medium-sized businesses. Across the country, we'll have a stronger middle class with higher incomes. We wouldn't have the dominance of so much top-heavy crony capitalism that the left complains about but enables with their policies and draconian regulations that small businesses find it hardest to survive.

With increased general business acumen and many more small entrepreneurs, include better ethics from our traditional morality, the faith that got us here, and so much scandalous poverty in our inner cities and pockets across the country would naturally end.

Part VI

Preparing Ourselves

"You will ever remember that all the end of study is to make you a good man and a useful citizen."

John Adams

17

Steps of Change and Your Children

"Happiness and moral duty are inseparably connected."

George Washington

HAVE YOU CONSIDERED enlightening your children from early on? From childhood, they should know about the relationship between their dreams and free enterprise. With their hearts right, teach them freedom, creativity, and all the possibilities that lie before them as entrepreneurs. Smart, honest, moral, hardworking free citizens mean a better future.

These days they'll hear a lot of bad things about our history. Don't skirt over or deny them; correct errors, and expose exaggerations, give them perspective. There is evil behavior within all political and economic systems, but there have always been honorable people, and none of us is perfect.

Today kids hear "capitalism is corrupt." Inoculate them against the attack; through their upbringing, get them to understand the idea of growth through free enterprise. As individuals, we must believe we're growing to flourish, so societies must too for general happiness, satisfaction, contentment, and more advancement. The truth of American history reveals how an economically and politically free country transforms struggling families into the middle class and sometimes into the wealthy.

The extreme ideological left will exaggerate and misrepresent anything they can, and they'll talk about the evils of capitalism against the supposed innocent, "different system" of Marxism. They speak with a false narrative. Your kids often won't hear half the story; they'll get a cynical misrepresentation on one side and a false glorification on the other. Listen to them and refute propaganda with a balanced historical perspective.

Compare the upward mobility in our culture to the stagnation and decay in Marxist societies; it's readily observable. Ask them what's better, if 90% of people struggle and 10% control the rest as in overly controlling countries, or if 10% struggle and 90% make a living like in economically free but civilized nations? Poke holes in the false narrative with an honest story.

The reality is, human corruption is no more prevalent in a free enterprise society than under a command economy or Marxism. Marxist countries have the highest death toll. It's easy to see when you add up the murders of Stalin, Mao, Pol Pot, and some other tinhorn dictators like the Castro brothers. Keynesian economics may not have the killings, but it is, at its core, crony capitalism and corrupt. Once it brings profound collapse from debt and inflation, it could lead to a murderous dictatorship.

The problem is human behavior, not our economic freedom. We see the wickedest deeds today in different cultures. You'll find evil wherever you find humans, even in our places of worship, but you'll also see the best of humanity. Living by the Golden Rule in our personal and business lives brings us a long way, and we should embrace our moral traditions. It's insane to throw away beneficial and wholesome things just because someone says they're wrong. Discernment works with knowledge and wisdom. As scripture says, "test everything; retain what is good (1 Thessalonians 5:21, 1987)."

There is and has always been a struggle for right over wrong. Humanity has had growing pains from ancient times, long before the Industrial Revolution to today; the answer is not to deny economic freedom or limit it through controlling regulations but to support our pursuit of happiness within a stable society with government-enforced rules of the road type laws. The highest potential for humanity comes with economic freedom within a moral and civilized society with simplified laws.

Policies controlling fairness take away God-given freedom and are always unfair. The test is what we do with our freedom; it defines who we are. We need it to grow and to live up to our potential. We need it to thrive. When your kids hear capitalism is corrupt, it's a misrepresentation and dishonesty because it isn't the system but people who commit fraud. Combat the propaganda with understanding.

The American experiment was to see if free people could govern themselves on a large scale. If we've done it for well over two hundred years and the whole civilized world has followed our example, isn't it a good thing? Point out how Adam Smith published his book, "The Wealth of Nations," in 1776. Ask them what significance this has, being the same year of the Declaration of Independence. Connect this with how we became so prosperous compared to other countries with different mentalities. Ensure the kids understand how our freedom, prosperity, and a free enterprise system are intrinsic to each other.

With our economic and political freedom interwoven in our public and personal lives, our view of history is often the difference in whether we're constructive or destructive. In the past, teachers taught about American exceptionalism and our noble history. It's one point of view our kids don't seem to hear much anymore. Don't ignore the bad, but give a fuller picture.

In America today, it appears too many schools teach our young the American way is enslaving people and stealing land. Putting history in context helps round this view. Human beings have migrated and encroached on others' territories since man could walk, and all nation-states result from it. People have enslaved others since prehistoric times. Our founding fathers struck out with a proclamation on which they risked their lives when they pronounced "all men are created equal." Today, some history teachers curl their lips and tell us they meant only all white men.

Is this what Thomas Jefferson meant when he penned this line? Show your kids the first draft of the Declaration of Independence and the paragraph Congress took out after much debate. Google "The First Draft of The Declaration of Independence" or "Jefferson's Draft" and save it to your computer. It removed the moral stain of slavery from the American experiment. He blamed the king with these words:

"He has waged cruel war against human nature itself, violating its most sacred rights of life & liberty in the persons of a distant people who never offended him, captivating & carrying them into slavery in another hemisphere, or to incur miserable death in their transportation thither. This piratical warfare, the opprobrium of *infidel* powers, is the warfare of the CHRISTIAN king of Great Britain. Determined to keep open a market where MEN should be bought & sold (Jefferson, 1760-1776) ..."

Give them perspective. Jefferson called them "MEN," capitalizing and emphasizing freedom for all is what he meant. Abolishing slavery was a brutal fight, but many had good intentions from the beginning.

The Declaration of Independence didn't claim all men will have equal outcomes; it said the government wouldn't play favorites. They were striking out against their ancestors' European caste system where your preordained place in society, whether low or high, was by religious or family privilege. The founding fathers set up a meritocracy, where "all men" would have the free opportunity to "pursue happiness" and achieve their life's dream; it's who we are as Americans.

Our modern political left's rhetoric tells us, even if they don't admit it, they want to impose more equal outcomes on us through government control; sometimes, the ones who acknowledge it say it's what the founding fathers wanted. You might hear, "so the country can become what the founders mean it to be." Is this lying or ignorance? Whatever it is, it's not true.

When the Democratic Party had what sounded like a majority yell, "NO," in a vocal poll about putting the word "God" into the Party Platform at the 2012 National Convention, did it tell us anything? Who are these people? Are these traditional American values? No, they're more like beliefs from the Progressive left's atheist idols, Marx and Keynes; our American heroes, like George Washington and Abraham Lincoln, frequently mentioned God in their speeches.

Sometimes people improve on a theme, but they can't when they throw out its essence. Marx rejected the economic foundation; he postulated that human evolution resulted in collectivism and preached forced socialism. He demonized entrepreneurs as thieves, stealing from the working class; he was precisely wrong because entrepreneurship is the genesis and driving force in economics. His system destroys the good instead of addressing problems.

Keynes did something similar because his theories, saying production doesn't come first, also devalue the entrepreneur. He claimed that people aspire to their higher potential in society when the rich, especially those who inherited it, have it taken from them and redistributed to those with less. This, he said, would drive the economy by consumer spending. The nanny state government with more control over the economy will bring prosperity?

With Keynesianism, we get confiscatory tax rates that look like Marx's demands in the Communist Manifesto, designed as one of the first steps to destroy capitalism. We get an inheritance tax to strip away family wealth, but we don't have an English caste system; we have a meritocracy. Ask your kids how they like that one. If you leave them assets when you die, the government could seize a significant percentage on top of their grief. You may not have enough for this tax to kick in because it confiscates from the very wealthy now, but a few years ago, the government stole the middle-class's family wealth too. Why does the left fight for an inheritance tax?

What kind of philosophy gives the government this right? Isn't this what the founding fathers rebelled against in 1776? If your children sigh and are glad because it doesn't affect them, ask if they mind their friends or even strangers getting robbed? If the left says they want the government to do good things, ask them what they call giving charity with a gun to your head? Is this practicing the golden rule? It's intrinsic to Keynesianism, but it's contrary to our founder's beliefs. How hard is it to say it's "un-American?"

One reason the left rhetorically pits the rich and the poor against each other is a divide and conquer strategy. Class warfare political tactics make low-income college students feel righteous when they vote for politicians that confiscate a child's inheritance. The irony! Your children may have to sell what you leave them to pay the government. Make it personal for them and ask them what's right. Are those telling them capitalism is corrupt themselves corrupt? Controlling others or being under control yourself is unnatural and should be unsettling to us. Younger kids get this instinctively. Give them and your older children concepts and personal examples.

On its face, control-oriented politics sounds right to many, with more justice for the oppressed. It often appeals to confused high school and college kids. They may have good motives, but becoming tools for the left is never noble. Tell them "safe spaces" are cowardly and ignoble. If you are "triggered" by something someone you disagree with says, you have emotional problems and need solid ethics and decency more than the person who said it. George Washington talked about "the battlefield of ideas," and he encouraged debate. Today college campuses seem to stifle or completely disallow "offensive" opinions. How dangerous! Ensure your kids know how Hitler, Lenin, and Stalin saw students as their "useful idiots." Political correctness is cultural manipulation, socialist tactics. We need objective, critical thinking to see and expose it and to persuade with our better ideas.

Both Keynes and Marx believed in controlling people to bring about justice. Bring about human freedom by taking it away? Does your creed include doing evil so good may come of it? Is it a coincidence both Marx and Keynes denied religious beliefs that espouse the Golden Rule? Religion extolling God as love and love, as "willing the good of the other," to paraphrase St. Thomas Aquinas, brought us Western Civilization. Would you prefer living in a more brutal, primitive society? Give your kids a choice after describing barbarism and its "strength being the norm of justice" ethic.

Wisely, the founding fathers often expressed a societal need for religious morality because human nature can quickly devolve into something ugly. Our blemished moral record is only conclusive evidence we need it. President John Adams summed it up quite well in a letter to the Massachusetts Militia:

"We shall have the Strongest Reason to rejoice in the local destination assigned us by Providence...Our Constitution was made only for a moral and religious People. It is wholly inadequate to the government of any other (Adams, 1798)."

Alexander Hamilton described the results of atheism driving the French Revolution. Prager University, in a video by Joshua Charles, called, "What Role Should Religion Play in a Free Society," describes, "The anti-religious force the French Revolution unleashed," quoting from Hamilton's papers:

"...annihilates the foundations of social order and true liberty, confounds all moral distinctions, and substitutes the mild and beneficent Religion of the Gospel, a gloomy, persecuting, and desolating atheism (Hamilton, 2017 [1794])."

The same Prager University video quoting from Washington's Farewell Address, 1796, shows him chastising those who claimed to be patriots while undermining the influence of religion in society:

"Of all the dispositions and habits which lead to political prosperity, religion and morality are indispensable supports. In vain would that man claim the tribute of patriotism, who should labor to subvert these great pillars of human happiness, these firmest props of the duties of men and citizens (Washington, What Role Should Religion Play in a Free Society, 2017 [1796])."

Today leftists try to drive any Christian expression from the public square. Let your kids see how opposed their attacks are to America's founding. History with a balanced perspective is invaluable to the kids and us. It reveals tremendous bravery and goodness, along with very human mistakes. We should not rashly judge others from times past without a fuller story. Introduce them to pivotal historical figures, but don't forget the basics of freedom and economics because they are inseparable. Immerse them in these things conversationally, even casually, from their youth.

Prepare your children; it is your "moral duty," as George Washington so eloquently said; they could become vulnerable targets for those peddling destructive disinformation. Far too few parents aren't doing this. In polls today, many high school and college kids want a socialist government. The change must first come within your home, starting early and consistently. Inoculate them from their poisonous peers, and unfortunately, from many of their teachers, especially their college professors.

Read with your children, *The Last Will and Testament of George Washington.* He freed his slaves upon Martha's death. He didn't discharge them upon his or in his lifetime because he would hate to see their families split up as some could leave but not others. He couldn't release the dower slaves, those willed down Martha's family line from her earlier deceased husband to his descendants, but they had intermarried with his slaves, who he could free. You can see his insistence his heirs take care of any too old or infirm to leave and that they educate the children (Washington, The Last Will and Testament of George Washington, 1992 [1799] 2-4).

According to a tour guide at Mount Vernon, I heard some years ago, Washington wrote it without a lawyer and only told those near his deathbed where to find it. It's striking how intelligent and knowledgeable he was.

Writing about dispersing his assets, addressing various legal contracts and entities, it's remarkable how upright and generous too. By forgiving debts and putting money aside for a school for orphan and destitute children, and freeing his slaves, it's clear he was a highly honorable man.

President Washington kept the slave's families together during his life and tried to do what was best for them; they had it relatively good on his plantation with plenty of food and no corporal punishment. Rather than fall into someone else's ownership after Martha's death, he made sure to free the ones he could.

Washington saw the inconsistencies of his newly founded constitutional republic and slavery, struggled with it, and sincerely desired their freedom. Still, he was afraid it could divide the country into war. He reflected in a letter to Robert Morris his frustration in not getting a legislative vote to abolish slavery:

"I hope it will not be conceived from these observations, that it is my wish to hold the unhappy people who are the subject of this letter, in slavery. I can only say that there is not a man living who wishes more sincerely than I do, to see a plan adopted for the abolition of it—but there is only one proper and effectual mode by which it can be accomplished, & that is by Legislative authority: and this, as far as my suffrage will go, shall never be wanting (Washington, From George Washington to Robert Morris, 12 April 1786)."

Let your kids know that Ben Franklin became President of the Philadelphia Abolitionist Society and petitioned Congress, although unsuccessfully, for complete emancipation for the slaves in 1790 (Benjamin

Franklin Historical Society, 2014). President John Adams spoke publicly and wrote in opposition to slavery, and his wife Abigale wrote her opinions to him condemning it. Our second President and the first, first family to occupy the newly built White House insisted on having no slaves on the staff (The White House Historical Association, 2018).

Alexander Hamilton, our first Treasury Secretary, produced economics papers arguing slavery was inefficient, and he was always against it. Hamilton became President of the New York Manumission Society, which advocated for slaves and free blacks, and it offered proposals for emancipation (Columbia University, 2018). There were other founders opposed to slavery. John Jay, the first Chief Justice of the Supreme Court, who wrote the Federalist Papers with Alexander Hamilton and James Madison, was the founding President of the New York Manumission Society (Ibid).

Abraham Lincoln gave public speeches calling slavery "evil" or "an evil" and calling for its abolition beginning in his twenties. Kids sometimes hear in school today that Lincoln didn't care about the slaves; he only wanted to preserve the union. I've heard some people on the cable news channels declare the utterly ridiculous statement that Lincoln owned slaves; he never did. Lincoln's letters and speeches, his whole life and death, blow these absurd notions apart.

Your kids may be able to cite facts to radical teachers or help friends understand a balanced perspective. Show them how courageous and honorable many of our historical leaders were. Don't deny bad things but put them in perspective; in an authentic and human context. Ask your kids to imagine they lived back then, born into a society where this was normal. What if they inherited slaves as children, like Washington, and grew up hearing it was the natural order. Would they change their minds about it as he did? What would they do to promote its end without having the country break out into a civil war?

It's obscene to choose the left's heroes, like Karl Marx, or John Maynard Keynes, over our actual heroes. The left may not openly celebrate these two men when it's not politically expedient, but their economic policies and political mentalities express the ideas. Their heroes were moral relativists and staunch atheists by whom people greatly suffered. Millions of innocent people died in the twentieth century under Marxist governments, and the Keynesian theories have our children facing a potential public debt Armageddon. Most traditional American heroes were heroes in reality and good people; this should be easy to see for anyone with an honest heart.

Read *George Washington's Letter to the Hebrew Congregation in Newport, Rhode Island*, and *George Washington's Letter to the Roman Catholics*. They're both readily available online. They show the father of our country walking the walk and openly opposing the prevalent bigotry of the time. You'll see him apologize for past wrongs, but now the government won't play favorites; there will be no bias against them.

He tells the Jews that the more they prosper, the better it will be for everyone. Washington understood economics and human decency (Washington, Letter to the Hebrew Congregation at Newport, 1790).

He tells the Catholics how he hopes their fellow countrymen will remember their bravery in gaining all of them their freedom in the Revolution (Washington, Letter to The Roman Catholics, 1790). According to the Mount Vernon website, Washington "frequently corresponded with John Carrol, the first Roman Catholic Bishop in the United States." And, "George Washington socialized with prominent Catholics both at Mount Vernon and during his presidency, attending a Catholic Church service while he was in

Philadelphia for the First Continental Congress, and donated money toward the construction of a Catholic church in Baltimore (George Washington's Mount Vernon, 2018)."

In Boston, in his General Orders, 5 November 1775, Washington forbade his troops to do something so popular in England, burning the Pope at the stake in effigy on the 5th of November. He explicitly argued that it was a monstrous insult to the French Canadians he hoped to get as allies against the British.

"As the commander in Chief has been apprized of a design form'd, for the ridiculous and childish Custom of burning the Effigy of the pope. He cannot help expressing his surprise that there should be Officers and Soldiers, in this army so void of common sense...to be insulting their Religion, is so monstrous, as not to be suffered, or excused (Washington, General Orders, 5 November 1775, 2018 [1775]);"

Get your children reading the founder's letters; read them aloud to them dramatically when they're young. Reading Abraham Lincoln will make anyone smarter; the compelling logic, lyricism, and poetry in his words are sublime; they'll become better writers and learn how to think. Read Ben Franklin, Thomas Jefferson, John Adams, and Alexander Hamilton. It'll give them pride in their country, an edge in school, form their minds, and help them develop an understanding of arguments within a historical context. They may pursue a classical education with a solid foundation.

Give them a basic familiarity with men like Adam Smith, a moral philosophy professor and an economist before he wrote what many consider the bible of modern economics, *"The Wealth of Nations."* Tell them who

Jean-Baptiste Say was and what "supply creates demand" means; that entrepreneurs drive the economy; when you make or do something valuable to others, you create demand because they want it! Explain Richard Cantillon's beautiful description of an "enterprise economy" and his rags to riches story rising above the oppression he faced. They'll see imperfect men achieving great things, and so can they.

Compare these men to Karl Marx and his demonizing of religion and the murderous dictatorships and general poverty his philosophy has wrought. Ensure they know of John Maynard Keynes' condescension towards Christian morality and that he was a eugenicist who flew in radical social circles.

The Communist Manifesto calls for workers to upend existing society forcibly. Ask your kids, lured by the left, if they want everything you've worked for, and they have confiscated violently? Tell them about the profound moral corruption intrinsic to the left's heroes and that today's leftist politicians' political and economic rhetoric comes from these villains. It's why they have no real workable solutions when you drill down into them.

When Bernie Sanders talks about the rich having too much of the wealth like it's a fixed pie and they're hogging it, it comes from fixed resources thinking, something Marxists embrace. Marx said the rich steal from the poor, but Marxism makes everyone poor but selected party members, destroying upward mobility. They'll hear Bernie doesn't want a system like that, but they must know *how* his ideas are Marxian and wrong. Bernie may also lean toward Fabian Socialism, but it's still about government manipulation and control, which robs freedom and has no productive force in it. His "Democratic Socialism" means taking away the system we want and telling us what's better for us. Listen to his words. Everybody is trying to sell something, and Bernie is trying to sell something that sounds too good to be true to young, idealistic ears. He may or may not be an evil man, but what he promotes portends a disaster economically and morally.

An excellent example of fixed resources thinking is when we hear we'll run out of oil in a few years. Tell them things don't work that way unless we have frozen imaginations! We're so far ahead of the curve technologically we won't come anywhere close to running out of it; we can already make it out of inert material by adding chemicals; until this is cheaper than taking it out of the ground, we'll continue pumping it. As time goes by, we'll discover many better ways of getting it out of the earth. We still use oil because it is so abundant, cheap, and the best option.

Gasoline and diesel in our cars and trucks are only accelerants to ignite oxygen for internal combustion engine explosions. We can use other accelerant fuels, like natural gas, hydrates, or synthetic fuels. There are other technologies, like, fuel cells or battery-operated electric cars. The most efficient fuel wins for a time until something better comes along. We could use nuclear power plants with modern, efficient waste recycling for all our electricity needs, including electric cars. Freedom, not force, spurs discovery!

Get them thinking with a broader perspective and dreaming instead of being stuck in a negative mentality of fixed resources thinking. The rich don't hog fixed resources. The affluent get that way by creating valuable things for others and receiving in exchange. Don't let your kids believe opportunities are limited. It's the left's control-oriented thinking that limits possibilities. Show them Venezuela before and after the Socialist Revolution! Give them understanding and get them dreaming about better times, so they take action and build a future, not about control or safety-oriented thinking. Get them going young and teach by example and word. Walk the walk yourself.

When you first prepare your kids, and they hear the complaints of people who quote Marxian or Keynesian beliefs, they'll know what it is. When Barak Obama or Joe Biden tell us we need to spend our way out of financial trouble, they'll see right through it! When Nancy Pelosi says food stamps and unemployment benefits give us the biggest bang for the buck in economic stimulus, they'll know why it sounds crazy.

Keynes didn't know if his ideas would work, but he wanted them tried. The left continues winning elections with them, our political leaders, like, Bernie Sanders, Nancy Pelosi, Chuck Schumer, Joe Biden, Elizabeth Warren, Barak Obama, too many politicians from California, etc. Am I getting too partisan? Listen to what they say; facts are stubborn things.

The "Progressive" theories have never worked, but today, they use them more than ever to get and stay in power. It hinders our political debate because they confuse the electorate with disinformation. Wouldn't it be better for us all if we got past these malfunctioning theories and had a productive competition between the parties? Republicans need clarity too!

Karl Marx's idea that religion is "the opiate of the people" was the idea that removed a moral basis from a Christian nation, Russia, and produced mass murderers like Lenin and Stalin, running a Godless government. Their Tsars may have been flawed, but their Communists were the worst monsters.

So which "jungle" brings out the worst in human nature, the man-controlled one of government mass murder or the free one of traditional Western Civilization, with values from religious underpinnings but with a percentage of wicked people running around hurting others? In the first case, the government killed the people. In the second case, the government can catch the murders and thieves and protect decent people.

If your child's deep concern is helping others, remind them they can't help without the ability to. Moral conscience is an excellent thing; everyone should live in obedience to a clear one. Show them that their freedom in a prosperous country will allow them far more opportunities to help people. If they say the government will supply the funds, remind them the government can't provide anything unless productive citizens and businesses prosper enough to support the government. Our better nature flourishes in freedom!

Economics students today need remedial training after graduation. There really is no free lunch, but we can show them why in basic theory and practice! We must produce before we exchange, is an immutable truth, like gravity! It's horrible after such an expensive education, but tell them their real learning now begins; you might call it "the realities of life in economics."

Required in college-level economics should be at least one course called "Entrepreneurial Activity, the Life Blood of Our Economy." How about "Entrepreneurs, the Driving Force in Economics!" The professors would likely botch it because they so often have no practical experience.

It's telling that economics degrees don't require such courses. The curriculum should include how the government can't do anything without entrepreneurs supporting it. When the government attacks the "business sector," it's attacking the economy, its lifeblood. How about these suggestions for introductory courses: "Economics is Trade, or Supply and Supply." Or, "Demand Does Nothing of Itself." How about "Demand Does Nothing to Drive the Economy, but the Concept is Important for Marketing, Analysis, and Price Theory," or "Demand only Wants, but Supply Provides (on both sides of any transaction)." Or, "The Reality of Say's Law of Markets."

The more we all understand these crucial distinctions, the more productive are our economic and political lives. I hope you discuss this book with your kids. Research it yourself. Read the Giants, read and observe the political left and the right, but "test everything; retain what is good."

18

Government and Society

"Thus, it is the aim of good government to stimulate production, of bad government to encourage consumption."

Jean-Baptiste Say

WHEN BUSINESS-FRIENDLY politicians come into office following anti-business ones, expectations of fairer regulatory policies will often result in quickly increasing production and exchange.

Businesses begin advertising, planning to expand, hiring more employees and consumers, expecting bigger paychecks from more profitable employers, start browsing and buying more freely. When the people believe he means it, a business-friendly political leader's rhetoric can make hopes soar, as we saw in the stock market just following President Donald Trump's election. President Ronald Reagan achieved this exceptionally well.

Following this through successfully is the tremendous opportunity President Trump and the Republican-held Congress have. It is their ticket to re-election, but I hope they would do the right things anyway. At this writing, Congress hasn't repealed the draconian laws in the last decade, and I am incredibly shocked they haven't repealed Dodd-Frank. Modification to that awful law is not enough. The problem looks like the sixty vote Senate threshold; Democratic Minority Leader Schumer told his caucus to vote no to beneficial, repeal and replace laws, and they're lined up behind him obediently.

Already economic growth is better than during the Obama years with only administrative policy changes, reducing red tape, and what the President can do through executive orders. Business tax cuts allow for expansion with reinvestment of working capital creating job growth, but we need to repeal many laws, and reckless spending is still a horrifying problem.

The better policy changes encourage the state of mind, or this concept of demand, that the entrepreneur creates, supported, and promoted, by the business-friendly government. It's confidence in substantial business activity and profits to follow because of government policy. Increased production and exchange then continue in a more complementary economy.

If the government prints excess money and overspends, will it get things going? It may create an initial fizzle, but nothing sustains it. Production and exchange depend on available value, knowledge, ambition, and general psychology. If politicians and bureaucrats slap on excessive regulations through new laws and bad policies, the business attitude will tend to remain cautious, as we saw under Obama.

Injecting necessary liquidity and loosening lending guidelines may help trade reach its potential, but only a "money crank" economist espouses printing and borrowing for prosperity. It creates imbalances and is a bad policy because, in reality, the economy grows by fundamentals in action.

The government has several very positive and invaluable roles regarding the economy, not to control it but to allow for its free facilitation by free people producing value and exchanging with each other. Promoting prosperity through sound policy, fair laws with actual enforcement, and allowing for increased productivity by intelligent infrastructure spending, protects and serves the economy, which is the people trading value. We must consider spending the people's hard-earned tax dollars is a sacred trust.

The people financially support the government; this gives them the natural right to control it. It should never be the other way around, where the government pays the people it directs, except for necessary government employees. Any State with too many government employees eventually fails because it can't support itself. Where is the Soviet Union?

The economy is the people and their actions, not the politicians and theirs. The government has a vital role in setting and supporting the stage, but it doesn't grow the economy; free people prosper with fair and limited laws. Keynesianism misses this entirely.

Watch out when you hear politicians say *they* will "build a fair economy," "build an economy that works for everyone," "create a fair system," "grow the economy," or "create jobs." Statements like these expose a control mentality; they are a political fraud.

Good government can set the stage by negotiating free and fair-trade agreements with other countries. Countries with many resources but without manufactured goods can get manufactured goods in trade for their abundant resources. Nations with cutting-edge pharmaceuticals can get cheap clothing in return; the consumers and businesses in both countries have more affordable consumer goods and materials to build and conduct more business. All the societies involved should achieve a higher standard of living.

The goal is free and fair trade, but it's a form of theft if one side cheats. The results don't have to be equal, but all must adhere to the same rules.

International trade is essential for us and our global associations and friends; it's economics in implementation; protectionism as an endgame is foolish.

Individual freedom and creativity cannot approach their potential without a conducive environment. Civilization depends on a civilized government, but the people organize it. It should not try to form the people. These are the United States' founding principles.

The government should never try to mold us into its image, as Socialists contend. Our personal beliefs should come from our faith in God and our families handing down the proper formation to us in love. We can then debate freely and associate as we choose, but not by government manipulation, control, or political propaganda. Increased efficiencies, growth, and moral goodness follow amongst free people in civilized societies. The government's role is not to form us but to protect our right to worship openly and freely and not discriminate against us if we don't.

Prosperous and advancing civilization depends on freedom, law, and order, with good honest political stewardship. Fair enforcement of reasonable legislation and regulations promotes growth, but restriction, interference, favoritism, and control only hinder. Economic freedom means creative freedom engaged in production. Although we'll never have a perfect world, we must aspire to open and honest free trade, striving as we fall short.

Just as a person who grew up in an abusive and violent family without love struggles, and often cannot reach his potential in life, so too with culture. Lawless, violent societies are poor. We see this in our own violent, lawless, and, therefore, impoverished neighborhoods. Nobody, no family, and no civilization is perfect, but how does justice prevail?

The first thing any society needs is law and order. We can then produce for each other and provide for our families and ourselves. When justice prevails, the potential for advancement and a higher standard of living exists. Societies that fail the moral test fall into a dictatorship not only because anarchy brings violence but because business activity needs stability. Freedom requires morality, which is an environment that fosters more prosperity. Economic theories designed to give up liberty to gain affluence are a big lie.

An overbearing, over-regulated society limits human potential, and it doesn't respect the citizens' humanity. It's cynical and immoral because it tries to control people's dreams, to force them to act in ways by design, denying them their God-given freedom and dignity. Extreme examples are communist societies. Even if the bureaucrats at the top have good intentions, they're in the first place by government structure acting in a corrupt, freedom robbing system.

Moral laws stop violent people from infringing on other people's liberty and safety. Someone might say yes, but one person's immorality is another person's freedom. It's precisely where social mores and society's moral code become so vital. Things are changing in America today; values are changing in the Western World. We must ask where we came from morally, what got us here, and where we're going.

Before Christendom, European peoples operated under the ethics of rape, pillage, and plunder; in fact, this is the story of mankind around the world. Governments consisted of warring clans and their warlord kings, and strength was the norm of justice. Good and evil were relative to victory or defeat. Western Civilization introduced right and wrong in caring for widows and orphans as religious duty through heaven in your heart and conscience. It's obvious we've been far from exemplary in many ways, but the change and the improvements are astonishing.

Has technology brought us beyond silly religious morality? Are we now more advanced innately as human beings? Do you think advanced technology prevents perverted values? With relative values, how does one define morality at all? If we lose our religious ethics and moral code, nothing does. There is good and bad religion. Love-based is good religion, the groundwork that brought us Western Civilization. The government should never hinder these traditional faith-based practices. If we lose them, we're in trouble.

Might would make right, and the more advanced the technology, the more dangerous things become. The strongest or most brutal would enforce their will. The one who could impose what they want, take what they want, force obedience on others, or kill them could do it faster and more efficiently.

Society may decline into constant warfare; advanced technology does not lead to morality. Little technology is better for humanity in this case because the combat would be more primitive. Advanced technology should warn us to keep the moral values that got us to a more civilized society, not to lose them.

No government can control a society of violent, dishonest, immoral people. Which comes first? Can corrupt people create an honorable civilization? In an extreme example of societal evil prevailing, a police state must arise, or chaos and destruction continue. When the population in any country becomes dishonest and immoral but still votes, the politicians will reflect the electorate before losing that right. With corrupt, greedy, and unethical politicians in place, a coup and a dictatorship usually follow. Observe history and look around the world at societies that can't achieve first-world status today.

Despite our moral failures, and although we'll never be perfect in this life, we must know what works overall. The people must first get along, be fair with each other, and rise to form a civil government. Civilization follows civilized people. When you trace things back, it wasn't the government that gave them the moral code. It was faith in a just and loving God. Secular government elites can't civilize the masses; an enlightened state rises from a righteous people.

The American experiment worked because of the shared moral code. Despite ethical failures and growing pains, we flourished because of the good, not the evil. Crooks may seem to win in the short run, but they can never build a prosperous society over time. Most people were decent and primarily wanted a system of voting rights with law and order. They also had many good leaders who knew a civilized society could only exist among people believing in a good God. Their goodness was a prerequisite for an operationally free country. How can any people maintain civility without a shared moral code and faith?

A few years ago, I had a chat with a security guard at one of the marinas in Marina del Rey, CA. He was about thirty years old and was only moonlighting on the weekends to make extra money; he also had a full-time day job. Any extra money he made went back to his father in Africa. I asked him why he came to America and how it was going for him. Why not just stay in Africa near his family?

To explain, he told me a couple of stories. He called his father a few days earlier, but his dad started crying after they began talking. A few weeks prior, he bought and delivered a big-screen television to his father, but the police saw it brought in, and they took it away. It was not in a rural area, but in a city where people could see what was happening. The Police there steal things for resale.

He didn't blame them because the government regularly ran out of money and couldn't pay them, sometimes for months. His kindness toward the police officer thieves was almost saintly. He then explained further with the story of a visit home.

He was a naturalized citizen, so he showed his U.S. passport when he went back to visit. One time, the authorities at the airport didn't believe him. He offered the usual bribes, but they took him away for intense interrogation. He demanded to see the U.S. counsel and warned them about the severe consequences; they were causing an international incident.

Very fortunately for him, they eventually checked with authorities. Someone from the U. S. Consulate came down, vouched for him, and took him out of there. Whenever he goes home to visit, the first thing he does is go to the mayor's house in his hometown to pay a bribe so he can move around freely without the police arresting him. Do you think businesspeople in such a country can rely on the enforcement of contracts? Is free and fair trade possible there? Lack of law and order is the first reason a state like this has no real economy.

One day, years ago, when I lived in Los Angeles, I struck up a conversation with a young man the landlord hired to paint in my apartment. It was a real human-interest story to me because he looked like maybe a small sixteen or seventeen-year-old, but also as if he had just snuck over the border the night before. He didn't speak English well and appeared afraid. Although cautious at first, he began speaking after I asked him some questions, sincerely.

I asked him the same type of things I asked the African guy. Why come here? Why not stay near your family? He said the police in his hometown would take him down an ally, frisk him, and steal any money he had in his pockets. They would tell him not to tell anyone, or they'd kill him. It was one of the ways the police acquired money. Making a living in Mexico was difficult, but after this happened to him a second time, he firmly decided to come to the U.S.

This essential matter of honesty and fairness impacts any society, from politicians to all citizens. What happens when the common man can't trust the authorities? An innocent person shouldn't be found guilty. Citizens must trust the police as they should expect an honest day in court. A vicious cycle begins when people can't believe government leaders or each other. There are many consequences when moral values become relative, but a big government can't impose moral values without tyranny.

In an unjust society, the politicians in power put their fingers on the scale, either for those they perceive as "more desirable" or "less fortunate." They rig elections, disheartening the people, and reducing voter turnout!

They have set-asides for those they deem worthy and freeze out those they think aren't. Let's say a single white male owns a real estate brokerage, and he applies to Fannie Mae for their real estate owned program to get listings when they have many repossessed properties for sale.

He knows many other real estate agents who continue getting a high monthly flow of REO listings, but there is a difference. They all have various shades of brown skin and or are female. He was distressed when he got to the bottom of the lengthy application that asked if he was of a race listed or female. He submitted it anyway but received nothing.

He found out they are "an affirmative action/equal opportunity employer." Not in his case. Can he trust the government? Like many real estate agents, he's not rich, but many others made big bucks because of their skin color or gender. Many of the right people, according to the government, did quite well through government set-asides of real estate owned listings after the real estate meltdown.

It's disheartening corruption to those not favored by the government, and I'm sure this true story happened to many others as it did to me. A white male in California is undoubtedly a minority, but not according to the government for its privileges. It's why many men put their businesses in their wives' names to circumvent this type of government evil.

Construction companies getting government contracts have done this for years. The wife doesn't even work there, but the company is in her name to compete for government contracts. What if the white male owner is not married? He's not the right widget in their social engineering scheme. He's not the favored race or sex, too bad, so nothing for him!

If a man has a marriage certificate to another man under the new laws, will the government discriminate against him? I won't be surprised if the government forms begin to include a sexual preference for favored treatment and not the traditional one.

What if a man grew up poverty-stricken, never knew his father, and his mother was a drug-addicted prostitute who didn't give him the love and example anyone needs, but he is single and white? According to the government, he is still in a privileged class, and they discriminate against him because of his gender and skin color. Why isn't this unconstitutional?

There are plenty of these types of scenarios in our country today. The government considers "privilege" because of skin color or sex, but it's the bureaucrats and politicians running our government, the set-aside specialists, who are racist and sexist. They demean those they give special privileges and hurt, especially the poor and those starting in life who aren't the proper sex or color.

The "less fortunate" can also be "more desirable" to crooked politicians who buy votes with campaign promises. They argue for the "more desirable" to get goodies off the backs of middle-class taxpayers. They may say they'll extend unemployment benefits forever or promise to use tax money to pay for other peoples' childcare. They may force bondholders legally first in line in a car company bankruptcy funded through a government bailout to get wiped out. Labor union stockholders that they rely on for votes get paid, even though the law says the opposite—the judge who approved it appointed by similarly corrupt politicians.

When tax money goes to well-heeled contributor friends for special tax breaks, low-interest set-aside loans, and loan guarantees or grants for business ventures the politicians deem worthy, it's affirmative action for the wealthy. Hillary Clinton said, "We can deploy solar panels," as part of her plan for a new energy economy when running for President. Whenever you hear things like this, watch for the next boondoggle. It's corruption and favoritism waiting in the wings. How catchy, the government will "deploy solar panels," but where? On her campaign contributors' mansions?

A young man from Eastern Europe I spoke with years ago told me he used to think America treated everyone equally until he lived here. He asked me why people get special treatment with a bitter tone because of their skin color. He didn't feel in a position of power as an immigrant with white skin. Is it evident to you how someone like him could have this perception? Struggling financially, alone, without any family on this continent, he sees others line up before him for job opportunities. The color of their skin or gender decides against him every time.

How do we still have a good reputation? Because we still have our Constitution, and we're very wealthy and powerful. Many foreign people don't understand or believe that Obama, G. W. Bush, and others before them signed into law an unfriendly business environment with unfair draconian laws and policies. We still have a good reputation in many ways, although our values and the founding fathers' intentions are under attack. We must ask how we became an exceptional country despite our flaws and moral failures.

People want to come to America because we're known as the land of opportunity; doesn't this suggest we are an exceptional country? I don't mean the way President Obama defined it—that we are because we feel we are, just like every other nation is because they think they are. The President's definition is precisely wrong.

Look at what the Mexican government did to one of our Marines, an Afghanistan combat veteran going to San Diego for a combat-related post-traumatic stress disorder. Is this an example of an exceptional county? Would we act this way? We heard his 911 call, he was just over the border after taking a wrong turn, but he couldn't turn around where he was.

He immediately turned himself into the Mexican authorities. Still, his antique guns on this side of the border became an excuse for them to arrest and abuse him in a Mexican prison for many months. After he was finally released and came home, he reported he was beaten by guards, tied to a post wholly naked, and made to stand there overnight. They also shackled him to a bed where he could barely reach the toilet but couldn't reach to flush it. Why do you think Mexican people continue fleeing the violence and poverty of their country?

What causes a moral and social breakdown in our country? How about a downtown Los Angeles Court freeing a former football star? A real-life drama broadcast on TV. The evidence didn't matter. His skin color released him in the jurors' minds before the sideshow began. Celebrity and ethnic privilege!

What about crime and poverty? How prosperous is the South Side of Chicago? How wealthy is South Central Los Angeles? Is anyone reporting prosperity in Camden, New Jersey? Detroit might feel bad if I leave them off the list. I could give you a long list of places in the USA with poverty and violence...or, is it violence and poverty? Which comes first?

The violence comes out of disorder, but you don't give people self-esteem and a disciplined life by giving them money and telling them they're victims—although it might get you their votes. They're prisoners in their communities, lacking freedom without safety. Low self-worth goes with a lack of morality. Corrupt government promotes immorality; it pays them more when they have babies out of wedlock, and it pays for their abortions, but we can't make moral judgments against the immoral secularists, or we'll be called racists? Who is this good for, but the corrupt politicians? Who runs these cities, and what values do they promote?

The one thing all these communities have in common is a moral breakdown. They were morally bankrupt before they were financially bankrupt, and virtually all their political leaders are Democrats. Sorry, that's just the truth. Who cares about these mothers and their children?

What are the answers from the left? They need better access to "free," taxpayer-funded abortions, uh, healthcare. Obamacare treats pregnancy as a disease, but what's the cure? Now, how's that for building up self-esteem, kill more of your preborn children? What about posterity? It conveniently vanished, leaving the mother emotionally and maybe physically damaged for life. Is this loving others and celebrating life? Who profits from all of this? Planned Parenthood "doctors" and executives. The politicians also tend to do well, often very well, with their starving constituents paying their hefty retirement pensions. Is it a surprise they continually demand more federal funding? You can bet they'd print and recklessly spend their own local currency if they could!

They also disproportionately send their young men to prison for violent and drug-related crimes. The left's solution? Leave them on the streets with the majority of low-income law-abiding citizens taking the brunt of it. How about our founding fathers' answer, a moral and decent God-fearing society starting with their fathers leading by example at home with their mothers? No, the secularists want to ban religion in the public square and promote transgenderism to the most innocent, prepubescent school children by giving them a "social education," as Karl Marx put it. What does that learning do but create disorder and destruction of our society as the communist founder designed?

Next, they'll claim it's all economically beneficial spending! With Keynesianism, we can print and borrow and give them money, cover their "medical care," or pay for their incarceration anyway.

Hope should mean different political leadership can at least tell them the truth and implement better policies. Social mores can change. Good religious leaders on the ground now are drowned out as the corrupt news media gives all the attention to high-profile con men who are in cahoots with the politicians. Why did President Obama have the "Reverend" Al Sharpton as an advisor? Why did MSNBC hire him? Please, take a moment to think about that one!

The politicians have scared the people in these neighborhoods against voting in Republicans, so the one-party state is usually easily re-anointed every election. The electorate must think the corrupt politicians care. They can feel their pain. Isn't re-electing these people and expecting different results the definition of insanity?

19

Curing Confusion

"When one side only of a story is heard and often repeated, the human mind becomes impressed with it insensibly."

George Washington

IF YOU ASKED someone on the street who they blame for our national debt explosion, what would they say? What are the odds they would point at John Maynard Keynes and his political friends?

After reading this, I hope you can describe how the "progressive" politicians who amended the Constitution to allow a direct federal income tax about a hundred years ago very quickly used it for an unprecedented federal power grab. The income tax became the vehicle for constant government growth, ever-increasing political control, and debt so enormous it's hard to imagine being able to pay it off.

Can you explain our changing mentality regarding debt, that "debt doesn't matter," and how this only occurred after adopting Keynesian economics? How we always paid down the national debt from major wars before the progressive era began? How the Great Depression brought fuller "progressive" implementation with massive government spending and extensive government control of the economy? The enormous increase in public debt in peacetime was unprecedented and has continued since. We used to keep our national debt very low proportional to our economy before the progressive era; our debt to GDP ratio is now over 100% and climbing!

Can you explain the difference between productive and unproductive spending? How money represents the value of our previous production held in a medium of exchange, and when we spend it, we destroy it as we don't have it or what it represents anymore. If we do it productively, in a production process, we transmute it into something more valuable we can sell for a profit; we create or have a part in making something worth more than what no longer exists. A tree becomes paper worth more than the raw materials and labor used in making it. The work is complete, the tree is gone, but more value exists for exchange in the resulting paper, the furniture, the finished product, etc.

If we provide more efficient business equipment or consultation (our paid expertise), others can then produce more quickly or more valuable products or services in any given period. We have a part in multiplying the value we destroyed (in our business operations) in what they produce. Like electric saws instead of hand saws, making more efficient tools accomplishes this multiplicatively when many people use them every day, and they can reinvest their additional profits. Efficiencies in business applications multiply.

Imagine making electric calculators, and you supply them to a society where everyone uses a pencil and paper. Merchants with your product perform transactions, say eighty percent faster than before. You destroy materials when making your product, you make a profit over your costs when you sell it, but each business person using it supplies far more goods to the public multiplied by all those to whom you sell calculators. They can continue growing their business with continually reinvested profits, and everything moves faster downstream. Modern computer technology increases our standard of living multiplicatively. The more we get done in any period, the more product we have, the more value we can trade for other things, and the wealthier we become.

When people consume but don't produce anything or enough to match their consumption, they destroy value they don't replace. You can cite Adam Smith. They run down their wealth and eventually live off other, productive people; he called them "prodigals" and "a public enemy (Smith, Wealth of Nations, 1991 [1776], 279-281)."

It's a profound reason why all spending is not worthy, and Keynesianism is absurd. Taking money away from producers and giving it to unproductive consumers to spend it to drive the economy is theoretically vacuous. In practical terms, unemployment benefits may help those in dire straits, but it provides no economic bang for the buck. Sorry, Nancy. Demand doesn't create its own supply; it does nothing on its own; it just wants. Supply creates value on both sides of a transaction that must come before any exchange unless we first borrow, print, or deplete wealth to trade.

Can you show how the post-war period had considerable economic growth from technological advances and more efficient production methods from WW II and beyond? How entire housing tracts went up in the time it previously took to build a few houses? Today we make sandwiches in a more efficient assembly line when we line up to get lunch faster, more efficiently, more consistently, and at a more reasonable price than we did before the war. Our standard of living went up because these things allowed us to produce and exchange more with each other. The war massively increased our production know-how.

Our competitive advantage in the world as the one big producer left standing helped us tremendously, but there is no proof of big government spending creating prosperity. Can you point out how the war on poverty hasn't had good results? If you can't, ask someone on the South Side of Chicago about the quality of life there.

Can you point out how countries worldwide have done "stimulus packages" without good results but only had debt explosions? Japan has the worst debt to GDP ratio globally at over 240% (Statista, 2017). They've done many stimulus packages but without impressive economic growth since the 1980s. Back then, their remarkable production and exchange created great prosperity. Today, their Keynesian economics is setting them up for disaster. Many European countries also approach the Keynesian cliff with higher debt than the size of their economies—there are a few worse off than we are at well over 100% debt to GDP!

Can you show how Barak Obama's economic policies and politics brought us back to increased Keynesianism? The massive stimulus attempts added immensely to the national debt, with only anemic growth through his two terms. If we didn't increase regulations and pass such controlling laws and didn't engage in such reckless spending, we would have done much better. More, better-paying jobs beat more government handouts. Valuable production and trade provide for perpetually increasing prosperity.

Can you point out that considering population increase and inflation, under Obama, we didn't have much if any economic growth, and we just about slid sideways when averaging his eight years? Do you realize that if Congress didn't go to the Republicans in Obama's first midterm election, he would have done more stimulus packages? Do you remember the election campaign when the only economic answer Obama and Biden had was more government spending? How their solution for "fixing the economy" included increased regulations on entrepreneurs across the economy, and how they seemed devoid of understanding how it limits growth?

Can you see the Keynesianism in Chuck and Nancy's response to President Trump's proposals? Schumer and Pelosi were initially falling all over themselves about Trump's trillion-dollar infrastructure rebuilding idea because they thought the workers spending their paychecks and government spending would drive the economy. They refused to go along with anything he wanted, however, for political reasons. They must believe they can wrest power through the obstruction. Typical of our politicians, but can you see Keynesianism in the debate?

How significant is it that Chuck was the Senate Minority Leader, and Nancy, the House Minority Leader, for the Democrats? What economic theory lies behind their politics? Did you see how they were for it (before they were against it) only through increased deficit spending, yet they always yell and scream at the suggestion of leaving more working capital in producer's hands through tax reduction? They can't see multipliers in working capital reinvestment and argue business tax cuts cause deficits but think increased government spending balances the budget. It sounds crazy because it is, but now you know why. It's because of Keynes' infamous and erroneous "fiscal multiplier."

Chuck Schumer said Trump should "forget about" repealing Dodd-Frank and other draconian regulations and laws because he'll block it. Can you explain why our politicians take these positions regarding economic theory? I hope it's becoming transparent to you now that Keynesians don't understand economics; everything is backward.

Republicans and Democrats grow the public debt in almost all circumstances because many Republicans are confused too. When the economy appears to be doing much better now under President Trump's policies, both political parties are going headlong into increased spending. The Senate budget dealings between Majority Leader Mitch McConnell and Minority Leader Chuck Schumer looked like they were expanding outlays in anticipation of more tax receipts. Isn't this like the salesman who spends his commission before he closes the deal?

Why do you suppose they act this way? Before the progressive era, especially with our current debt, we would've paid it down with higher tax receipts. Not now when debt doesn't matter! Not when government spending creates multipliers in confused and childish Keynesian minds!

Do you know when debt doesn't matter? When we've paid it off or down so low that we can pay it off any time like the U.S.A. always did before the "progressive era," economic confusion began; when we acted like adults!

Can you see how too much government control forced crazy lending policies through Fannie Mae and Freddie Mac? They set the guidelines and purchased the loans, even subprime loans in the end, that pushed housing costs up to absurd levels bringing on systemic financial implosion?

As a mortgage broker through those times, I experienced it personally. The Government-sponsored enterprises' lending guidelines became more liberal each year as house prices went up and appraisals came back higher and higher. Those running the GSEs did the politicians' will to make too expensive homes affordable, and instability resulted. If conservative rules governed these organizations by charter and political caprice had no place, we wouldn't have had the mess.

The politicians most at fault blamed everyone else, especially mortgage brokers and appraisers, who followed their laws and policies. They set reckless guidelines, then attacked and continued their assault against the smallest shops with their awful legislation and regulations. Is it a coincidence they attack those least able to fight back?

In the past, borrowers had to prove their income, put a reasonable amount down, and have acceptable credit. Fannie Mae and Freddie Mac began offering stated income and assets or the NINA (no income, no asset) loans. No money down loans became the industry norm through the GSEs because Congress wanted it that way. When house prices were near their peak, Freddie Mac rolled out NINJA loans—no income, no asset and no job data or questions with cash out to 70% LTV, and with low interest rates! What could these be but a vehicle to bail out homeowners who had taken money out from their inflated home values and wanted more but really couldn't afford it? Reckless applications by government design create defaulted loans.

Do you remember Franklin Raines, the head of Fannie Mae and initially a President Bill Clinton appointee? He sat before Congress admitting they loaned out one hundred dollars for every one they kept on hand while he gave himself millions of dollars in bonuses on the enormous volume.

How about when Representatives Maxine Waters and Gregory Meeks accused the Republicans who questioned him of being racist because Mr. Raines was black? A reasonable reserve ratio might be about seven or eight to one, but if you suggest one hundred to one is reckless, you're a racist!

Congress pressured the banks to lend in low-income neighborhoods with very marginal applicants through the Community Reinvestment Act and other laws, people who really couldn't afford to buy. FNMA and Freddie even facilitated subprime lending, purchasing blocks of these loans after pension funds and other investors worldwide lost faith in them, attempting to shore up the crazy home prices. They caused tremendous damage with their meddling and engaged in political grandstanding while blaming everyone but themselves before passing draconian laws to hurt us all.

Why won't the government release Fannie and Freddie from conservatorship with more conservative lending guidelines after many years of holding them captive? Why do they continue stealing the stockholders' profits when they're doing well while keeping the stock value to almost nothing? Shouldn't those American stockholders get some of their money back? The government has already taken far more from their profits than it cost to bail them out. An entirely private or wholly public system wouldn't facilitate funding mortgages better. The infrastructure is already in place. Why not be wise, set better guidelines, and let them operate?

Congress approved corrupt bureaucrats running Fannie Mae and Freddie Mac and had legal oversite over them, yet they refused to do it. Wall Street investment banks invented instruments they could sell like snake oil— mixing pieces of reckless mortgage instruments with portions of car loans and student loans, conveniently having no recourse on their inflated profits in resale. Somehow no one could see this public and private corruption working together for what it was, but the laws the politicians passed after it all did more harm than good. Where was oversite? Where was effective regulation? Oversite means being unafraid to look at them, oversee them, and act when wrongdoing appears. It doesn't mean attacking sound business practices by politically progressive meddling and manipulation.

The government caused the need for the bailouts; they created and exacerbated the problem. Then they blamed small mortgage brokers and appraisers but bailed out their campaign contributor big bank friends. They passed laws making business uncomfortable for the big banks while making it extremely difficult to nearly impossible for small brokers and lenders—giving their big bank friends far more market share. Brokers quit operations all over the country under government caused stress—giving consumers fewer choices.

Can you explain how government debt only grew from great wars before the progressive era? There were no debt explosions in peacetime, even during previous recessions or depressions. How we paid war debt down to little or nothing afterward, every time? Even though the debt to GDP ratio improved in the post-war period because of economic growth, the national debt has increased almost every year without the political will to pay it down since Keynesian economics took hold.

Can you explain the Keynesian infiltrated societal mentality among the elitists? These elitist Keynesians educate our children and control the news media. Their ideas are now so pervasive, even somewhat conservative commentators and writers pass them along without understanding, and no one questions it publically. What about Keynesian political rhetoric? Can you show how our politics is dripping with it? Do you see the big picture and how we got here? Can you point out that even the Republican answers tend to result in more of the same?

Can you debunk the Keynesian theory of demand creating its own supply? How about the fiscal multiplier? Explain how economics is trade or value exchanged between parties, and therefore, supply and supply or produced value traded and win the debate! Economics is not supply and demand, although they are critical analytical concepts for price theory, efficiency in markets, and other business-related things like marketing, planning, and government information compiling. Can you point out how demand is an entrepreneurially created state of mind and how it doesn't exist without a valued supply? Repeating these things brings clarity; it helps us advance the conversation and find real solutions to stop the debt spiral.

Do you remember the government shutdown just after the Republicans first took control of the House of Representatives during President Obama's first term?

The polls indicated most people blamed the Republicans, but why? Weren't both political parties at fault? Neither could agree on the budget. Wasn't this a shot across the bow of those politicians who only wanted to expand Keynesian economic policies to "jump-start the economy" or "create jobs" because they think consumer spending drives the economy?

Weren't the Democrats more at fault for the reckless Keynesian government spending? Don't the Republicans at least deserve some credit for trying to face the issue? Hadn't the people just hired the Republicans to stop the insane Keynesian policies? If the Republicans increase our national debt massively like Obama and the Democrats attempting to stimulate the economy, won't they also deserve the blame?

If I were a man on the street with the media microphone up to my face during the government shutdown, my answer might be something like this: Government shut down? Isn't that a mail truck delivering over there? Of course, they'd have to admit it's only a partial shutdown, and they probably wouldn't know what percentage is open or closed. I might then question why the media calls it a "government shut down" when just a small portion isn't operating.

I might ask them how much our federal budget deficit is currently. Is it hundreds of billions or over a trillion dollars annually? Again, they probably wouldn't know. Unfortunately, these days, who cares? I might then say, well, isn't it a good thing part of the government is shut down, given the politicians' incredible financial irresponsibility? Shouldn't we save some money? They probably wouldn't have an answer for this either.

I might then ask if they believe voting for politicians who run on spending more than we take in tax receipts is irresponsible? It makes the voters as reckless as the politicians they elect. I might then say, isn't the better question which politicians deserve credit for shutting down part of the government? Isn't that the responsible thing to do?

Maybe we could shut down parts of the government until we have a balanced budget. Doesn't life work that way for the rest of us? Don't you think that if government employees lose pay, even if any government contractors lose money, the politicians should lose their pay first? How about we dock their benefits too? Isn't that fair, given they caused the problem?

Although I admit I haven't done the test myself, reports say our national debt, not including unfunded liabilities, if stacked in one-dollar bills, would reach the moon, go around it, and reach halfway back to earth. When you read this, it'll probably have circled Earth and gone back to the moon again.

It's nothing to be proud of, but when President G.W. Bush left office, the national debt, if stacked that way, would have reportedly reached halfway to the moon. Isn't this vast federal debt evidence Keynesian economics doesn't work? How come after years of expanded Keynesian policy under Obama, we couldn't pay the debt down? The Keynesian answer is the Republicans were obstructionists. Why? They wouldn't let them do more stimulus packages!

I heard President Obama's Labor secretary, Tom Perez, on NPR, giving the host an economics lesson. He said customers and businesses are "partners," and the companies need more customers to prosper, so we should have a higher minimum wage—he thought it would drive the economy and create more jobs when they spent their higher paychecks. The incompetence of these people is insanity defined. Perez went on to become the head of the Democratic National Committee!

He spoke doctrinaire Keynesianism with everything flipped on its head. He gave the standard misrepresentation that the economy is 70% consumer spending, and therefore the higher minimum wage would create more customers. He claimed he asks all around the country "all the time," what can we (the government) do to help businesses, what do you need? They tell me we need more customers! They should've said, "laissez-faire (let us be)!"

Won't there be consequences for producers and likely job cuts from forced wage hikes? NPR had an analyst point out some potential negative business ramifications after the interview, which I admit, I didn't expect.

What if some businesses close because they can't pay the higher wage? Some companies won't start up, and many may fire or not hire employees. Shouldn't we acknowledge that either profit shrinks, meaning less investment and fewer new hires, or the cost gets passed along to consumers whose minor increase in pay now can't buy as much? Inflation means everyone makes less in real terms. The left's deception is that wealthy owners pay for it, so attack them! But what about aspiring entrepreneurs?

It could drive more manufacturing out of the United States, especially in garment production and other lower-skilled sectors, because foreign companies will have a competitive advantage. All the employees for those concerns and those they couldn't hire won't have jobs or spending money, at least until they can hopefully do something else.

Secretary Perez followed the typical Keynesian pattern. His initial mistake? Demand creates its own supply. His following error flows from the first. Consumer spending drives the economy. He supported it with the marginal propensity to consume, advocating putting more money in low-income people's pockets, so they'll spend it quickly to drive the economy, and it's all off a cliff with slow growth and increasing national debt.

Where does the consumer's disposable income come from in reality? It comes from business, whether their own or someone else's as an employee. Government employees' pay comes indirectly from successful entrepreneurial activity because government revenue comes from taxed profits and out of their employees' paychecks.

In the Labor Secretary's wild Keynesian world, business concerns consistently pay out more money in wages, and some of it might come back to them in the form of consumers with a little more money in their pockets. Does that sound like a good deal to you? Where will they spend it? Will it create prosperity? Since Keynesians constantly argue in the aggregate, maybe it will drive the unemployment rate up as fewer people have jobs, which means less overall consumer spending.

This country has always been a meritocracy. Low and minimum wage positions were considered entry-level. Someone starts low with an incentive to do a good job and rise to a managerial position with more pay. It gives them a good reason to go back to school and get a better education or better, more marketable skills for a more lucrative job. The idea is to follow our dreams and better ourselves by moving up within the same or a different organization, or perhaps even start our own business.

The living wage idea creates people comfortable flipping hamburgers, and they become less aspirational. When naturally, in practice, young people without work experience learn work ethics and job skills starting at the bottom. What if the government forces an increase in adult pay but not for kids? Won't businesses avoid hiring adults and mainly employ young people for simple tasks? Government interference and ineptitude always cause problems. The answer is straightforward rules of the road laws and enforcement, not bureaucrats attempting to control us.

Look at the results of illegal immigration, especially in our cities. Not only does it drive wages down for low-income Americans, but it reduces our opportunities overall. Our kids get frozen out of learning work ethics because the kitchens in fast food restaurants only hire Spanish-speaking foreigners. Young Americans often can't get bank teller jobs because they only hire Spanish/English speakers. The same is true of customer service jobs. The thing is, they often can't speak English functionally, but they can speak Spanish, so they get the job. Effectively the political left now fights for higher wages for illegal immigrants, and our teenagers who can't find work are home playing video games. I live in California, and I see this especially in the big cities. It didn't use to be this way. Teenagers did these jobs historically.

Since the left always "wants to do more," why not have the government set the ages people can have certain types of employment and pay? Maybe the government can review each applicant before any business hires them to ensure they place them appropriately and at the correct income. Does this sound crazy? Confused "progressives" may think these sound like good ideas.

The truth? Government control raises business costs, hurts efficiencies, profits, and morale. It kills dreams. Not only lower profits, lower tax receipts for the government, and job losses follow, but many people go out of business if they can't raise their prices enough, which would cause inflation.

Given all the inefficiencies Keynes has wrought, the debt trap, existential danger, political deception, and moral degradation, shouldn't we finally cure the confusion, once and for all, and call for more than his banishment from our culture and economic thought, but for his total demise?

20

Preparing Ourselves for Keynes' Death

"If your actions inspire others to dream more, learn more, do more and become more, you are a leader."

John Quincy Adams

WHAT WOULD THE world look like if we never mentioned John Maynard Keynes anymore—if we thoroughly exorcized his theories from our economics departments, political arguments, think tanks, financial reporting, and from general discourse?

Imagine all people, but especially children in low-income neighborhoods learning from the time they are young about the value of what they've done. Through their parents, schools, and osmosis from shared knowledge in society and their communities around them, they'll learn that any money in their pockets and bank accounts is a little piece of what they created. It represents the value of what they made.

When they buy gum, it's a tiny bit of them getting a buck for sweeping someone's front walk or mowing someone's lawn; they made an exchange of value. When a person trades a little piece of a job well done, of labor and skill, of valuable production, don't you think work then represents something wholesome? Parents won't bark at them to get a job, develop discipline, or need money to buy things because both the parents and the kids will see the money as a medium of exchange holding the value of their previous production. They won't "have to" work because creating is inspirational.

Mowing someone else's lawn now becomes valuable; they can help the other person, get the value of what they did for someone else, hold it in their hands, and trade it. They can invest it or use it to make something more valuable to someone else and then exchange it for more value. Can you see the power in this?

Do you think kids will grow up having more pride in what they do when creating value for others means they can receive it in exchange? Do you think they will save and invest more, starting at a younger age? Won't they understand how supply creates demand when they do a good job and receive more job offers? Seeing value in finished products and services develops into higher quality goods and services for us all.

It might occur to them how they can organize people and invent or copy systems at a young age but make them more efficient. The younger they realize this, the more it develops in their minds. Increased efficiency adds to their profit. They can split that additional income with their customers, giving them a lower price and thereby grow their business. The more these ideas crystalize, the more they develop, whether their dream is to make surfboards, bicycles, computer technology, electric cars, or build new spaceships. The more they implement actions toward their goals, the more they do in life, including the more they can do for others. They might believe they can change the world. They may invent, produce, and create jobs from early on. Think of all the personal growth potential when we never think demand drives the economy ever again.

Opportunities follow for everyone around them who learns or works and trades with them. Store owners will respect their customers, spending their creation of value through a medium of exchange or money. Customers will be more careful about how they destroy their hard-earned production, and entrepreneurial activity gains more respect than before. People won't grow up blowing money over the bar but will frugally save and invest young.

More trade ensues with more reinvestment, and a better societal work ethic develops. People will see money as an asset, something valuable for underlying reasons, and used for productive purposes. They'll more likely invest, save, and build a business. They will no longer learn through osmosis from the culture around them to spend what they have so frivolously. We all gain better ethics, cleaner living, and more discipline from understanding valuable production power with these "old fashion" values.

Before Keynesian confusion came in, these old fashion values were staples of American culture. The "progressive" era gave us an artificially slow debt-ridden economy with risks of catastrophic inflation and our confused culture. The left thinks Keynes' ridiculous-sounding theories are sophisticated, but this only exemplifies their confusion.

For a window into American values before the progressive era, read Ben Franklin's autobiography. His life was discipline, experimentation, discovery, and implementation. He wrote, worked, and invented from childhood. He made daily schedules for himself and made up prayers he would say at set times every day.

Franklin became the most famous writer in the colonies, studied many issues and topics, and published the most read periodical, Poor Richard's

Almanac. He invented a printing franchise system and had partnerships in print shops up and down the East Coast, from New England to the Deep South, and he retired in his early forties. He then experimented with electricity and invented the lightning rod that saved European towns and cities from the terrible fires that often destroyed them.

People around Europe had paintings of Ben Franklin over their fireplaces because they were so grateful he saved them from this most horrible scourge. He became a much loved and admired international celebrity. He invented other things, including the Franklin Stove, and later in life, he joined the anti-slavery movement and became the leader of the Philadelphia Abolitionist Society.

He was a statesman and diplomat: a founding father of the United States. It was all possible because supply created demand from his childhood to early middle age when he retired from his business enterprises. He then did many great things we remember. He did those things for us, and we still benefit from them. Do we need more Ben Franklins?

Keynesians teach us the government can make the difference. It can cause more general prosperity by giving people jobs and handing them money, and they spend it to drive the economy. Does this sound stupid yet? In other words, the Keynesians believe they can give a boy a fish and feed him for life because they can keep giving him fish every day with money they print, borrow in the citizens' names, or take from other citizens by government force through taxation. Does that sound like a functioning economy? Remember what he wrote: he believed his system would be the norm going forward, not a cyclical exception as many try to sell it. He gave us what we have on an ongoing basis, and the government debt keeps piling up.

Won't we help our children, including those in low-income neighborhoods, when we remove Keynes from their thinking? Instead, we must discuss wholesome, practical values. How valuable will it be for them when their parents know this and teach by example? When their father or mother hands them a buck, they'll see it as a bit of their parent's hard-earned labor, of whatever honest work they did to have the value in hand. Will kids think as they grow up how they can't wait to create value like mom or dad? Will they learn to be more careful with money? Will they respect it more than seeing it as something the government owes them but doesn't give them enough of so they're always short of it?

If more of us know and practice these things, parents will more likely be good examples, or if their parents aren't, kids can learn from other relatives, volunteers, friends, and the community around them. We'll also have less unethical behavior, fewer ungrateful kids, and less drug use from our middle class and wealthier neighborhoods; they'll be more eager to work or find a calling younger.

In our low-income neighborhoods politically run by "progressives," these days, the boy resents you and the government as he becomes morally degraded. He does poorly in school and gets used to other people giving him things. Instead of being thankful, he gets angry, demands more, accuses you of keeping him down. He then riots, vandalizes, steals, kills (especially other boys in his neighborhood), and goes to jail. The left pushes for his early release, then for felonious voting rights. More moral degradation follows.

What Ben Franklin wrote so famously in Poor Richard's Almanac, "Let not a lender or a borrower be," becomes the infamous Keynesian inspired ideas, "debt doesn't matter," and "in the long run we are all dead." It becomes a Federal Government with a 105% debt to GDP ratio built up mainly in peacetime, in other words, for no good reason, with pension and other obligations of much more.

Until Malthusian theory, we saw population increases as an essential part of economic growth; it equaled more hands to work on the farm or family business. With his demand-driven theoretical arithmetic, Keynes saw no moral problem in his controlling ideas. He argued for population control for a better future without seeing human beings as individual economic engines. In his confused mind, demand created its own supply, and supply didn't create demand. He was wrong. We need more productive people!

Today our social security system faces implosion because we have stunted population growth. With Keynesian deceptions gone from our minds, we'll have more children raised in more productive and wholesome family atmospheres, and our schools will no longer teach the overpopulation myth that threatens our civilization. The truth is, America is a very rural continent. The one thing we have for sure is wide open spaces.

For today's problems, as in times past, it turns out, growth is the answer, not population stagnation or reduction. Trade with more people able to produce valuable things leads to a better future. We should teach our people to fish to feed themselves and others for life, not continue giving them fish. They'll learn the most when they can freely interact with others. Poorer countries first need morality leading to free and safe societies with stable governments, and they'll gain self-respect and be able to feed and teach others when we all produce and trade freely.

Talk about old-fashioned values; these are biblical teachings: dignity in work, taking care of yourself, and working hard so you can take care of others. You can reference St. Paul as he refused money for his preaching and teaching, which he admitted would be legitimate income, but did other work besides to feed himself to set an example for others. My guess is St. Paul would have highly supported Abraham Lincoln's statement, "the change must come from within; it cannot come from without."

People need free interaction with those with better technology and better production methods. When they learn to do it better than those who traded them, they can feed themselves and others through their hard work and inspiration and teach others by trading and interacting with them. Call it practical, productive experience. They learn from us, and we learn from them. We need freedom, not a controlling government! Keynes' death means killing the manipulative nanny state and celebrating liberty and innovation from the smallest to the largest enterprise.

Eradicating Keynes, Marx, and Malthus and those like them means we can have a more honest political debate. The politicians can take their positions and make their economic arguments on reality and not fraud, with the financial information we receive from the news networks, newspapers, magazines, and websites based on truth.

It means we'll never say the economy is 70% consumer spending again because it's ludicrous, it's misleading, and it tees up Keynesian arguments. It's a prerequisite for fraud. Nancy Pelosi will never again say, "food stamps and unemployment benefits give us the biggest bang for the buck in economic stimulus." Joe Biden will never again say, "we need to spend our way out of trouble." Our youth will laugh at Bernie Sanders' fraudulent ideas.

It'll be a foregone conclusion that the government forcing redistributed tax money is counterproductive and immoral. It can cause a short-term fizzle of activity and economic disequilibrium, but with moral degradation and resentment in those who receive the redirected money and those forced to give it up. It hurts morale when people have their hard-earned money confiscated while paying for too much regulation. You can ask many business people today, especially those in the mortgage industry over the last few years, with Dodd-Frank, the Mortgage Safe Act, and all the additional power given to the Federal Reserve Bank for implementation. The only reason we still prosper is technology keeps our productivity up in the face of it.

When Keynes is dead, politicians will know, everyone will know that business production drives the economy, it must come first, and consumer spending is a way to measure activity. The economy consists of trade between producers. It's ironic Keynesians call themselves behavioral economists when their very program hurts producers' morale.

We won't fall into the deficit spending trap, into the allure of more government spending to solve our economic and budgetary problems. Our more level-headed politicians will pay down our debt with the additional tax receipts when we have surplus years, just like they used to. We won't have the magnetic pull of "deficits don't matter" or "redistributive justice," which is a lie, telling us to confiscate from the rich and give to the poor as if we have fixed resources, or it's justice.

We'll understand that stifling government control hinders everyone's aspirations, and the poor and middle class suffer from it the most. The wealthy increase opportunity for all others in a free society because we can trade, sell to them, and enjoy the products and services they supply that made them rich. We'll know that low overall living standards come from government control and over-regulation, especially on small businesses.

Kids will learn in school, and adults will know that businesses create jobs; jobs don't create businesses. Economics is the valuable production of goods and services traded. We need the results from our production on hand to sell and buy. In the big picture, we need a profit or a paycheck before we can buy anything.

The world without Keynes and leftist indoctrination in our society mean we'll better discern right and wrong. We'll see our debt as immoral, as undoubtedly evil, and that roughly 40% of the general population and 70% of those with African ancestry born out of wedlock are awful. We'll see a child deserves a mommy and daddy and that the government engineering the natural law because of modernist beliefs is absurd.

We can renew our traditional values, including loving those with whom we disagree. Society won't force the immorality of a few, or their psychological problems on us all, as if our kids are bigots when they naturally realize the behavior is wrong. We'll have much less demonization and personal attacks on others; discernment and caring will replace relativism, self-indulgence, and lack of restraint. We'll laugh at ourselves again.

A Christmas tree will be a Christmas tree in a world without Keynes, and a Christmas party will be a Christmas party. Our government, schools, and courts will stop forcibly changing society into a sterile secular paradise where progressives never get offended. They'll cease this horrific and insidious brainwashing of our kids.

Why won't the indoctrination police let us openly celebrate our traditional values? Have you noticed how much "progress" they've made? There are atheist clubs and now some Satan clubs popping up in American public schools. They hate and discriminate against Christianity, but these are okay in the name of tolerance? They undoubtedly play to win over time, but they also strike hard at opportunities and have advanced their social causes quickly in recent years. They violently protest and "resist" when they perceive timeless values are ascending. When they ferociously object, it's evidence we're doing the right things.

When we've come to our senses, never again will we ignore the character of people who come up with new theories that contradict time-tested foundational truths. Keynes was confused about much more than economics; there is a record of his many dalliances into perverted sexual behavior in letters to friends who engaged in the same things.

There are books and articles about things he did that are so twisted; it's hard to believe. Keynes listed the prep school boys he successfully corrupted in his diary (Farlex, 2018). A "same-sex" child predator who glorified in grooming and molesting kids, never expressing a guilty moment about it, and was close to others like him in radical socialist circles? Really? Can't the Democratic Party find a better economist and political philosopher? He is their main guy, but some Republicans are confused and follow him too!

With John Maynard Keynes dead, the political left will no longer have the economic theory they use to engineer society to their beliefs. We'll see reasons for right and wrong rooted in timeless values we can openly embrace in a world without Keynes.

John Maynard Keynes and his "progressive" friends led us to a society with a Supreme Court that legislates from the bench. When the court changes laws by interpreting words to mean something different than they explicitly say, instead of sending them back to Congress to make changes or to clarify ambiguous language, then our system gets a little more poisoned. They make up laws from their perception of modern social mores. They say marriage is something different than it has ever been before. Getting married becomes about how consenting adults feel or define pleasure for themselves instead of being society's foundation. Getting a license from your state or local government becomes a federal constitutional right? Next, they'll use "equal protection under the law" for immediate family members, or groups of anything, "marrying." When this bond applies to anything, it becomes meaningless, and a bit more of society collapses. Fewer confused young people step to the altar for a lifetime commitment or do it without religious vows, thinking they can always get divorced. More babies born out of wedlock and or abortions follow.

Often the mainstream left won't go along with radical social beliefs before it's politically expedient, like President Obama and Hillary Clinton were for maintaining marriage as we've always understood it until "Progressive" lawyers won court cases. They and the news media then jumped on board, and public opinion slid that way. Their success and hypocrisy are systematic. So, what happens? Now we must let men dressed as women into the Lady's Bathroom because a minuscule fraction of the population has a specific diagnosed mental disorder, gender dysphoria.

We've reached societal insanity in the name of not wanting to hurt anyone's feelings. The floodgates are open. What's next? Will we give hormones to children stopping their puberty because they are tomboys or confused kids after watching cartoons and being taught in school from the youngest age that switching genders is heroic? Will we celebrate doctors who surgically mutilate mentally ill or objectively confused people? Oh, we already are? Isn't it better to speak the truth in love and help those with problems?

Supreme Court justices shouldn't put their personal social beliefs over the law declaring anything constitutional they feel should be, Justice Kennedy. They become unelected morality legislators reading in legal rights that do not exist, matching their immorality, and they disenfranchise most

Americans who believe in the rule of law. Originalists should apply the Constitution and overturn prejudicial modernist interpretations.

Science tells us we have the instructions that make an individual's eye color, skin color, size, looks, personality, and physiology stamped in our cells; this is a distinct human life. Everything that makes an individual is there in our forty-six chromosomes at conception, but we're confused about taking someone else's life because of an erroneous Supreme Court decision? The most innocent among us who we should protect the most have their life taken for our convenience. New York State Politicians rejoice in allowing it up until birth. Isn't someone you can't see just as much a person on the other side of a door if you shoot through it and kill them? Isn't the baby on the inside the same person when they come out?

There is no "right to privacy" in the Constitution, but they invented or "construed" one, then further stretched their "progressive" construal, leading to millions of lives slaughtered in the womb. Are we a moral or immoral society? Are we still an exceptional country?

When Supreme Court decisions do not follow the Constitution, the first steps of an unraveling occur. When they construe their previous construals, they pass the law down through the generations in sort of a "telephone game." It ends up meaning something very different than originally intended.

Instead of embracing "be fruitful and multiply," we may have aborted the next Ben Franklin, Enrico Fermi, Nikola Tesla, or Albert Einstein. We may have killed the next guy to save us before he was born. Think about it. What would that genius have invented? The future energy or transportation technology breakthrough? We'll never know. What have we lost?

What is right and wrong? What would have happened if George Washington's mother decided to "choose" differently? Most of us wouldn't have been born because our ancestors wouldn't have come and met here. Our leaders, judges, and economic philosophers affect our children and us more than we know. We need discernment and clarity.

How do we build a prosperous society? The highest possible business freedom and morality. What's the best balance? Striving for the good and not demonizing those who fall short, including ourselves. Through a loving and just God, we pick ourselves up and help others after our moral failures. We go back out on the playing field of life and play the game ethically.

We don't win by immoral standards and cynical choices with constraining micromanaging laws, but with higher personal and societal morality, political liberty, and the freedom to pursue happiness. Rules of the road, moral, common-sense legislation, and policies that allow rewarding production and exchange get us there. Adding ethical values to business freedom is the right recipe.

With Keynes gone for good, there will be no more "public sector" and "private sector" talk. The difference between the economy and the government will be evident to all. Politicians will consider it foolish to try to spend our way out of trouble, and both political parties will see that controlling regulations are harmful and immoral. We'll all see that controlling others is wrong and bad for everyone. Consistent enforcement of common-sense laws and repealing draconian ones becomes valuable and necessary.

With a revitalization of ethics, morality, the traditional family, and pride in what we make, we'll make better quality products and be better people for it. More kids in poor communities will have good examples from two-parent households, and generational cycles of poverty will finally end.

Judging and categorizing people into groups will become less frequent by power-grabbing politicians because it won't work on an informed populace. People will get along better. There will always be bad behavior, but with new clarity, we'll see it quickly. With more law and order, naturally, we'll spend less on investigations and police because of better behavior.

The Keynesian debt trap will vanish as we responsibly grow our way out of it and pay it down. When government spending becomes a smaller percentage of the actual economy, tax rates will decrease as our debt payments come down. We'll have more overall prosperity, and our responsible government will be able to do the things it should, even help those in dire circumstances. What an irony. With our debt paid down to little or nothing, the government will be able to afford things we can't now.

I'm making a statement for a compassionate, not a self-centered society. Keynes' view of money as something you get given you, borrow, or print, with no moral value, leads to a decline in moral values throughout society. Keynesian thinking creates a greedy and selfish culture. Money has moral value when it represents the excellent work we do for each other. Ill-gotten gains, getting something for nothing, selfishness, and conveniently disregarding others' lives are all destructive. Greed is not good!

The whole world will have a higher standard of living. There is always a danger of greed with prosperity, but if we follow our Founding Fathers' vision for us, a moral and religious society will help guard against it. People will give more to charity and help more locally, not only because they'll have more to offer, but because it will become more popular, and by the Grace of God, a good conscience leads one to give.

I may have given you some hyperbole about life without Keynes. Still, he is the "progressive" economist that enables the economic and political confusion that propels us toward the cliff financially and morally. We can become much better people if he is never heard from again.

Conclusion

"The future doesn't belong to the fainthearted; it belongs to the brave."

Ronald Reagan

I T'S OFTEN DELICATE talking to friends, neighbors, and family members who profoundly disagree with you—especially those staunchly politically opposed or with very different personal values—yet the debt we're leaving, and our societal breakdown are inherently moral issues. They stem from confusion, and understanding how and why we got here is vital.

When you're tying decency, debt, and the government's role into economic and political questions, the stark truth can hurt, but does denial ever help? We must bring clarity to this dangerous situation, so the next generation doesn't suffer immensely.

How important is this, especially now, when socialist movements have such cache' with our youth? Our political parties should have an honest debate rooted in sound moral values and true economic principles from both sides. Personal, slanderous attacks must stop, and honesty must prevail.

How do we tax equitably without reckless spending and a debt explosion? First, understanding the economy foundationally, as I have repeated so often, the fundamentals: it's an exchange of value from both sides of a transaction or trade, and government burdens slow and restricts it. It's not government spending. Public policy should support growth by understanding the economy by protecting our freedoms and private property rights. It must create an environment with law, order, and effective and efficient infrastructure; it should never control or restrict it.

If higher incomes have a higher tax percentage, it must only support the necessary government, and a light burden is best. Taxing progressively to drive the economy through a redistribution of wealth and income is wholly discredited; Keynesianism. It hinders advancement, and we must reject and disregard it entirely. Demand does not create its own supply!

The government is not part of the economy; there is no "public sector." The economy is production and trade; it's not 70% consumer spending! Redistributing wealth for social engineering is not helpful to anyone. Freely interacting with the wealthy and with everyone else is the answer. Education and mobility, freedom, ideas implemented with persistence, and a successfully executed vision win.

Which came first, the chicken or the egg? Businesses create jobs; jobs don't create businesses! Just knowing valuable production, which is supply, is the economy's action and comes before demand, so we have something others value for trade, makes the difference. It's the foundation for your arguments. Talk to anyone who'll listen! Enough people understanding this is the difference between Western Civilization financially imploding or not. Otherwise, the Keynesian politicians will eventually spend us into collapse. If they speak or campaign with this faux economic theory, don't vote for them and tell them why!

Reckless government spending reflects upon our control-oriented politicians, but we share the blame if we're passive. It feeds their egos to think they can control prosperity. We must win the argument and vote for the right leaders. How do we rein in the insanity? With an educated electorate! Enough of us must understand these basics. It's not complicated. When we believe their con, that says we can deficit spend and not worry about it, it's how politicians prey on us; they get our votes and set our kids up for a disaster. Tell your friends to read this book so we can stop them!

Imagine if we had a major war now with our debt to GDP ratio already over 100%. We could lose the war and our freedoms from printing and borrowing into an inflationary catastrophe. Having low government debt with a strong economy must always be our goal for safety, security, and prosperity—we must get this right for our children's future.

Some people throw around numbers saying the administrative state, including the federal, state, and local governments are about 50% of the economy. I say it's not part of the economy. Counting spending as output exposes a Keynesian bias; they don't produce but only control, restrict, and redistribute.

Effective government is vital for societal stability. Congress giving administrative agencies with unelected bureaucrats direction to freely add governing rules can't be what our founders wanted. But the Federal Reserve Bank and government agencies do it through the Community Reinvestment Act, Dodd-Frank, the Mortgage Safe Act, the Patriot Act, and Obamacare, to name a few. Can you imagine the founders debating whether 2,500-page laws can become 12,500 pages of regulations with the full power of administrative law? It's the people losing sovereignty over the government and a recipe for out of control government growth, hindering entrepreneurialism that drives the economy, and building public debt!

We must kill the administrative state and stick to the Constitution, or we will surely continue going the wrong way. Politicians must be accountable to the people. As I've already expressed, we need term limits on Congress, and we should consider other ideas with The Convention of States movement, for example. We have problems we must address.

Leftists have emotional reactions to these answers, but the key is we must produce value to trade, even to help others, and government control fails. A free society creates prosperity from the bottom up as small creative enterprises become large. We don't create wealth collectively, as Marxists, like Sen. Sanders, try to delude our children. Top-down structures and production by committee with forced rules and planning stifles competition; creative freedom wins. Economic and political freedom go hand in hand. We will win the argument with these ideas, but we must be moral people.

In nineteenth-century congressional debates, Republicans and Democrats sometimes argued over who was more conservative. We don't see this now. Keynesianism is a stubborn economic heresy that feeds leftist thinking and leads to Marxism; we notice this explicitly within the Democrat Party. Within their political spectrum, to the left, you have Bernie and AOC; they're Marxist; to the right, with Nancy and Joe, it's all Keynesian. They compete in socialist ideas, with radicals pulling them to the left and calling everyone racist who disagrees with them! Unfortunately, the Republicans aren't much better when it comes to Keynesianism and spending. We must shift this mindset!

How do the astronomical deficits and debt naturally end in a free, fast-paced, productive society? With fiscal discipline! We don't have to make drastic moves, but we must take the right actions consistently. Sen. Rand Paul's "Penny Plan" looks pretty reasonable. A rough summary is, we cut 1%

for each of five successive years, and we achieve a balanced budget. Spending then can't increase more than 1% annually after that, allowing the economy to grow faster over time, enabling debt reduction. Is it that easy to move in the right direction? Not when Keynesian "economists" tell our leaders that spending cuts cause recessions! With the business tax cuts and lessened regulations resulting in a better economy, even if we had to cut a little more because the deficit has grown from necessary military spending increases, we won't feel it! Painless!

What happened when it went to a vote? No Democrats and just a few Republicans voted affirmative. Forget a tiny successive cut; they can't even agree to reduce built-in increases! Sometimes Republicans suggest reducing additional spending, but the Democrats attack, saying the GOP wants to starve babies and kill people. They run ads showing Republicans throwing grandma off a cliff! To foreigners or anyone who doesn't watch the American media, they do these things; it's not hyperbole! How can we expect our children to act like adults when our political leaders act like children?

A Balanced Budget Amendment is another idea, if we must, but realize, we didn't need one before we began building up debt in peacetime in 1931. It was before leftist economic theories, especially Keynesianism, gripped our society! The Penny Plan (and sticking to it), reforming entitlements, getting a balanced budget amendment, or possibly even a new precious metal standard don't stand a chance until we exorcise ourselves of these economic heresies. We must kill John Maynard Keynes before he kills us!

Our lives reflect our values. In the last eighty years, the most impactful economist openly embraced radical personal beliefs as he promoted, and his followers continue expanding contrarian economic ideas. Weird men sometimes come up with strange theories. When political extremists gravitate to them, it could mean something much more sinister. Those behind the scenes use it as the "gateway drug" to implement even harsher government control philosophies. Why are these forces constantly pushing for more economic control and more socially libertine beliefs? How do they go together if someone were building a society? They are opposed to it. It eerily seems someone wants to destroy our civilization, not build it up.

We must understand who invented such a lauded and pervasive economic "general theory," principally because it's a deception, it doesn't work, and it's leading us to disaster. Where Keynes came from philosophically, socially, and morally, and who gravitates to his thinking today can help us see where we're going. Why are we sociologically breaking down as we don't seem concerned about the extreme growing danger of our national debt? Why is there a connection with Marx's ideas from the *Communist Manifesto* to destroy capitalism in our excessive tax system?

Disagreement from people who see the world through a different lens, and in my experience, especially convinced left-leaning people pinches what is like raw emotional nerves; broaching a subject so ingrained and intrinsic to their whole identity creates an almost existential dilemma for them.

No one likes their core beliefs challenged. It's why religion and politics are out of bounds in polite company, but we don't get anywhere if we don't broach the subject. Those who trust us, those willing to talk, and those in the middle without strong biases, might be the most receptive.

There is finesse involved in persuasion. You must plant seeds. It takes time and consistency, but clarifying the economic basics first allows you to build an argument—the underlying theories matter.

In my experience, elitist leftists almost always read Keynesian propaganda articles if they read about economics at all, and they think they're very erudite. They've seldom read Keynes, but others explaining how economics works using Keynes for their positions. When you bring up Say's Law attempting to explain how we create value before we trade, they often lose their composure, shout you down before you get half the sentence out, their eyes blazing and their fists clenched, declaring, "Say's Law doesn't work!" Marxian and Keynesian political and economic jargon usually follow. Their data is often wrong, and they can't tolerate you making a compelling point; they're skilled at quickly changing the subject or attacking you personally. These are tough ones.

We want to reach everyone, but like Paul Revere on his midnight ride, we can perhaps take but one road at a time. Trying to sway vicious leftists may well be casting your pearls before swine. We need a majority, not 100%.

You are your children's primary educator, don't trust those running the schools to do it! Talk to your grandchildren consistently, too, especially if their parents don't. Immerse them in constructive, logical, practical thoughts and make them good citizens who add to society. I wrote the chapter on enlightening your children because we, and they, can't afford the Keynesian economic and political "progressive" deception to continue building debt and destroying our society. We must slay Marx for good too. Our kids must stand up and win the argument, but we must lead by example; ugly things are in their future if we stay on this road too long.

I hope this book helps prepare you for what George Washington called "the battlefield of ideas."

God's speed.

Jim Malloy

Bibliography

1 John 4:8. (1987). *The New American Bible.* Iowa Falls, IA: World Catholic Press.

1 Thessalonians 5:21. (1987). *The New American Bible.* Iowa Falls, IA: World Catholic Press.

ABC News. (2013, December 15). *'This Week': Round Table on Pope Francis.* Retrieved from youtube: https://www.youtube.com/watch?v=Av63Q4JkFFE

Adams, J. (1798, October 11). *From John Adams to Massachusetts Militia, 11 October 1798.* Retrieved July 10, 2018, from National Archive Founders Online: https://founders.archives.gov/documents/Adams/99-02-02-3102

Adolphsen, S. (2017, May 17). *LePage's Welfare Reform: Good for Maine, a Model for the Nation.* Retrieved from National Review: https://www.nationalreview.com/2017/05/paul-lepage-reforms-maine-welfare-good-model-nation/

Akerlof, G. A., & Shiller, R. J. (2009). *Animal Spirits.* Princeton, NJ: Princeton University Press.

Amadeo, K. (2018, July 31). *Unemployment Rate by Year Since 1929 Compared to Inflation and GDP.* Retrieved from The Balance: https://www.thebalance.com/unemployment-rate-by-year-3305506

Benjamin Franklin Historical Society. (2014). *Slavery and The Abolitionist Society.* Retrieved from Benjamin Franklin Historical Society: http://www.benjamin-franklin-history.org/slavery-abolition-society/

Blake, A. (2016, June 20). *More young people voted for Bernie Sanders than Trump and Clinton combined—by a lot.* Retrieved from Washinton Post: https://www.washingtonpost.com/news/the-fix/wp/2016/06/20/more-young-people-voted-for-bernie-sanders-than-trump-and-clinton-combined-by-a-lot/?noredirect=on&utm_term=.3b0ccea64a9c

Bureau of Labor Statistics. (2018). *United States Department of Labor*. Retrieved from Tables & Calculators by Subject: https://data.bls.gov/pdq/SurveyOutputServlet

Cantillon, R. (2010 [1755]). *An Essay on Economic Theory*. (M. Thornton, Ed., & C. Saucier, Trans.) Auburn, AL: Ludwig von Mises Institute.

Church History. (2017, Sept. 7). *Church History: Complete Documentary 33 AD to Present*. Retrieved from Youtube: https://www.youtube.com/watch?v=xFIXMM1KWyc

Collaborative project of George Washington's Mount Vernon and the Center for History and New Media at George Mason University. (2018). *Martha Washington and Slavery*. Retrieved from George Washington's Mount Vernon: http://www.mountvernon.org/george-washington/martha-washington/martha-washington-slavery/

Columbia University. (2018). *The Manumission Society, Colonizationists, and Abolitionists*. Retrieved from Columbia University & Slavery: https://columbiaandslavery.columbia.edu/content/manumission-society-colonizationists-and-abolitionists

Complementary Currency Resource Center. (2007, 10 1). *Youtube*. Retrieved from Silvio Gesell: https://www.youtube.com/watch?v=hxdPIOUTd2k&list=PLfyoTWmrz-1YRLBFkxeo4nyGb0TJ7l4Pg

Constitutional Rights Foundation. (1995 Updated 2000, July). *The Income Tax Amendment: Most Thought It Was a Great Idea in 1913*. Retrieved from Constitutional Rights Foundation: http://www.crf-usa.org/bill-of-rights-in-action/bria-11-3-b-the-income-tax-amendment-most-thought-it-was-a-great-idea-in-1913.html

Copp, T. (2018, April 11). Why The Number Of Military Aviation Accidents Has Sharply Increased. (A. Cornish, Interviewer) National Public Radio. Retrieved from https://www.npr.org/2018/04/11/601630170/why-the-number-of-military-aviation-accidents-has-sharply-increased

Court, M. J. (1976, May 24). *Virginia State Board of Pharmacy v. Virginia Citizens Consumer Council, Inc. (No. 74-895).* Retrieved from Cornell Law School Legal Information Institute: https://www.law.cornell.edu/supremecourt/text/425/748

Democratic Socialists of America. (2018, August 17). *Home.* Retrieved from Democratic Socialists of America: https://www.dsausa.org/

Dictionary of American History COPYWRITE 2003 The Gale Group, Inc. (2016). *Wage and Price Controls.* Retrieved from Encyclopedia.com: https://www.encyclopedia.com/history/dictionaries-thesauruses-pictures-and-press-releases/price-and-wage-controls

doctorzebra.com. (2018). *Dr. Zebra.* Retrieved from George Washington: Eyewitness Account of his Death: http://www.doctorzebra.com/prez/z_x01death_lear_g.htm

Engels, F. (1883, March 17). *Karl Marx's Funeral.* Retrieved from Marxists.org: https://www.marxists.org/archive/marx/works/1883/death/dersoz1.htm

Esolen, A. (2015, January 26). *How Dark Were the Dark Ages?* Retrieved from Prager University: https://www.youtube.com/watch?v=Cqzq01i2O3U

Fabian Society. (2018). *Our History.* Retrieved from Fabian Society-The Future of the Left Since 1884: https://fabians.org.uk/about-us/our-history/

Farlex. (2018). *The Sex Diaries of John Maynard Keynes.* Retrieved from The Free Library: https://www.thefreelibrary.com/The+sex+diaries+of+John+Maynard+Keynes.-a0181820760

FDR Presidential Library & Museum. (2016 [1937]). *Federal Government Employee Unions.* Retrieved from FDR Presidential Library & Museum: https://fdrlibrary.org/unions

Federal Trade Commission. (2016, August). *Q&A for Telemarketers & Sellers About DNC Provisions in TSR.* Retrieved from Federal Trade Commission: https://www.ftc.gov/tips-advice/business-center/guidance/qa-telemarketers-sellers-about-dnc-provisions-tsr

Franklin, B. (1729, April 3). *The Nature and Necessity of a Paper-Currency*. Retrieved from National Archives Founders Online: https://founders.archives.gov/documents/Franklin/01-01-02-0041

George Washington's Mount Vernon. (2018). *Washington and Catholicism*. Retrieved from George Washington's Mount Vernon: http://www.mountvernon.org/george-washington/george-washington-and-catholicism/

German Propaganda Archive. (1938). *The KdF Car (Volkswagen)*. Retrieved from German Propaganda Archive : http://www.bytwerk.com/gpa/vw.htm

Gesell, S. (1918). *The Natural Economic Order*. (T. b. Pye, Ed.) Retrieved 06 29, 2018, from Natural Money: http://www.naturalmoney.org/NaturalEconomicOrder.pdf

Gordon, J. S. (2017, April 21). *Smoot-Hawley Tariff: A Bad Law, Badly Timed*. Retrieved from Barrons: https://www.barrons.com/articles/smoot-hawley-tariff-a-bad-law-badly-timed-1492833567

Grice-Hutchinson, M. (1952). *The School of Salamanca*. London: Oxford University Press, Amen House.

Hamilton, A. (2017 [1794], July 2). *What Role Should Religion Play in a Free Society?* (Charles, Joshua) Retrieved from Prager University: https://www.youtube.com/watch?v=sm8oGUXomHc

Hayek, F. A. (2007 [1944]). *The Road to Serfdom*. (B. Caldwell, Ed.) Chicago, IL: University of Chicago Press.

Hayek, F. A. (2012, 09 29). Hayek on Keynes's Ignorance of Economics. (L. Ralston, Interviewer) Malthus0. Youtube. Retrieved from Malthus0 youtube Channel: https://www.youtube.com/watch?v=y8l47ilD0ll

Herbert Hoover Presidential Library and Museum. (2018). *The Great Depression*. Retrieved from Herbert Hoover Presidential Library and Museum: https://hoover.archives.gov/exhibits/great-depression

Higgs, H. (Vol. 6, No. 4 (July 1892)). Cantillon's Place in Economics. In ". o. JSTOR.", *The Quarterly Journal of Economics* (pp. pp. 436-456). ITHAKA is an authorized agent of Artstor Inc. doi:10.2307/1882513

International Encyclopedia of the Social Sciences. (2018). *Wage and Price Controls.* Retrieved from Encyclopedia.com: https://www.encyclopedia.com/social-sciences-and-law/economics-business-and-labor/economics-terms-and-concepts/wage-and-price

Investopedia. (2018). *Gross Domestic Product - GDP.* Retrieved from Investopedia: https://www.investopedia.com/terms/g/gdp.asp

Jefferson, T. (1760-1776). *Jefferson's "original Rough draught" of the Declaration of Independence.* Retrieved from The Papers of Thomas Jefferson, Princeton University: https://jeffersonpapers.princeton.edu/selected-documents/jefferson%E2%80%99s-%E2%80%9Coriginal-rough-draught%E2%80%9D-declaration-independence

Jensen, E. M. (2002, October 4). *The Taxing Power, the Sixteenth Amendment, and the Meaning of 'Incomes'.* Retrieved from Tax Analysts: http://www.taxhistory.org/thp/readings.nsf/ArtWeb/736DB4705B4EE21D8 5256F2B00548FA3?OpenDocument

Juan de Mariana, T. b. (2011). *A Treatise on the Alteration of Money.* Grand Rapids, MI: Christian's Library Press.

Kain, E. (2011, August 3). *The Inexplicable War on Lemonade Stands.* Retrieved from Forbes: https://www.forbes.com/sites/erikkain/2011/08/03/the-inexplicable-war-on-lemonade-stands/#297415d22a52

Keynes, J. M. (1933, 12 31). *An Open Letter to President Roosevelt.* Retrieved from University of Texas: http://la.utexas.edu/users/hcleaver/368/368KeynesOpenLetFDRtable.pdf

Keynes, J. M. (1936). *The General Theory of Employment Interest and Money.* New York, NY: Harcourt, Brace, & World, Inc.

Keynes, J. M. (1938, February 1). *Private Personal Letter*. Retrieved from FDR Library:
https://fdrlibrary.org/documents/356632/390886/smFDR-
Keynes_1938.pdf/e6a5bbc6-db07-4d65-8576-e4ea058c5641

Krugman, P. (2009, July 7). TimesTalks: Paul Krugman: How Government Helps in
Recovery | The New York Times. (A. Rosenthal, Interviewer) Retrieved
August 11, 2018, from NY Times You Tube Channel:
https://www.youtube.com/watch?v=h3WRs06j_XU

Lear, T. (1799, December). *George Washington: Eyewitness Account of his Death*.
Retrieved from Dr. Zebra:
http://www.doctorzebra.com/prez/z_x01death_lear_g.htm

Leuchtenburg, W. E. (2005, May). *When Franklin Roosevelt Clashed with the
Supreme Court – and Lost*. Retrieved from Smithsonian Magazine:
https://www.smithsonianmag.com/history/when-franklin-roosevelt-
clashed-with-the-supreme-court-and-lost-78497994/

Liberation School. (2006, May 11). *What is Suplus Value*. Retrieved August 17, 2018,
from Liberation School: http://liberationschool.org/03-what-is-surplus-
value-html/

Lind, B. (2000, 02 5). *The Origins of Political Correctness*. Retrieved from Accuracy in
Academia: https://www.academia.org/the-origins-of-political-correctness/

Lux, M., & Greene, R. (2015, February). *The State and Fate of Community Banking*.
Retrieved from Harvard Kennedy School Mossavar-Rahmani Center for
Business and Government:
https://www.hks.harvard.edu/centers/mrcbg/publications/awp/awp37

Marx, K. (1887 [1867]). *Capital Volume I*. (F. Engels, Editor) Retrieved from
marxists.org:
https://www.marxists.org/archive/marx/works/download/pdf/Capital-
Volume-I.pdf

Marx, K. (1970 [1859]). *Critique of Political Economy*. (M. Dobb, Ed., & S.
Ryazanskaya, Trans.) Moscow, USSR: Progress Publishers.

Marx, K. (1999 [1844]). Contribution to the Critique of Hegel's Philosophy of Law. In K. Marx, & F. Engels, *The Communist Manifesto with Related Documents* (p. 126). Boston, MA: Bedford/St. Martin's.

Marx, K., & Engels, F. (1998 [1848]). *The Communist Manifesto.* New York: New American Library, a division of Penguin Group.

Marx, K., & Engels, F. (1999 [1848]). *Manifesto of the Communist Party with Related Documents.* Boston, IL: Bedford/St. Martins.

McIntyre, K. &. (2009, January 21). *Get Over It: New Deal Didn't Do the Job.* Retrieved from The Heritage Foundation: https://www.heritage.org/budget-and-spending/commentary/get-over-it-new-deal-didnt-do-the-job

McMahon, T. (2018). *Inflation and CPI Consumer Price Index 1920-1929.* Retrieved from InflationData.com: https://inflationdata.com/articles/inflation-consumer-price-index-decade-commentary/inflation-cpi-consumer-price-index-1920-1929/

McMahon, T. (2018). *Inflation and CPI Consumer Price Index 1930-1939.* Retrieved from InflationData.com: https://inflationdata.com/articles/inflation-cpi-consumer-price-index-1930-1939/

Minneapolis. (2018). *City of Minneapolis.* Retrieved from Door to Door Sales: http://www.ci.minneapolis.mn.us/www/groups/public/@communications/documents/webcontent/wcms1p-096805.pdf

Mises, L. V. (2005, 07 14). *Mises Daily Articles.* Retrieved from Mises Institute: https://mises.org/library/stones-bread-keynesian-miracle

Morgenthau, H. (1939, May 9). *Henry Morgenthau Diary.* Retrieved April 19, 2018, from Franklin D. Roosevelt Presidential Library and Museum: http://www.fdrlibrary.marist.edu/_resources/images/morg/md0249.pdf

Mussolini, B. (1932). *The Doctine of Fascism.* Retrieved from San Jose State University: http://www.sjsu.edu/people/cynthia.rostankowski/courses/HUM2BS14/s0/The-Doctrine-of-Fascism.pdf

Office of Management and Budget. (2018). *Historical Tables*. Retrieved from White House Office of Management and Budget: https://www.whitehouse.gov/omb/historical-tables/

Peck, I. (2016). *The Decline of Real Estate Appraisers*. Retrieved from Working RE: http://www.workingre.com/the-decline-of-appraisers/

Pelosi, N. (2011, December 16). *Nancy Pelosi Says The Way To Create 600.000 Jobs Is Unemployment, Food Stamps*. Retrieved from Ambushroxx Youtube Channel: https://www.youtube.com/watch?v=q06u0n9UfWO

Peter G. Peterson Foundation. (2018, March 22). *Federal Deficits And Surpluses, 1800 To Present*. Retrieved from Peter G. Peterson Foundation: https://www.pgpf.org/chart-archive/0023_federal-deficit-surplus

Phillips, M. (2012, November 13). *The Long Story of U.S. Debt, From 1790 to 2011, in 1 Little Chart*. Retrieved from The Atlantic: https://www.theatlantic.com/business/archive/2012/11/the-long-story-of-us-debt-from-1790-to-2011-in-1-little-chart/265185/

Proverbs 29:18. (1987). *The New American Bible.* Iowa Falls, IA: World Catholic Press.

Rothbard, M. (2006, 11 10). *New Light on the Prehistory of the Austrian School*. Retrieved from Mises Institute: https://mises.org/library/new-light-prehistory-austrian-school

Say, J.-B. (1971 [1964,1880,1821]). *A Treatise on Political Economy.* New York, NY: Augustus M. Kelley, reprint of 1880 Edition: Claxton, Remsen, & Haffelfinger: Philadelphia.

Shea, F. J. (2016, April 21). *Myths About the Catholic Church I, Pagan Mixing Myth, Dark Ages Myth. The University Series.* Retrieved from Jim Malloy Youtube Channel: https://www.youtube.com/watch?v=Etf0I428E2U

Sheckler, E. (2018, January 20). *How the appraiser shortage is affecting homeowners*. Retrieved from Inman: http://www.inman.com/2017/01/20/how-the-appraiser-shortage-is-affecting-homeowners/

Skinner, A. S. (1997). *Adam Smith: The French Connection*. Retrieved from University of Glasgow: https://www.gla.ac.uk/media/media_219021_en.pdf

Skousen, M. (2007). *The Big Three in Economics, Adam Smith, Karl Marx, and John Maynard Keynes.* Armonk, NY: M.E. Sharpe, Inc.

Smith, A. (1764, July 5). Letter to David Hume from Toulouse, France. Toulouse, France.

Smith, A. (1986 [1764]). Letter to David Hume from Toulouse, 5 July 1764. In R. L. Malone, *The Essential Adam Smith* (p. 327). New York: W. W. Norton & Company.

Smith, A. (1991 [1776]). *Wealth of Nations* (Great Mind Series ed.). Amherst, NY: Prometheus Books.

Sowell, T. (2001). *Basic Economics A Citizen's guide to the Economy.* Retrieved from altfeldinc.com: www.altfeldinc.com/pdfs/BASICECONOMICS.pdf

Statista. (2017). *The 20 countries with the highest public debt in 2017 in relation to the gross domestic product (GDP).* Retrieved from Statista: https://www.statista.com/statistics/268177/countries-with-the-highest-public-debt/

Steindl, F. G. (2008, March 16). *Economic Recovery in the Great Depression.* (R. Whaples, Editor) Retrieved from Economic History Association: http://eh.net/encyclopedia/economic-recovery-in-the-great-depression/

Tax Foundation. (2013, October 17). *U.S. Federal Individual Income Tax Rates History, 1862-2013 (Nominal and Inflation-Adjusted Brackets).* Retrieved from Tax Foundation: https://taxfoundation.org/us-federal-individual-income-tax-rates-history-1913-2013-nominal-and-inflation-adjusted-brackets/

Tax Foundation. (2018). *U.S. Federal Individual Income Tax Rates History, 1862-2013 (Nominal and Inflation-Adjusted Brackets).* Retrieved from Tax Foundation: https://taxfoundation.org/us-federal-individual-income-tax-rates-history-1913-2013-nominal-and-inflation-adjusted-brackets/

The White House Historical Association. (2018). *No Slaves on the Adams' White House Staff.* Retrieved from The White House Historical Association:

https://www.whitehousehistory.org/no-slaves-on-the-adams-white-house-staff

Tomlinson, L., & Griffin, J. (2018, April 6). *String of US military aircraft crashes in 2018 continues deadly trend.* Retrieved from Fox News: http://www.foxnews.com/us/2018/04/06/disturbing-string-aircraft-crashes-in-2018-continues-deadly-trend-for-us-military.html

U.S. Department of Commerce. (2017, October 27). *GDPCHG-Excel.* Retrieved from Bureau of Economic Analysis: https://www.bea.gov/national/xls/gdpchg.xls

U.S. Federal Labor Relations Authority. (2018). *50th Anniversary: Executive Order 10988.* Retrieved from FLRA.gov: https://www.flra.gov/50th_Anniversary_EO10988

U.S. Senate. (2018). *Art & History Party Division.* Retrieved from U.S. Senate: https://www.senate.gov/history/partydiv.htm

U.S.Department of Education. (2017). *About ED Overview and Mission Statement.* Retrieved from U.S.Department of Education: https://www2.ed.gov/about/landing.jhtml

United States Census Bureau. (2017, September 8). *Historical Poverty Tables: People and Families - 1959 to 2016.* Retrieved 2018, from United States Census Bureau: https://www.census.gov/data/tables/time-series/demo/income-poverty/historical-poverty-people.html

United States History. (2018). *Unemployment Statistics during the Great Depression.* Retrieved from United States History: http://www.u-s-history.com/pages/h1528.html

United States Holocaust Memorial Museum. (2018). *INDOCTRINATING YOUTH.* Retrieved from Holocaust Encyclopedia: https://www.ushmm.org/wlc/en/article.php?ModuleId=10007820

United States House of Representatives. (2018). *The Ratification of the 16th Amendment.* Retrieved from History, Art, & Archives United States House of Representatives: http://history.house.gov/Historical-Highlights/1901-1950/The-ratification-of-the-16th-Amendment/

University of California Berkeley. (2018). *Robert Reich*. Retrieved from University of California Berkeley: https://gspp.berkeley.edu/directories/faculty/robert-reich

Washington, G. (1786, April 12). *From George Washington to Robert Morris, 12 April 1786*. Retrieved from National Archives Founders Online: https://founders.archives.gov/documents/Washington/04-04-02-0019

Washington, G. (1790, March 15). *Letter to the Hebrew Congregation at Newport*. Retrieved from Teaching American History: http://teachingamericanhistory.org/library/document/letter-to-the-hebrew-congregation-at-newport/

Washington, G. (1790, March 15). *Letter to The Roman Catholics*. Retrieved from Teaching American History: http://teachingamericanhistory.org/library/document/letter-to-the-roman-catholics/

Washington, G. (1992 [1799], July 9). *The Last Will and Testament of George Washington* (Sixth Edition Revised 1992 ed.). Mount Vernon, VA: The Mount Vernon Ladies' Association of the Union. Retrieved from George Washington's Mount Vernon: http://www.mountvernon.org/education/primary-sources-2/article/george-washingtons-last-will-and-testament-july-9-1799/

Washington, G. (2017 [1796], July 2). *What Role Should Religion Play in a Free Society*. (Charles, Joshua) Retrieved from Prager University: https://www.youtube.com/watch?v=sm8oGUXomHc

Washington, G. (2018 [1775]). *General Orders, 5 November 1775*. Retrieved from National Archives. Founders Online: https://founders.archives.gov/documents/Washington/03-02-02-0279

Wolfensberger, D. (2004, March 16). *Woodrow Wilson, Congress, and the Income Tax*. Retrieved from Wilson Center: https://www.wilsoncenter.org/sites/default/files/ACF18.pdf

Your World with Neil Cavuto-Stuart Varney. (2011, January 5). *Pelosi Says Food Stamps & Unemployment Insurance Helps Economy* . Retrieved from Cesar Cota Youtube Channel: https://www.youtube.com/watch?v=xbqW4qYmYG8

Zaru, D. (2015, June 11). *Texas cops shut down girls' 'illegal' lemonade stand.* Retrieved from CNN: https://www.cnn.com/2015/06/11/politics/lemonade-stand-shut-down-texas/index.html

www.ingramcontent.com/pod-product-compliance
Lightning Source LLC
Chambersburg PA
CBHW072259210326
41519CB00057B/1835